Britain, France and the Unity of Europe
1945–1951

Britain, France and the Unity of Europe

1945-1951

John W. Young

LEICESTER UNIVERSITY PRESS

1984

First published in 1984 by Leicester University Press

Copyright © Leicester University Press 1984

All rights reserved. No part of this publication may be reproduced,
stored in a retrieval system, or transmitted, in any form or by any means, electronic,
mechanical, photocopying, recording or otherwise,
without the prior permission of the Leicester University Press.

Designed by Douglas Martin
Set in Linotron 202 Garamond
by The Word Factory, Rossendale, Lancs.
Printed and bound in Great Britain by
The Pitman Press, Bath

British Library Cataloguing in Publication Data

Young, John W.
Britain, France and the unity of Europe, 1945–1951
1. European federation.   2. Great Britain – foreign relations – 1945—
3. France – foreign relations – 1945–1958   4. Great Britain – foreign relations – Europe.
5. Europe – foreign relations – Great Britain.   6. France – foreign relations – Europe.
7. Europe – foreign relations – France.
I. Title
327 1'7'094 D1060

ISBN 0–7185–1246–4

Contents

Part III. The Demise of 'Western Union', 1948–50

Part IV. Divided Visions, 1950–1

Illustrations

Abbreviations

Note Places of publication are given only for works published outside the United Kingdom. In abbreviating less frequently cited periodical titles, commonly accepted abbreviations such as *J.* for *Journal, Rev.* for *Review*, have been used; other abbreviations are listed below. For abbreviations used in the citations of official sources, see p.217 below.

A.C.C.	Allied Control Council (Germany)
C.E.E.C.	Committee of European Economic Co-operation
C.F.M.	Council (or Conference) of Foreign Ministers
C.G.T.	Confédération Générale du Travail
C.O.S.	Chiefs of Staff
C.U.S.G.	Customs Union Study Group
E.C.A.	Economic Co-operation Administration
E.D.C.	European Defence Community
E.P.C.	Economic Policy Committee
E.R.P.	European Recovery Programme
F.G.	British official committee established to investigate the 'Franco-German coal-steel authority' (Schuman Plan)
M.R.P.	Mouvement Républicain Populaire
NATO	North Atlantic Treaty Organization
N.E.C.	National Executive Committee
O.E.E.C.	Organization for European Economic Co-operation
R.P.F.	Rassemblement du Peuple Français
T.U.C.	Trades Union Congress
U.N.	United Nations

In memory of
my father,
John Frazer Young
(1935 – 1980)

Preface

THIS BOOK analyses the British government's policy towards France during the post-war Labour administrations with a view to answering one particular question: why, after emerging from the Second World War with something of a 'blank cheque' for their future co-operation, did Britain and France become united as members of the Western alliance, but fundamentally divided on their approach to European unity by 1951? Using evidence from British official files, the work challenges the traditional thesis on British policy in Europe after 1945. It is generally believed that London was 'anti-European' in this period; that at best she wanted European co-operation to encourage American aid to the continent, and that she wasted the goodwill towards her that the liberation of Europe had brought. The French, meanwhile, are held to have led a far-sighted and successful movement towards European union. The psychological reasons for this division are said to have been laid in the war: British institutions survived triumphant in 1945, with no need to be fused in a wider framework; but continentals emerged from defeat and occupation, willing to unite with one another.

These psychological forces were certainly important in separating Britain from Europe, but the mechanics of the division of Britain and France were far more complex. Most countries emerged from war more willing to co-operate with one another – hence the hopes for the United Nations. From the moment he took office, Labour's Foreign Secretary, Ernest Bevin, wanted close Western European co-operation, based on an Anglo-French alliance; and when Russia became a threat in 1947 he developed a new policy of Western European co-operation in the Western Union. In 1947–8 he even favoured a customs union with the continent. The French, on the other hand, were far from being European idealists before 1948: they delayed an Anglo-French alliance by demanding concessions to their nationalist ambitions in Germany and the Middle East; and in 1948 they preferred bilateral treaties with other Western European powers to the multilateral Brussels Pact. Certainly some Frenchmen wanted greater economic co-operation in Europe, but this was mainly because of their need for economic supplies from abroad, rather than European idealism.

The reason Britain and France divided on European co-operation after 1948 was because the interests of each led them to radically different *approaches* to the question. Bevin had a 'European' vision, and even contemplated the creation of a European 'state' in the long term, but his vision was pragmatic, and he wanted to develop it gradually, catering, as he advanced, for co-operation with America and the Commonwealth. The French, however, wished to move quickly to a European federation – an approach which Bevin saw as premature and unrealistic. Bevin's doubts seemed justified by the impracticality of French schemes which emerged, especially their idea of a 'European Assembly', and in 1949 he turned more towards co-operation with America and the Commonwealth. In 1950, when Paris finally emerged with a practical scheme for European unity, in the Schuman Plan, Britain refused to join it. Even then British policy was to seek co-operation with the continentals, but a gulf was opened between Britain and France which in the following years proved hard to close.

During 1945–51 many people interchanged such words as unity, union, integration and federation with little regard to their precise meaning and thus added to Anglo-French misunderstandings. In this book the words unity and integration are used to refer to all types of close co-operation between states; inter-governmental co-operation refers to the traditional type of co-operation between nation-states, involving at most voluntary restrictions on sovereignty; functional co-operation is used with regard to the policy of gradually building up close links between states, possibly involving the surrender of sovereignty over an area of policy, with the intention of forming a mesh of commitments among states; and finally, the words federal, supranational and union (except in reference to specific bodies, such as Western Union) refer to co-operation involving a formal loss of sovereignty by member-states.

The present text is a development of my Ph.D. thesis, 'The Labour government's policy towards France, 1945–51', which I completed at St John's College, Cambridge, over three years, 1979–82. Although it consists entirely of my own work, there are many people without whose help it could never have been completed. My greatest thanks go to Dr Christopher Andrew, of Corpus Christi College, Cambridge, my Ph.D. supervisor, whose readiness to guide my work, give advice and read over the drafts of the text was invaluable. Great thanks too, to Colonel Robert Frazier, of Nottingham University, my tutor as an undergraduate, who first suggested that I research into Anglo-French relations at the dawn of

the Cold War. The book would not have appeared but for the
encouragement of Professor Geoffrey Warner of the Open
University, and Dr Henry Pelling of St John's College, Cambridge,
both of whom pressed me to seek its publication. It was also thanks
to the good offices of Professor Warner, and by kind permission of
Lady Younger, that I have been able to use Kenneth Younger's
diary and papers for the later period. Professor Alan Milward, of
UMIST, was kind enough to discuss the economic aspects of
European unity in the late 1940s with me; Pierre-Olivier Lapie,
René Massigli and Maurice Couve de Murville allowed me to
interview them when I visited Paris in 1981; and I have Christian
Pineau and Maurice Schumann to thank for helpful written
information on the period. Ruth Ripley-Duggan and Anne-Marie
Riley carried out the laborious but vital work of typing, and Peter
Boulton of Leicester University Press gave all the assistance
required by a newcomer to the world of publication. Finally, thank
you to my wife Elizabeth, for all her support and practical help
through three busy years. Whatever assistance and influence other
individuals have had, however, the views expressed in the work are
my own, and I bear the responsibility for any flaws that remain in it.

JOHN W.YOUNG

Introduction:
Bevin's inheritance

July 1945

ON 26 JULY 1945 the Labour Party entered government with its first and greatest overall majority. The new Prime Minister, Clement Attlee, soon left London for the last great wartime conference at Potsdam, accompanied by his Foreign Secretary, Ernest Bevin. At Potsdam America, Britain and Russia – the 'Big Three' – were planning the post-war world; final victory over Japan was only weeks away. Yet one major power, Britain's most important ally when the war began, had no share in the deliberations: France had still not recovered from defeat by Germany in 1940. She was, however, to play an important role in Bevin's foreign policy, and on returning from Potsdam he quickly outlined what that role should be. The occasion allowed the Foreign Office to gather their thoughts about their continental neighbour.

Britain and France had long had a love-hate relationship. In retrospect 1815 marked the end of centuries of conflict, and heralded a more positive association: they became the 'liberal', Western states facing the authoritarian East, were allies in the Crimean War and later formed the 'entente cordiale'. But bitter rivalries remained, as seen in the war scare of 1860 and the Fashoda Crisis of 1898. Despite triumphant co-operation in the First World War, which left them at their peak as world powers, strains were again apparent in the 1920s: there were colonial disputes, tensions in the Middle East, and differences over how to treat the former enemy, Germany. Totalitarian threats drove them back together in the 1930s but only in a one-sided relationship where France, terrified by internal divisions and economic weakness, tied herself to Neville Chamberlain's policy of appeasement and followed him to the abyss of war in 1939. By mid-1940 the two countries were working closely together, hoping to build the post-war world on their co-operation, but in June came France's sudden defeat. Before France surrendered, however, the British offered her an 'indissoluble union' (including a single leadership and common citizenship).

Proposed by officials of both sides, notably Jean Monnet, this idea appealed to Britain's new Prime Minister, Winston Churchill, and France's Under-Secretary of Defence, Charles de Gaulle, as a way to keep France in the war. But the French Cabinet rejected it, certain of Germany's ultimate victory. Again, at the moment of their greatest need, Britain and France were divided.

After France's surrender Marshal Pétain, a hero of 1914–18, became the leader of a pro-German regime based at Vichy. But General de Gaulle refused to accept defeat, fled to London (where the British, desperate for allies, gave him assistance), and boldly declared his own Free French movement to be the true government of France. De Gaulle was a passionate nationalist, who wanted France to be a strong, independent Great Power – to exhibit *grandeur* as he put it. His beliefs were based on an interpretation of French history, about which he admitted a degree of irrationality: 'All my life I have thought of France in a certain way. This is inspired by sentiment as much as by reason ... I have the feeling that Providence has created her either for complete success or exemplary misfortunes. If ... mediocrity shows in her ... it strikes me as an absurd anomaly.'[1]

For de Gaulle, greatness was part of France's inner self: Vichy, subservient to Germany, could not represent the true France. And so, comparing himself to Joan of Arc and Clemenceau, the general set himself up as the representative of the 'real' France with a simple programme: first, to gain recognition as leader of France by the Allies; second to win French popular support; and finally to restore France to *grandeur*. In 1940 this programme seemed impossible to achieve: de Gaulle lacked resources and relied entirely on British goodwill. But after France's defeat Churchill had expressed the hope 'that life and power will be given to us to rescue France from the ruin ... into which she has been cast.'[2] France's restoration was both a promise by and a necessity to the British. She had always been a vital balance in Europe, and recently an ally and friend, and British leaders repeated their aim of restoring her strength throughout the war. In September 1943 Churchill declared, 'I regard the restoration of France ... as a sacred duty ... it is one of the most enduring interests of Great Britain in Europe that there should be a strong France.'[3] The Foreign Office, under Anthony Eden, firmly believed in France's future importance and in de Gaulle as her leader.

Yet Bevin did not inherit a clear position on France, mainly thanks to the personal relationship between Churchill and de Gaulle. The former understood de Gaulle's stand as the representative of French *esprit*, and both men had common characteristics – especially a strong mixture of realism and romanticism. At first, too, they were good friends. But in contrast to the Frenchman, Churchill was emotional and gregarious, he had greater concerns than France, and he questioned whether de Gaulle genuinely represented the French people. Most influential on Churchill, however, was the American attitude. From 1942 America was the dominant military power in the West, and short-term realities made her concerns more vital to the British than the restoration of France. Furthermore, Churchill and Roosevelt developed a close friendship. This had a marked effect on France because Washington supported the Vichy regime, believing it could resist Hitler. American diplomats viewed de Gaulle as a vain upstart and Roosevelt greatly disliked him: when de Gaulle claimed to be another Joan of Arc the President thought it hilarious, and he refused to recognize the general as leader of France, arguing that the French people must elect their own leader.

Despite the Foreign Office's pro-Gaullist line, from 1941 there was a series of Anglo-Free French crises, notably in the Levant. France had had links with the Levant since the medieval Crusader States, and she bitterly resented the fact that the First World War left Britain predominant throughout the Middle East, while France was restricted to the 'mandate' of Syria–Lebanon. There, ignoring the fact that mandated territories were supposed to be led towards self-government, she enforced firm rule and proceeded to 'civilize' the Arab inhabitants. In contrast, in their sphere of influence, the British came to respect Arab feelings, and even acknowledged some local powers – as in the Anglo-Iraqi Treaty of 1930. This contrast reflected radically different colonial philosophies: the British had always established local bodies in their empire, and even granted sovereign rights to the Dominions in 1931; the French pursued a 'civilizing mission' in their empire, came to believe in an 'indissoluble link' between Paris and the colonies, and considered that the natives gained so much from French rule that they could not possibly want independence. Outside influences (usually the British) were blamed for any nationalist feeling. But 1940 shattered French prestige in the Levant, and in 1941 the Gaullist General Catroux (an experienced colonial administrator) promised the natives eventual independence. The British (who had done most to win Syria–Lebanon from Vichy control) associated themselves with Catroux's promise – and here trouble began. De Gaulle immediately condemned the British action, because he was certain that their real aim was to seize the Levant for themselves. After bitter arguments, an Anglo-Gaullist agreement was made which confirmed the promise of independence but recognized France's predominant interest in Syria–Lebanon. This reduced friction but did not end it; de Gaulle was reluctant to work towards independence and some local British representatives, led by Churchill's friend and emissary, Edward Spears, remained critical of French rule. The Foreign Office became torn between the two halves of the 1941 agreement: Arab independence, respect for France. In November 1943 there was more trouble, after the French imprisoned the nationalist Lebanese government. This further harmed French prestige with the Arabs, invited universal condemnation, and eventually forced France to surrender most of her rights in the mandate.

Perhaps the worst single crisis with de Gaulle came in November 1942, after Anglo-American forces invaded French North Africa and turned to anyone but the general to lead the government of the 'liberated' territory. In 1943 the Americans even considered seizing French strategic bases such as Dakar and establishing military rule in France, after its liberation. Influenced by this, Churchill proposed that Britain should try to overthrow de Gaulle, but Eden – helped by Bevin and Attlee – countered that suggestion, declaring that Britain should have her own policy.[4] This had little effect: a year later, as the liberation of Europe began, de Gaulle was told bluntly by Churchill that he would always put America first.[5] By then, however, events were moving the Frenchman's way: he had eliminated all his rivals and, when the liberation began, he was seen to have immense popular support in France. In October he finally received full Allied recognition as leader of France. It was a great triumph for the general (and for the Foreign Office's support for him), but it marked only one stage in his pursuit of *grandeur*.

In 1944–5 Anglo-French relations were increasingly influenced by planning for the post-war world. British hopes here centred on the 'Four-power Plan' which aimed to maintain future peace through a global security system – the United Nations – based on the unity of the Big Three and China. In Europe the British hoped to see a Commission of Allied states, under the U.N., set up to handle political and economic issues (although Churchill had wanted a 'Council of Europe' as part of a series of organizations which would emphasize regional organizations rather than a central U.N. body).[6] More important for Anglo-French relations, however, was another idea for Western European security, the 'Western bloc'. Ironically, this was first suggested by the Soviet leader,

Joseph Stalin, in 1941, when he told Eden that after the war Britain should have military facilities in Western Europe to counterbalance Russian predominance in the East.[7] However, various Western European governments, exiled in London, developed similar ideas after 1940, designed to prevent another German conquest of their homelands: Norway's Trygve Lie wanted to see Anglo-American bases in post-war Europe; Holland's Eelco van Kleffens wanted a Western European security system; and, most important, the Belgian Paul-Henri Spaak wanted Britain to lead a more united Western Europe for the sake of its political and economic well-being.[8] The Foreign Office studied these ideas in 1944 and decided that a Western bloc, led by Britain, was desirable for three main reasons: to share the burden of containing Germany after the war; to provide Britain with a defence-in-depth, should war occur again; and to increase British influence in the world by making her the representative of Western Europe. Vital as the cornerstone of such an arrangement would be France – the major continental power west of Russia, once Germany was defeated. But, importantly, the Western bloc was seen only as being subsidiary to the Big Three alliance: the Foreign Office did not want it if it antagonized Russia (by seeming a potential threat) or upset America (by detracting from the global approach of the U.N., of which Washington was an avid supporter). Some British officials hoped to counter Russian power via a Western bloc, but Eden quashed these ideas. The Western Europeans were delighted at British interest in the scheme, and even America and Russia expressed no official objections to it (although in 1944–5 the Soviet press attacked the idea as an 'anti-Soviet' alliance). Firm opposition came from Churchill, however, who prevented moves towards a Western bloc because he feared wasting scarce British resources: unless a strong French army was rebuilt and a viable U.N. created, he believed Britain would have to pour aid into Western Europe to make it militarily useful. The Foreign Office remained eager to see a Western bloc but were quite unable to pursue it.[9]

British plans in 1944–5 for maintaining their power and influence may be summed up as follows: the creation of a world security system, the U.N.; co-operation with America and Russia; development of the Commonwealth relationship; the rebuilding of France, both as a world and a European power; the (possible) creation of a Western bloc; and controls on Germany – the major enemy – to prevent another war. Controls on Germany would include external security arrangements such as the Anglo-Soviet Treaty of 1942, and

internal measures: a long occupation, denazification and dis-
armament (which all the Allies wanted). The important point for
Anglo-French relations was that France, with similar interests to
Britain as a democratic, colonial, European power, shared all these
aims to some degree, but with inevitable differences in emphasis:
whereas Britain sought to rebuild French power gradually, de
Gaulle wanted instant recognition as a Great Power; the French
wanted American co-operation, but lacked Britain's personal relationship with Washington; the French wanted the U.N. to succeed
but de Gaulle saw the potential for Soviet-American tension once
these giants had defeated Germany.

Two areas where Britain and France shared general ideas, but not
detailed approaches, were to be especially important in future. The
first was in Western Europe, where de Gaulle's officials began
producing some imaginative schemes in Algiers in 1943. These
included Hervé Alphand's project for a Western European economic
union, René Mayer's suggestion of a North West European coal-
steel area, and Jean Monnet's proposal of a European Federation
(Monnet of course was involved in the 1940 'indissoluble union'
idea). The Free French foreign minister, René Massigli, however,
found these ideas rather unrealistic, and the general himself disliked
plans, like Monnet's, that would limit French independence: de
Gaulle preferred to see a French link with the nascent Benelux
customs union (of Belgium, Holland and Luxembourg). By late
1944 these ideas, like Britain's Western bloc, were pushed into the
background: each continental country concentrated on its own
economic problems, Benelux encountered practical problems, and
the Benelux leaders showed a preference for British, not French,
leadership. (France's 1940 defeat and de Gaulle's arrogance were
contrasted unfavourably by continentals with Britain's war effort.)
But these events revealed important differences between British and
French thinking on Western Europe. Most obvious was the
question of leadership: de Gaulle believed Britain would leave
Europe, in her traditional way, after the war, allowing French
domination; but the British, after their wartime experience, were
now willing to be tied to the continent. A second difference was the
accent of French officials on dramatic schemes for European political and economic union. Men like Monnet firmly believed, after two
world wars, that new forms of international co-operation must be
pursued and the old nation-state abandoned. Inside France too, in
1944-5, there was sympathy, bred by the Resistance, for a new
internationalism: there were high hopes for the U.N.'s success,

closer European unity, and a reborn France acting as a 'moral force' in the world. To de Gaulle such ideas were anathema – he continued to pursue *grandeur* – but if he lost power this internationalism might return to the fore. Economic arguments for European co-operation had their own force for French planners because of the memory of French economic weakness vis-à-vis Germany in the 1930s: Alphand's and Mayer's ideas were adaptations of pre-war schemes to ensure France's economic security by linking her to other European economies. Again, for the moment, these ideas did not become French policy: de Gaulle saw draconian limitations on German industry as the way to ensure French economic security. But ideas existed which could be resurrected in future, and they were ideas shared more by the Benelux countries than by Britain: Spaak wanted the Western bloc to include close political and economic co-operation, but Whitehall thought mainly in terms of a military alliance. The reason for this difference was simple: the continentals had been conquered by Hitler and their political continuity broken, so that customs unions and political federation no longer seemed extreme ways to ensure their future survival; for Britain, Hitler's advances were predominantly a military threat, though they had shown the need for close co-operation with Western Europe.[10]

The second important area of Anglo-French differences was in Germany. Though Britain and France both wanted firm controls on post-war Germany, there were arguments over how to do this. Of the four powers who shared the occupation of Germany – Britain, France, America and Russia – only France developed a full 'thesis' on how to treat the former enemy in 1944–5. This included five major aims: to abolish centralized German government and emphasize local powers; to separate the Ruhr – which contained the bulk of German industry – and place it under international control; to separate and occupy the Rhineland, Germany's traditional invasion route into France; to tie the Saar, an important coal-mining area, into France's economy; and to force high reparations from Germany to pay for French recovery.[11] Some Frenchmen, notably René Massigli (ambassador to London from August 1944) and Jean Chauvel (head of the foreign ministry) thought this too harsh, but the French had a deep-seated terror of Germany after three invasions since 1870, and the thesis was seen as a vital complement to de Gaulle's policy of *grandeur*.[12] But in early 1945 the British were thinking on very different lines: they had been given a German occupation zone which included the industrial Ruhr, and they were concerned at the huge costs which could fall on Britain if this zone's economy were crippled by draconian controls.[13] More important in the short term, Britain simply refused to discuss Germany's future with de Gaulle, partly because Whitehall had no detailed plan of its own, partly because she wanted to work in unison with her two main allies, America and Russia. De Gaulle found this refusal to talk offensive.

In 1944 de Gaulle had high hopes of restoring French power by playing a major role in Germany's defeat, but France simply lacked the economic and psychological strength to do this. So the general had to rely on diplomatic success. First he turned to Britain for help. The Foreign Office hoped to impress him in November 1944, when Churchill visited Paris, with a frank discussion of policy and promises of support. But for de Gaulle this was not enough: he wanted to be treated as a Great Power immediately.[14] Therefore he turned to Russia, visiting Moscow in December. Russia and de Gaulle had a paradoxical view of each other: Stalin was contemptuous of France's 1940 defeat and did not want to rebuild her strength, but supported de Gaulle as an alternative to Vichy; de Gaulle hated communism but wanted a Russian alliance to pin Germany down after the war, please the French Communists, and prove that he did not rely only on Britain and America. But in Moscow Stalin would not treat de Gaulle as an equal any more than Churchill would, and as the price of a Franco-Soviet Treaty the Russians tried to force France to recognize a communist puppet government in Poland. Although such a treaty was signed the talks did not augur well for future Franco-Soviet relations.[15] De Gaulle got little further with French status in 1945 when he was excluded from the Yalta and Potsdam summits. But in fact there were gains to show, mainly because of Britain's policy of rebuilding French power. In early 1945 Britain expected American forces to leave Europe after the war, and therefore a strong France in Europe became even more vital to her. At Yalta, Churchill and Eden 'fought like tigers for France'.[16] (The U.S. State Department also adopted the British attitude of rebuilding France for the good of Europe.)[17] As a result she received an occupation zone in Germany, had her empire fully restored and became the fifth permanent member of the U.N. Security Council. But for this de Gaulle was completely unthankful: after Yalta he snubbed Roosevelt by refusing to meet him.

On their side the British were upset by the lack of progress on an alliance with France. While opposing a Western bloc Churchill had proved willing to pursue such an alliance and, during the talks on a Franco-Soviet Pact in December, the Foreign Office had suggested that a tripartite treaty, including Britain, be made. But de Gaulle refused, arguing that before making a treaty Britain and France should agree a common policy in Germany and the Levant.[18] In early 1945 the Foreign Office still wanted a treaty and anglophile diplomats, such as Chauvel and Massigli, supported the idea. But de Gaulle was too suspicious of the British and did not see a formal Anglo-French link as a vital necessity. So he continued to use the Foreign Office desire for an alliance to press for agreement with French aims in the Levant (where he continued to believe that British machinations rather than Arab nationalism threatened French rule) and in Germany (where, as seen above, it was impossible for Britain to agree to France's thesis). For de Gaulle such agreements were necessary to prove British goodwill and prevent a return to the unequal partnership of the 1930s. But again he was overvaluing France's importance: the British were simply not prepared to answer such demands. There was a bid to make a treaty in April, when de Gaulle's mood seemed to change, but it came to nothing.[19]

However, the issue which dominated relations when Bevin came to power was another crisis in the Levant. Since 1943 France had clung on to her few remaining rights there, the Arabs continued to demand complete independence, and the British still tried to balance their commitments to both sides. But in May 1945 the French sent troop reinforcements to the area and enraged the Arabs, who believed they were about to be coerced by force of arms. Violence erupted and the French shelled Damascus. The British, as ever, were terrified of trouble spreading to their own sphere and they intervened with troops to separate the antagonists. This episode came less than a month after Germany's defeat, when Anglo-French cooperation should have been close. Instead a furious de Gaulle declared that, if only France had the resources, there would be war with Britain! Weeks of petty insults and vain attempts to find a settlement followed.[20] Fortunately the crisis did not greatly affect British popularity in France, where the Levant seemed an obscure problem. The French Assembly even passed a resolution favouring an Anglo-French alliance, and the Foreign Office now considered it would be best if de Gaulle were to lose power.[21] But the crisis did create a complex situation where British troops were lodged between two bitter antagonists, with no obvious route to a peaceful settlement.

Especially at the personal level of Churchill and de Gaulle the

Second World War saw the continuation of the traditional love-hate relationship between Britain and France. Now the two countries faced the different, but no less difficult, world of peace. De Gaulle's conditions for a treaty, and the Levant crisis, left difficult problems for Bevin, but there were positive elements at work: both were democratic, imperial, Western European states; an alliance between them was a popular idea in both countries; and Britain had helped to restore French power. At Potsdam France seemed to regain her long-sought equality with the Big Three by joining a new body, the Council of Foreign Ministers (C.F.M.), which was intended to make a comprehensive peace settlement in Europe through a series of meetings. The question, as labour entered office, was whether these favourable factors could be turned to lasting good – or whether Britain and France would again find that their different interests brought as much division as unity.

Part I

YEARS OF
FRUSTRATION

The long road to an Anglo-French alliance
August 1945 – March 1947

1

The 'grand design' of 13 August 1945

ALTHOUGH France was hardly mentioned during the British 1945 election campaign,[1] both main parties supported her recovery: in 1943 remarks by Jan Christian Smuts that she was finished as a Great Power caused an outcry in the Commons.[2] The Labour Party supported France's revival and wanted an Anglo-French alliance to provide Britain's basic link to Europe.[3] Labour's leader, the deceptively quiet but able Clement Attlee, had gained a wide knowledge of foreign policy as Churchill's deputy Prime Minister, and supported French revival, the Western bloc and an American commitment to European security.[4] Ernest Bevin too, whose long trades union past had brought wide international experience, took a keen interest in wartime foreign policy, and though he never expected to be Foreign Secretary, he came to the fore on international issues at the Party Conferences in 1944–5. On France he was an unashamed Gaullist – always opposing Churchill's criticisms of de Gaulle – and he was referring to France, at the 1945 Party Conference, when he remarked that Labour could manage foreign policy because 'left understands left'.[5]

Despite some initial fears about the unexpected socialist victory, the Foreign Office quickly came to like the new Foreign Secretary.[6] The Conservatives too saw Bevin as an excellent choice.[7] He certainly had many gifts: a strong-minded, pragmatic and hard-working character, he was highly intelligent, though lacking a formal eduction; he was both an instinctive decision-maker and a great visionary; and many of his abilities pointed to his being a good Foreign Secretary, including an ability to grasp essentials, experience in negotiations (from the hard school of trades union disputes), and an appreciation of the international community. He soon settled into his new job, taking on the essential burdens, developing

consistent aims, and pushing his policies through Cabinet (helped
by his strong position in the party and by Attlee, who did not
greatly interfere in foreign affairs). Bevin could certainly prove
egotistical, intolerant, even jealous; and on a practical side he never
mastered parliamentary procedure, wrote badly and suffered increasing ill-health. But his only major critics were Labour left-
wingers who accused him of pursuing Tory policies, and he was to
prove a great Foreign Secretary.[8]

Soon after Potsdam Bevin requested an early meeting with the
Western Department (which handled Western European affairs),
and the ambassador in Paris, Duff Cooper, on France. He wanted to
know how to improve Anglo-French relations in general, and he
particularly wanted to look at two areas: the Levant, the obvious
crisis area, and trade, a reflection of his economic interests.[9] The
Department felt little could be done on trade, but they pressed both
for the idea of a Western bloc and for a conciliatory policy in the
Levant, and these became the main subjects at the meeting on 13
August.[10]

Despite its problems the Western bloc was still popular with the
Foreign Office as a way to increase British influence in the world
and provide security in Europe. Officials hoped Bevin could end the
delays, bring a French treaty, and move on to wider Western
European links, though obviously there first had to be talks with
France on the Levant and Germany.[11] Bevin, who had already been
briefed about the Western bloc for Potsdam, did not disappoint
them: at the 13 August meeting he declared his long-term aim to be
extensive political, economic and military co-operation throughout
Western Europe, with an Anglo-French alliance as the cornerstone.
The Big Three relationship was still paramount in British thinking,
however, and Bevin was concerned at criticism of a supposedly
'anti-Soviet' Western bloc in the Russian press and wanted to delay
action on a French alliance while he explored the Russian reaction.
(In all this, in fact, Bevin continued Eden's policy.) But support for
Western European co-operation, based on an Anglo-French
alliance, was to remain a foundation of Bevin's foreign policy. The
long-term plan of 13 August was dubbed the 'grand design' and the
Foreign Office looked forward eagerly to being able to pursue it.[12]

However, even without the Soviet problem, there were
difficulties to overcome. Here too Bevin was very positive. He
declared himself free of the animosity generated by the
Churchill–de Gaulle feud for example, and was even willing to
consider French views on Germany. But the main problem re-

mained the Levant, where British troops still kept the peace between Frenchman and Arab. Bevin already had the views of Eastern
Department officials (who handled Middle Eastern relations) on the
Levant. They still sought to balance Britain's commitments both to
Arab independence and to French rights. On one side they hoped
the Arabs would let a French presence remain in the area (perhaps
with a military base under U.N. auspices); on the other they hoped
to dissuade the French from returning to Syria (which they had
almost abandoned). But the dangers remained grave, and the
Eastern Department believed that the only genuine long-term
solution for Britain was a mutual Anglo-French troop withdrawal:
this would please the Arabs by removing French armed forces,
without humiliating the French (since the British would also be
leaving). From now on such a withdrawal became the Foreign
Office's basic aim in any settlement.

Bevin quickly recognized that a Levant settlement was needed
before his general policy of co-operation with France could
succeed. And on 10 August he was told of a hopeful development:
Count Ostrorog, France's political representative in Syria–
Lebanon, had said that a mutual Anglo-French withdrawal was
possible.[13] At the same time the defeat of Japan removed the last
good excuse – the necessities of war – for Allied troops to be in the
Levant, and made a settlement even more necessary.[14] So at the 13
August meeting the Eastern Department's ideas were forged into a
formal peace proposal. This had a mutual withdrawal as its
centrepiece, but the British added other points to help French
acceptance: they would support France's retention of cultural and
economic rights in the area, and would even allow French troops to
intervene there if disorders broke out in future. The Foreign Office
felt there were enough concessions here to tempt even de Gaulle:
hopefully the first steps towards an Anglo-French treaty could soon
be taken.[15]

The Western Department was very pleased with the 13 August
meeting and Duff Cooper felt all the differences with France could
now be easily removed. He returned to Paris and told France's
foreign minister, Georges Bidault, that an Anglo-French treaty
might soon be possible. This upset the Foreign Office because Bevin
had not yet explored the possible Russian reaction to a treaty,[16] but
it was not the first – or last – time that the ambassador exceeded his
instructions and tried to push a formal alliance along. Duff Cooper,
a popular and brave pre-war minister (he resigned over
appeasement) had failed to impress as a wartime Minister of Infor-

mation, and so he looked to the Paris embassy as the pinnacle of his career. Furthermore he desperately wanted to crown the appointment with an Anglo-French treaty, and despaired over all the delays to this. As a Conservative he was fortunate to retain the desirable Paris post, but Bevin liked Duff Cooper and his wife Diana, who were popular in France and made the embassy a glittering social centre. Besides, the Labour and Conservative Parties were largely united on international issues in the post-war years.[17]

The Foreign Office kept knowledge of their long-term grand design tightly restricted, though Parliament was told that policy towards France was under review.[18] For the moment Bevin concentrated on the Levant problem, putting Britain's peace proposal to the French ambassador, Massigli, on 16 August. Massigli was both an experienced diplomat and an anglophile, and as keen as Duff Cooper to make a treaty. He considered de Gaulle's belief that France could demand a high price for an alliance a 'dangerous illusion' and, like everyone else, he was very pleased on hearing Bevin's views about Anglo-French co-operation.[19] Encouraged by Massigli's positive attitude, and by Ostrorog's talk of withdrawal, Bevin confidently took his Levant proposals to the Cabinet on 23 August, and easily had them approved.[20]

Relations with France seemed off to an excellent start. With Churchill gone the Foreign Office line was in the ascendant and already the Levant problem looked likely to find a swift solution. This was part of a general hope as the war ended. The British, after six years of war, knew their world position was threatened by economic decline, military overextension, and the rise of America and Russia; and they feared Soviet expansion and non-co-operation. But it was hoped that an international community under the U.N. would allow Britain to withdraw safely from areas she could no longer hold, and Bevin believed a frank 'cards-on-the-table' approach would keep Russia content. Like other powers Britain was determined to ensure lasting peace and security, principally by avoiding past mistakes: just as America pressed for a new League of Nations, and Russia for old, Tsarist security aims; and just as France sought an improved version of the 1919 peace settlement; so Britain wanted an American commitment to Europe and sensible treatment of Germany (both of which failed to emerge in 1919), the development of the Commonwealth (a proven success story), and close links to Western Europe (to prevent another 1940).

But the Great Powers soon found more problems in the world than they expected, problems which radically altered old concepts: America's one-world ideal and Russia's search for security did not mix well, for example, in a situation where both possessed unprecedented might, and the old European powers had largely disintegrated. For Anglo-French relations the grand design of 13 August 1945 was to provide a sound long-term plan in fact. But the situation in which it was carried out was to change enormously, and in the short term relations were to be dogged by two problems that had troubled Britain and France since the 1920s: the Levant and Germany.

2

A settlement for the Levant

August 1945–March 1946

DESPITE the high hopes of the 13 August meeting for a swift settlement, the Levant problem was to dominate Anglo-French relations for another six months, largely because of de Gaulle's insistence that France could remain a Middle East power. The very day that Bevin put his Levant peace proposals to the Cabinet in fact, Massigli delivered an unfavourable reply to the British ideas. The French, instead, wanted Britain's full support for their 'special position' in Syria–Lebanon, and insisted that a French garrison must remain there – a condition which ruled out all hope of a mutual withdrawal.[1] Despite the change of government in London and moderate counsels in the French foreign ministry, the Quai d'Orsay, de Gaulle was as stubborn as ever.[2] At first the British were undaunted: their response to the French note was to confirm their support for French rights in the Levant, point out Massigli's and Ostrorog's positive views, and insist on mutual withdrawal as the only way to a settlement.[3] But in early September the Levant problem sank sadly back into stagnation. Massigli could offer no hope of altering France's insistence on reaching a satisfactory agreement in the Levant before an Anglo-French treaty was made, and de Gaulle's view, if anything, seemed to be hardening. A visit by him to America in late August went surprisingly well, notably in talks with Roosevelt's successor, President Truman. To de Gaulle, Americans seemed as arrogant as ever, and he was certain they would clash with Russia, but Roosevelt's death in April removed the main anti-French element in Washington. Truman quite liked France (he had served there in the First World War) and even told de Gaulle that America was too pro-British in the Levant.[4] The general returned to Europe confident of U.S. friendship and ill-disposed to Britain. He condemned the moderation of Ostrorog and Massigli, declaring that a mutual withdrawal would only justify British policy, and he refused to discuss France's position in the Levant unless Britain's position in the Middle East was also discussed. The idea that France's treatment of the Arabs and the erosion of her power by the war made her position untenable did not occur to him.[5]

Fortunately this situation improved in mid-September when the Council of Foreign Ministers (C.F.M.), established at Potsdam to make peace treaties in Europe, met for the first time in London. Bidault, the French foreign minister, wanted to discuss an Anglo-French alliance at the conference,[6] and just before it opened de Gaulle gave an interview to *The Times* which, though insisting on solving the Levant and German issues before an alliance, was friendly towards Britain. (The general probably wanted to please his own people in doing this: France's first post-war elections were due soon, and an Anglo-French treaty was popular.[7]) The C.F.M. itself was mainly noteworthy for its arguments between Russia and the Anglo-Americans. But Anglo-French relations were strengthened during the conference by Russian tactics. On 22 September Molotov, Russia's foreign minister, declared that France should have no say in making any European peace treaties other than the German and Italian ones. But when the conference had opened France had been allowed into *all* the discussions, including treaties with Finland and Hitler's Eastern European allies, and Bevin (supported by James Byrnes, the American Secretary of State) refused to reverse this position. Days of argument on this problem led to the C.F.M.'s adjournment in early October. This dispute was actually an excuse for a breakdown – even Molotov admitted its triviality – but British support for France (in the tradition of Yalta and Potsdam) contrasted with Russia's treatment of her as a secondary power.[8] Against this background, the way to a Levant agreement was paved.

On 13 September Massigli and Chauvel, the leading anglophiles in the French camp, were reminded that Bevin wanted a mutual withdrawal, and three days later Attlee, Bevin and Bidault discussed the Levant at Chequers. Away from de Gaulle, Bidault proved surprisingly forthcoming: he said France would withdraw if her 'special position', and a single military base in the Lebanon, were assured. This, alongside the behaviour of Ostrorog and Massigli, showed that de Gaulle's diplomats did not generally share his views on the Levant problem (though they did hope to maintain a presence in the area) or his cavalier attitude towards a British alliance. But how they could win the general over to their approach remained a major problem.[9] French officials maintained their positive approach over the next week and, on 25 September, Chauvel pre-

sented two memoranda to the Foreign Office which were to be of
central importance over the next months. The first memorandum
proposed a mutual withdrawal, though with a token French force to
remain in Lebanon until a French military base was formally established there (as they hoped) under the auspices of the U.N. The
second memorandum, however, proposed an agreement whereby
Britain and France would respect each other's spheres of influence
in the Middle East in future, thus guaranteeing that Britain would
not replace France in the Levant, in the way de Gaulle feared. The
first memorandum seemed a reasonable plan, and a revised version
of it was soon provisionally accepted by officials on both sides.[10]
But the second memorandum caused some debate in the Foreign
Office: the Eastern Department (looking to British interests in the
Middle East) argued that France had destroyed her own position in
the Levant and could not expect Britain to stay out of the area
entirely now; but the Western Department (looking to Western
Europe) were willing to follow what they called a 'self-denying
ordinance' in Syria–Lebanon.[11]

Bevin and Bidault had begun their relationship well in London,
though the Frenchman was a very different character from his
British colleague. A small, frail, nervous man, of an academic
background, Bidault was nevertheless politically ambitious and personally courageous, rising to be head of the Resistance during the
war. Like de Gaulle he was an ardent nationalist and a student of
history, but he and the general disliked each other and frequently
differed over international issues. Bidault's power base was France's
new christian democratic party, the Mouvement Républicain
Populaire (M.R.P.), which he had helped to establish. He was quite
young, very interested in foreign policy and, though the Foreign
Office had little love for him, he seemed likely to be important in
international affairs for some time.[12]

On 9 October the British Cabinet approved the evacuation plan
that officials had drawn up, but the second French memorandum
was not fully discussed, simply because Chauvel and Massigli (to
British surprise) had said it was *not* a condition for a French
withdrawal.[13] The next day, however, Massigli changed his line on
the second memorandum, informing Bevin that it would be 'helpful' to have such an agreement on Middle East policy: Bidault and
Chauvel were unwilling to suggest a withdrawal to de Gaulle without some important British concession. Given the general's previous views this was understandable, but Bevin was upset by the
shifts in French policy, and Duff Cooper doubted anyway that

de Gaulle would be impressed by a general agreement based on the second memorandum.[14] Suddenly the situation seemed to be returning to stagnation: Ostrorog talked of consolidating French rule in Lebanon; the Arabs were restless; and Paris now seemed to be playing for time. Bevin still hoped for a swift settlement in the Levant, however, and his exasperated officials searched for some new initiative to resolve the problems.[15] Duff Cooper suggested that a unilateral British declaration-of-intent to leave the Levant would convince de Gaulle of their good intentions; but this might only have panicked the Arabs into believing that Britain would abandon them to the French army.[16] Some sort of general agreement, based on Chauvel's second memorandum seemed the only way forward and Oliver Harvey (the Assistant Under-Secretary, and an expert on France) ruled that one should be attempted. Talks on this were held with Massigli, but since the Foreign Office still refused to form an Anglo-French 'front' in the Middle East, the result was an innocuous document, by which the two sides merely promised to exchange information and to refrain from 'injuring' each other in the region – there was not even any formal British support for France's claim to a military base. The agreement seemed unlikely to impress de Gaulle, but Bevin approved it on 29 October.[17]

Then, however, even hopes of an early French reply to the proposals were disappointed. First Bidault shrank from putting the proposals to de Gaulle. Then on seeing the agreements the general proved cautious, though not, as Whitehall feared, completely negative. Next came France's first post-war elections (for a Constituent Assembly) which were followed by long political wranglings, as the communists, who emerged as the strongest party, pressed de Gaulle to give them key Cabinet posts.[18] Movement on the Levant only restarted in late November when Bidault apologetically requested some changes to the evacuation plan. Fortunately, however, these were of a minor nature (and the British had some of their own) and suddenly an agreement was completed and signed on 13 December: military experts were to meet and organize a mutual withdrawal; some French troops would remain in Lebanon until a regional security system was formed under the U.N. (with, of course, a French military base); and the general agreement of October was accepted by Paris. For the moderates on both sides it seemed a major success. Unfortunately the success was shortlived.

Within a few weeks it became clear that the 13 December agreement satisfied neither de Gaulle nor the Arabs. De Gaulle's approval of the evacuation plan was not given because of the general agreement, which never looked likely to impress him, but because his officials interpreted the withdrawal agreement to mean that a token French force *alone* would remain in Lebanon, awaiting the foundation of a military base, while all the British forces withdrew. In this de Gaulle sensed a chance to reassert France's position without British interference. But Whitehall had a different interpretation: they argued that since the withdrawal was to be mutual, *some* British forces should remain alongside the French, until a U.N. base was established. Actually the agreement itself was at fault: it was based on a mutual withdrawal (Britain's aim since August), but only spoke specifically of a French force remaining in the Levant, awaiting a U.N. base. It was a costly oversight, because on 7 January de Gaulle broke off discussions. Bevin saw this as another example of France's unrealistic hope of remaining a Middle East power.[19] In the French Cabinet, on 17 January, de Gaulle launched into a tirade against British 'machinations' in the Levant, while Bidault vainly sought to make a moderate voice heard.[20]

The Arabs disliked the agreement for very different reasons. Since August, Anglo-French negotiators had avoided the complication of introducing Syria–Lebanon into the talks on their own future; but now the Europeans were to be given a lesson in the impossibility of dictating terms to the Arabs on the pre-1940 scale. The Arabs' simple aim had always been to end French influence, and Britain could not afford to ignore this because the Middle East – strategically placed and with huge oil resources – was vital to the Empire's security. It was an area of constant worry for Bevin, and in September he had told British officials that he would not press French privileges in the Levant to the point of alienating Arab opinion.[21] This principle guided him throughout the long Levant negotiations. Initially, in fact, Syria and Lebanon welcomed the 13 December agreement as a way to remove the French, but on reconsidering, they grew suspicious about the retention of some French units in Lebanon and over the agreement on long-term Anglo-French co-operation. Britain tried to counter these doubts by assuring the Arabs that their independence was certain and that some British troops would remain alongside the French. But Arab doubts gradually hardened into opposition and then, in early January, the Syrian Parliament voted for an appeal to the U.N., which was due to meet in London (for its first Assembly since being established), to remove the French forces. This showed that the Arabs could find new ways to achieve their aims, should the Europeans prove difficult.[22] Thus by early January, after months of trying to satisfy both the Arabs and the French in the Levant, British efforts (in the words of the Permanent Under-Secretary, Alexander Cadogan) had 'got nowhere'.[23]

The apparent deadlock of early January was broken far more quickly than the British dared hope, mainly thanks to three factors. The first was the strengthening of Anglo-French friendship when France's great power status was threatened by another meeting of the Big Three, in December at Moscow. This meeting was hastily called by the American Secretary of State, James Byrnes, to try to resolve the differences with Russia which had arisen at the London C.F.M. But in organizing it, Byrnes – a born improvisor, with little international experience – simply left the French out (to prevent a repeat of the London arguments over her role), and even threatened to attend without Bevin. Bevin, however, was determined to defend France and went to Moscow only on condition that Germany and other issues of interest to her were not discussed.[24] The meeting's results were not unfavourable to France: on the European peace treaties it was decided that she could discuss all the treaties (though she could help to draft only the German and Italian ones); and it was decided to hold a formal peace conference on the 'minor' European treaties (that is, excluding the German peace treaty) in Paris. De Gaulle was enraged at France's treatment, but Bidault managed to have the Moscow decisions accepted by the Cabinet. Once again Britain had defended French interests from the 'super-powers'.[25]

Far more important was the sudden resignation of de Gaulle on 20 January. Though in mid-1945 British officials would have welcomed such an event, in early 1946 they were better disposed to the general, particularly because he seemed the best barrier against the French communists. But de Gaulle was tiring, France's economic problems were unsolved, and his hopes of achieving a semi-authoritarian constitution (with himself as President) were opposed by the political parties. The de Gaulle myth, founded in 1940, was now stained by reality. So, after warning a few people, he resigned. His memoirs portray a world waiting for his departure, eager to take advantage of France. But while there were rumours of his likely resignation, when it came most people were taken by surprise, including Duff Cooper. Almost everyone expected that he planned to return; they could not guess how far away his return would be. After the resignation, London expected much improved relations with France. De Gaulle's attitude to Britain was always ambiguous: he admired her stability and relied on her wartime aid;

but he resented her too, believing that France and she were in a state
of peaceful, but bitter, rivalry. Nowhere did his views cause more
damage than in the Levant, and his resignation did more than
anything else to bring about a settlement there.[26]

The third factor was the use of the U.N. which, with all the
world's hopes for peace centred on it, provided a new, respected
forum for settling disputes. In January the Syrian and Lebanese
delegations arrived in London and confirmed that they would put
the Levant issue to the U.N. Assembly. They wanted to concentrate
their attacks on France, not Britain (which had been defending
them, effectively, since June) – and the moderate Lebanese even
kept the Foreign Office informed about their plans – but British
officials were very upset at being taken before a world tribunal
where, in the complexities of the Levant situation, they would
inevitably appear as a 'colonial' power alongside the French.[27] In
fact the British and Bidault hastily tried to resolve the problem
before the U.N. debates began. Ostrorog was sent to talk with the
Lebanese delegation, but failed to reach an agreement with them,
principally because the French still refused to set a date for their
final withdrawal.[28] Meanwhile, at an Anglo-French level Bevin and
Bidault agreed to restart talks on the basis of the 13 December
agreement.[29] But events had gone too far for such a solution to
succeed: a U.N. resolution was about to end European power in the
Levant for ever.

On 4 February Bevin told the Cabinet that he would adhere to
any U.N. decision on the Levant. The British wanted to respect the
new world security body wherever possible, and were thoroughly
disenchanted with the whole Levant situation; and Bevin's
approach seemed the best way to extricate British forces from a
difficult situation with honour.[30] In the Security Council Britain's
main aim was to avoid criticism of herself. This was made easier by
the fact that on 13 December she (and France) had agreed to a
withdrawal in principle, anyway. Several proposals were put in the
U.N. before a moderate American resolution, which simply expressed the hope that European forces would leave the Levant, received
majority approval. Although the Russians vetoed this resolution,
Britain and France agreed to carry it out.[31] U.N. supporters saw this
as a great success.[32]

The British immediately decided to withdraw from the Levant as
soon as practicable, and to cancel all parts of the 13 December
agreement contrary to the U.N. resolution. Ironically, this upset
both the Arabs and the French. The Arabs feared that the British

would leave while the French did not; the French feared that all the 13 December agreement was lost (actually the parts of the agreement based on Chauvel's second memorandum of September 1945 still survived). It took several days before Bidault agreed to draw up entirely new arrangements for a withdrawal, and even then the French caused delays.[33] Although British troops finally left the Levant in June – one year after their original intervention – the French claimed that they could not leave until April 1947. But, to the end, Britain remained true to the principle of placating the French: help was given to them with shipping facilities, and the Foreign Office refused to be drawn into public criticism of the French delays.[34]

In March 1946 the Levant problem was effectively settled. The Arabs had their independence; the British had safeguarded their own Middle East position; and France had ceased to be a Middle East power. (With French troops gone the Arabs had no reason to grant her any rights in the region.) De Gaulle's hopes of remaining in the area had made it a hesitant settlement, but once he had resigned Bidault's moderate line had won through. For Anglo-French relations the Levant issue had brought long arguments, on an issue which had existed since the fall of the Ottomans, and which was largely irrelevant to the British and French people. The Levant problem certainly required a solution in 1945–6, but not single-minded attention to the detriment of wider Anglo-French co-operation. There were positive elements in the situation: the two foreign ministries always pursued a moderate line and the British did not swerve from their intention to rebuild French power. The Levant, however, was only one problem which de Gaulle wanted to solve before making an Anglo-French treaty, and unfortunately the other – Germany – was also the cause of grave Anglo-French disagreements in 1945–6.

3

The Western bloc, the German problem and the stagnation of Anglo-French relations

February–July 1946

WHILE Britain and France concentrated on the Levant problem the idea of a treaty between them slipped into the background. But Bevin's great aim of Western European co-operation remained and in late 1945 he had explored the Russian attitude to this (as he had decided to do at the 13 August meeting). He raised the idea of an Anglo-French treaty with Molotov during the London C.F.M. and was assured that Russia had no objections to it.[1] But British officials still feared that a wider Western bloc would offend Moscow and in November, when Oliver Harvey drafted a Cabinet Paper (ready to use should a French treaty soon become possible) he opposed the idea of a Western bloc because of the Russian complication. This upset some officials, including the Permanent Under-Secretary, Alexander Cadogan, who felt a Western bloc was needed regardless of Russian views: but for the moment Big Three unity was more vital to Bevin than regional security in Western Europe.[2] Then, however, during the Moscow C.F.M., Stalin himself told Bevin that British links to Western Europe were quite understandable. This was very reassuring to the British, who told the French of Stalin's view, but actually Soviet policy was confusing: they never officially opposed a Western bloc, but the Moscow press showed a deep suspicion of it.[3]

Meanwhile de Gaulle revived his own ideas of 1943–4 for Western European co-operation. In *The Times* interview in September he spoke of Western Europe as a geographical and political whole, with Britain and France at the centre, and in October he declared the Rhine to be an 'artery' uniting Europe. He continued such speeches on a visit to Belgium, and even revealed a positive side to his German policy – hoping that the new, weakened Germany would play a positive role in Europe. But his ideas remained imprecise, and seemed to contradict his policy of French *grandeur*; like Bevin, he feared offending the Russians with any Western bloc. (Furthermore the French people showed little support for his schemes.)[4] However, there were many other enthusiasts for Western European co-operation: in Britain in late 1945 and early 1946 Lord Vansittart (a former head of the Foreign Office and a great believer in the French alliance) and various M.P.s expressed disappointment with Bevin's failure to form a Western bloc;[5] and the Belgian foreign minister Spaak again in November pressed London to take up the leadership of Western Europe, proposing the formation of a series of military committees in the region.[6]

The Western bloc continued to be delayed, however, not so much by Bevin's insistence on placating Moscow, but because the vital cornerstone of any Western bloc – the Anglo-French treaty – still faced de Gaulle's twin conditions of satisfactory agreements on Germany and the Levant. In 1945–6 London vainly tried to persuade Paris that an alliance and the German problem should be treated as entirely separate issues. The British certainly had good reasons for arguing this: in late 1945 they had no comprehensive plans of their own for Germany's future and, anyway, had to consider Soviet and American views; and Germany was a *four*-power issue, on which Britain and France could not dictate a settlement. But de Gaulle was unswayed by such considerations. He was determined to enter an Anglo-French alliance on his own terms, and he wanted British support for his thesis to improve its chances of acceptance.

The most important issue for Anglo-French relations in Germany in 1945–6 was the Ruhr, which lay inside the British zone and which, of course, de Gaulle wanted to separate from the rest of Germany because of its economic importance. In September 1945, at the London C.F.M., Bidault presented a memorandum to explain French views on the Ruhr, but the C.F.M.'s agenda was so crowded that this memorandum could not be discussed. Instead Bidault was asked to express French opinions through normal diplomatic channels.[7] (It became clear at London in fact that because of the workload of making the peace treaties, the German treaty – the most important and complex – would not be discussed until last. For France this meant an exasperating wait before her views could be fully discussed.) The last months of 1945 were spent in these diplomatic explanations of France's case. In fact it had already been decided to hold talks between Anglo-French experts on the Ruhr: Attlee, Bevin and Bidault had decided to do this on 16 September, during the same discussion that began progress on the Levant problem.[8] These experts' talks were held in October and Anglo-French differences on the problem were soon apparent. The French pressed for the creation of an independent Ruhr state to weaken Germany's economic and military strength decisively. But the British, with responsibility for the Ruhr, feared the economic chaos that would result from separating Germany's industrial heart: they believed that Britain, already financially exhausted by the war, might then have to pour huge amounts of money into Germany to stabilize her economy. Since these were preliminary discussions, however, serious Anglo-French arguments were avoided.[9] Later, in November and December, French views were also put to Washington and Moscow.[10]

The Ruhr became a more openly divisive issue for Anglo-French relations in 1946 as the Levant problem reached a settlement. On 4 January a Foreign Office meeting decided that even if the Levant problem were settled, the Ruhr would require a full discussion before an Anglo-French treaty could be made. The Western Department hoped that British views on the Ruhr might be ready in February, so that Bevin and Bidault could discuss the issue during the U.N. Assembly in London. Meanwhile all other moves towards a Western bloc had to be delayed: Spaak's latest schemes were given a non-committal response, and moves were made to stop Lord Vansittart criticizing the government over the issue in the Lords.[11] But hopes of swift progress on the Ruhr, as on the Levant, increased enormously with de Gaulle's resignation. There were signs that the general's successors would reverse his hard-line foreign policy: the new premier, Felix Gouin, even publicly declared himself in favour of an Anglo-French treaty.[12]

The U.N. conference did not dash these hopes. Although, unfortunately, the British were unable to have a detailed Ruhr plan ready in time, Bevin's views were now clear. Most importantly, he favoured the retention of the Ruhr-Rhineland in Germany, and sought to prevent future German aggression by stiff industrial controls on the Ruhr (to limit its production levels, forbid the manufacture of armaments, and so on). The British felt that the separation of the Ruhr, as France wanted, would cause unacceptable economic chaos.[13] Bevin and Bidault discussed their respective views on 1 February, and Bidault immediately pointed to the root of their differences: the French, terrified of yet another German invasion, wanted the more extreme, political solution of Ruhr independence; the British, more removed from the German menace and concerned with their own financial problems, preferred economic controls.[14] On 18 February the two men met again and Bevin said it was impossible for him to support France's view on the Ruhr in international discussions. Their conversation then went off at a tangent about the Soviet threat: Bevin suggested that an independent Ruhr would so weaken Germany's rump that Russia could easily take it over; but Bidault replied that Russia might well seize Germany anyway and that it was best to separate the vital Ruhr area and keep it in Western hands. This was the first important indication London had that the French feared Russian as well as German expansionism.[15]

Despite these differences, the Levant settlement at the U.N. conference left Britain very confident about Anglo-French relations. On 7 March the Lord Chancellor told the Lords that an Anglo-French treaty might soon be possible, and Gouin now said that a treaty could be signed without prior agreement on the Ruhr. Thus encouraged, one official, Anthony Rumbold, took Oliver Harvey's draft Cabinet Paper of November 1945 out of storage, and sought action upon it. (Notably Rumbold felt that support for a Western bloc should still be avoided in the paper, not only because of Soviet suspicion, but also because Holland and Norway had shown no enthusiasm for a bloc since the war ended.)

Duff Cooper too, as always, wanted to make a treaty, but importantly, *he* felt that the German problem must still be resolved first. This view caused some debate in the Foreign Office. Many officials wanted to pursue a treaty immediately because more French elections were due in June and the British wanted to encourage an anti-Communist vote: a treaty might have been useful for this because it was still a popular idea in France. On 29 March a Foreign Office meeting decided to resolve the Ruhr issue *before* a treaty was negotiated, but on 3 April, at a high-level meeting of Bevin, Harvey and Orme Sargent (who had succeeded Cadogan as Permanent Under-Secretary in February) this earlier decision was reversed, and instead it was decided to send Harvey to Paris to see whether an Anglo-French treaty was possible or not. The precise reason for this was that Gouin had now gone further than ever before, and spoken

of controlling the Ruhr by economic controls – as Britain wanted –
not political independence. This, coming after de Gaulle's resignation and the Levant settlement, encouraged the British to believe that de Gaulle's successor was about to reverse the general's
policy on Germany and allow a treaty.[16]

But Harvey's mission was to end in a minor humiliation. When
he arived in Paris on 4 April, it was clear he had run across a deep
political argument in the French Cabinet. Gouin and the Socialists
did want to abandon de Gaulle's German policy in favour of a
moderate line, but Bidault and the M.R.P., anxious to attract
'Gaullist' votes and to appeal to the French people's deep-seated
fear of Germany, did not. Bidault, in contrast to his moderate views
on the Levant, was a genuine supporter of a hard-line policy
towards Germany. On 5 April Bidault's line won through in the
Cabinet because of support from the third main party in France's
'tripartite' government, the Communists. At first Bidault said that
an Anglo-French treaty might still be possible without a German
agreement (and the Foreign Office actually warned Washington and
Moscow to expect a treaty). But on 9 April the French Cabinet
announced that a treaty must still await the settlement of outstand-
ing differences. The British felt snubbed by this blunt and unexpected announcement, which seemed to make a mockery of
Bidault's supposed support for a treaty, and they returned to the
position they had held in early 1945: they would not go 'begging'
France for a treaty again. Even some French diplomats were upset
by Bidault's behaviour, but Duff Cooper was critical of his own
side: he pointed out that Harvey had rushed across to Paris with
little preparation even though London knew that French politics
were confused and that Germany was an emotive issue in France. A
little more care and patience would have made all the difference.[17]

After the April fiasco, and only weeks after the successful Levant
settlement, Anglo-French relations began to stagnate. The new
French government had decided to continue with de Gaulle's
German thesis but the British were still no nearer to liking this.
World interest now centred on Paris where the peace conference on
minor treaties (July–October) was preceded by another long
C.F.M. in two sessions (April–July). The workload of these conferences would have made Anglo-French treaty negotiations
difficult anyway, but on 17 April the British Cabinet made a treaty
even less likely by finally rejecting the French Ruhr plan in favour
of economic controls. Bevin did hope to please France with some
special political arrangements in the Ruhr, such as the creation of a

new Ruhr province to help enforce the economic controls on the industries there, but otherwise there was little to offer France.[18] At the Paris C.F.M. the Big Three continued to avoid formal talks on a German treaty until the lesser treaties were finalized.

Bevin and Bidault met in Paris on 26 April and again discussed the Ruhr. Bevin was anxious to please the French, and although he was unwilling to hold formal four-power talks on the issue he did offer to give an informal outline of British views on the Ruhr to France. Two days later Harvey held such informal talks with French officials and got a very positive response. For a time the optimistic British even believed that an Anglo-French agreement on the principle of economic controls rather than political separation of the Ruhr might still be possible.[19] But on 9 May Bidault repeated his support for an independent Ruhr to Bevin, arguing that mere economic controls would gradually be eroded by a future German government. A full report on the Ruhr was drawn up by Anglo-French experts in May, but it simply outlined the two sides' differences, and could provide no basis for agreement.[20] At a personal level relations were close enough, and on 15 May Bidault again insisted that he wanted a treaty.[21] But on Germany there was deadlock.

In mid-1946 Anglo-French exchanges in Germany became completely confused by American and Russian actions. During the C.F.M. there were some talks on the German problem and in them Molotov followed an obstructive, even sinister, policy. He refused to begin any preparations for a German peace treaty, he demanded a share in controlling the Ruhr, and he scotched all discussion about an important, new American initiative for a four-power treaty to guarantee Germany's demilitarization in future. (Known as the Byrnes' Treaty, this idea appealed to Britain and France as a way to ensure European peace and get a long-term American commitment to the continent's security.)[22] Finally, on 10 July, Molotov made a public appeal for popular German support: he declared that Russia wanted to rejuvenate Germany's economy. To Americans this seemed like a clear attempt to win Germany for Moscow, and Byrnes responded by inviting any other occupying power to unite with the American zone in order to salvage German unity. Britain, who was eager to share the huge cost of her zone with someone better able to afford it, accepted this invitation. Eventually, in September, Byrnes made his own appeal for German support at Stuttgart and, among other things, declared that American troops would now remain in Europe until Germany's future was settled.

In retrospect, it was clear that these events divided Germany between East and West, and increased Soviet-American tension. The effect on Anglo-French relations was threefold. First, the vanity of the hope that Britain and France, even together, could shape Germany's future was fully revealed. British and French opinions were reduced to irrelevancies – in stark contrast to 1919 when America withdrew from Europe and Russia was in revolution. The hopelessness of French aims was especially clear: Russia and America now wished to win the Germans over to their side, not to force a harsh peace on them (though, for the moment, both East and West preserved some of their original hard-line views). Second, Britain's decision to unite with the American zone separated her from the French. Some elements in the Quai d'Orsay wanted to join the new Anglo-American 'bizone', and London and Washington hoped this could be done, but, as early as June, Chauvel had warned the Americans that France could not take sides if East and West divided in Germany: the French people, with their deep-seated anti-Germanism, were far from ready for a mild policy towards their recent conquerors, such as Byrnes now wanted; and the communists in the French government made a break with Russia impossible. So Bidault adhered to the French thesis, steered a middle course between Russia and America, and continued to hope for four-power talks on a German peace treaty.[23] Meanwhile, at the Paris meetings, he collected prestige both as the host and as a mediator. This did not offend the Anglo-Americans, however: instead Bevin and Byrnes strengthened their support for one part of the French thesis: in December they allowed Paris to erect a customs barrier, around the Saar, as a step towards its economic juncture with France.[24]

The third effect of the mid-1946 events was to reduce Anglo-French talks on Germany to uselessness. In late April Bidault had been able to restate the French thesis to the C.F.M. but with no result.[25] In late May Duff Cooper sent a spirited defence of French plans for the Ruhr to London, and Bevin considered it 'interesting' enough to present as a Cabinet Paper, but it did not change British policy.[26] On 4 June Bevin told the Commons that though he favoured the Saar's economic union with France, he could not accept French views on the Ruhr.[27] Undaunted, Duff Cooper tried to raise the subject of an Anglo-French treaty again in July. First he went to Bidault, who was not interested; then he appealed to the Foreign Office, only to have Harvey declare that Britain 'need not run after the French'. Harvey was still smarting from the April rebuff and now viewed a treaty as a very long-term affair, which would have to await the formation of a stable French government and a German peace treaty.[28] In September Anglo-French experts again discussed the Ruhr, but these were the first such talks since May and neither side had changed their position in the meantime.[29]

In the summer of 1946 the German problem looked likely to delay an Anglo-French treaty indefinitely. The hopes raised by de Gaulle's resignation and the Levant settlement had been dashed; Bidault had maintained de Gaulle's German thesis and London and Paris had disagreed fundamentally on the Ruhr issue. The British tried to placate the French wherever possible in Germany but there were limits to how far they could go in doing this, especially because of their own financial liabilities in the Ruhr. The French, for their part, had adopted positions in Germany which looked reasonable enough – that the country should be prevented from making another war, and that Britain should show her goodwill towards France before a treaty was made – but they overvalued their own strength, refused to compromise, and showed an exasperating inconsistency by claiming to want a treaty while refusing to negotiate one. A year after Labour's election victory, René Massigli was very concerned with the failure to progress on an Anglo-French treaty. He was also concerned at Britain's suspicion of the Communist influence in Paris, and at France's disappointment with the scale of British economic assistance since the war.[30] It was in the field of economics, however, that Bevin was about to bring a much-needed fillip to Anglo-French relations.

4

Economics, politics and an unexpected advance

July–September 1946

AT THE MEETING of 13 August 1945, Bevin had pressed for economic as well as political co-operation with France and Western Europe. In 1945 all the world's leaders, having experienced the terrible results of the 1930s depression, had economic policies to parallel their political aims. It has already been seen that Spaak and de Gaulle's wartime planners wanted Western European economic links after the war. And the Americans, supported by the British, wanted to create a new world economic system, known as 'multilateralism', in parallel to the political system of the U.N. Multilateralism sought a freer world trading system in which all countries would compete on equal terms (reversing the pre-war economic nationalism) to maximize the use of resources and avoid another depression. In 1944 an International Monetary Fund (to maintain stable exchange rates) and a World Bank (to finance reconstruction and development) had been formed as part of this policy, and it was intended to form an international trading body to stimulate world commerce and replace the clumsy bilateral trading arrangements which had developed.

Unfortunately economic, like political, plans faced enormous problems in the post-war situation. Much of the American global economic plan never emerged, and even in the more limited area of Anglo-French trade there were serious problems. The basic difficulty for Bevin's bold hopes of an active economic policy (not only in Western Europe, but in the colonies and Middle East), was that Britain, strained enormously by the war, was simply incapable of using resources to help others. The Foreign Secretary often despaired over this situation to Attlee.[1] The problem had, in fact, been seen before the war ended when the French, seeking to revive their shattered economy, had asked for British aid. Britain had been able to help rebuild the French transport system, but (to her own disappointment) could offer Paris almost no food or raw materials.[2] After the war, when all Europe faced inflation, food and fuel shortages, and the destruction of housing and factories, Britain herself had to turn to America for a large loan. It was to America too that France turned in 1946.

The French were always disappointed with the limits of British economic help. The most important area where Paris expected aid was coal, which was desperately needed to heat homes and fuel industry, and which France was unable to supply herself. By mid-1945 Britain, through her occupation zone, controlled the great Ruhr coalfields, and all Europeans hoped to see these tapped for themselves. Inter-Allied bodies were established to do this in fact, and France became the main recipient of Ruhr coal exports, but the volume of supplies never satisfied Paris. Many factors limited the exports from Germany: some coal had to be used in Germany (much of it for consumption by Allied troops), the mines had to be restored to working order after the war, and there was a lack of skilled labour.[3] Furthermore Britain's zone soon became such a financial burden that coal was retained there to help revive the Ruhr economy and minimize the British costs in keeping the population content: in June 1946 a moratorium on the coal exports was suggested to allow the zone to recover.[4] The British constantly tried to familiarize the French with these problems, but the French were unsympathetic and accused London of putting the Germans before its Allies.[5] The situation only grew worse: late in the year London decided to attempt a decisive resolution of the zone's economic problems, and this, inevitably, meant new, tighter limits on coal exports. These were introduced at the end of the year, but Bevin, realizing the likely effect of this on the French public, delayed a public announcement of British intentions until after the French elections.[6]

French political difficulties were one factor which encouraged the British to try to help France's economic problems in 1946. After de Gaulle's resignation, there were two main political problems in France. The first was the existence of a weak, coalition government in which three large parties – the M.R.P., the Socialists and the Communists – looked to their own interests, united only by the need to draft a new French constitution and by fear of de Gaulle's return. Originally all three parties were quite radical, but they became more and more divided in 1946 as the M.R.P. began to draw right-wing support, while the others competed for working-class votes. The second problem was the strength and importance of the communists who, helped by their role in the Resistance, had gained more than a quarter of the vote in October 1945 to become the largest party. Inevitably, for the sake of national unity, de Gaulle had had to include the Communists in his Cabinet, but they remained distinct from the other parties and practically owed allegiance to a foreign power – the Soviet Union. This was of great concern to many Frenchmen and to the British, especially when East–West tension increased during 1946.

Whatever his faults, General de Gaulle had provided a semblance of order and strength in France. When he left some British observers felt France could no longer play the role of a great power.[7] Duff Cooper was soon approached by Frenchmen who feared that the economic problems and Communist influence in France were a recipe for civil strife. One, General Billotte, asked Britain to support a new party he claimed to be forming.[8] In the Foreign Office concern about France's internal problems centred on the Communist threat. Some officials argued that the M.R.P. and Socialists would control the Communists and that Britain must co-operate with any French government, but others feared the communists might soon dominate the French government and pursue an anti-British policy under Moscow's direction. There was general agreement that Communist support should be discouraged if possible. The lack of intelligence sources makes a full appreciation of this issue impossible, but in countering the communists the British apparently ruled out direct involvement in French politics (there was horror when Duff Cooper passed Billotte's request to London without rejecting it), and used indirect means to try to raise the standing of Western-style democracy in France and lower communism's appeal. Specific aims for achieving this were the successful resolution of the Levant and German problems, and increases in economic aid to France.[9] In March 1946 Western Department officials argued forcefully that major economic aid must be provided to France to improve the standing of the pro-Western parties before the next (June) elections. France's position was discussed in terms of the 'domino theory': if she fell, it was said, the rest of Western Europe would follow, leaving Britain as the last democratic bastion in Europe. France was the key to Europe.

However, when, on 29 March, the Foreign Office looked at what economic aid could be given to France it was very limited: all that could be suggested was a loan of fats, more discussions on the Ruhr coal problem, and encouragement to America to give France a large loan (negotiations for such a loan were currently under way). This appalling situation was a major reason why, in early April, the British seized the chance given by Gouin's speeches to rush Harvey off to Paris to see if an Anglo-French treaty was possible. As officials admitted, a treaty was the cheapest thing Britain could offer to publicize the cause of democracy in France.[10] The Americans and Russians also tried to interfere indirectly in French politics in 1946: Washington (like London) used economic aid;[11] Moscow during the Paris Conferences reversed its position of September 1945, and allowed Bidault into all the peace treaty discussions.[12] The effect of such propaganda is hard to judge but the Communists received a severe setback when the first draft of France's new constitution (largely shaped by them) was defeated in a referendum.[13] After this a new Constituent Assembly had to be elected, to draft another constitution. Before these elections Gouin made another request for British economic aid – for openly political reasons – but was turned down. Attlee had now ruled out all such loans on the grounds that Britain could not afford them.[14] However, again this British failure did not harm the democrats: the June elections left the M.R.P. as the largest party and Bidault became premier as well as foreign minister.

After this French politics remained confused, especially since de Gaulle returned to active politics in mid-1946, attracting right-wing support. The British viewed his return as unfavourably as they would a Communist government.[15] But the Communists remained the main problem: Massigli sensed that their influence made the British wary of co-operation with France;[16] and in the summer Bevin told Bidault that Britain and France could not 'carry on a conversation ... with a third Great Power in the cupboard' (a reference to Soviet influence in Paris via the Communists). In September Bevin said that the Communists' power made it more necessary to await a French initiative on a treaty, rather than to go 'begging' them for one.[17] Despite Bidault's attempts to reassure Bevin, the Foreign Office were convinced that there was widespread Communist infiltration in the Quai d'Orsay.[18] By late 1946 political instability and the Communist influence seemed engrained into French politics. They would continue to harm Anglo-French co-operation in future.

In late July 1946, when Massigli became very concerned about the general stagnation in Anglo-French relations, economic problems seemed as difficult as ever. On 26 July Ashley Clarke, Minister at the Paris embassy, discussed economic relations with Hervé Alphand, now the Quai's economic chief. Alphand's specific concern here was Britain's failure to import more French goods. This problem had been growing for months because Britain was unwilling to take more of what were basically luxury products from France, at a time of economic austerity. But Alphand did not dwell on this issue. Instead he moved to more grandiose ideas and declared that if Anglo-French co-operation was to be genuine, they should help each other's economic reconstruction by integrating their economies. Alphand, of course, had proposed in 1943 in Algiers that there should be a European economic union after the war. Since then events had only confirmed his belief that since France relied heavily on economic supplies – especially coal – from abroad, an economic juncture with other countries could bring important benefits.[19]

Such ideas were to become increasingly important in post-war Europe. (Already a similar principle was being pursued in the Benelux customs union.) Plans for economic union had been seen before, between the wars and, in the 1920s, one man who had taken an interest in them was Ernest Bevin. At the Trades Union Congress in 1927 he successfully pressed a motion in favour of a European customs union, after seeing the advantages of a large, competitive market during a trip to America. By 1930 he had changed his views, arguing that racial, language and economic differences made European union difficult, and preferring greater co-operation within the British Commonwealth. But in the late 1930s he returned to the idea of European unity, with links to the Commonwealth and America, and in 1940 spoke specifically of an Anglo-French imperial customs union. These schemes showed Bevin's imagination and marked early attempts by him to develop a relationship between Europe, the Commonwealth and America – three areas that were to be vital after 1945 – but his ideas were imprecise and idealistic, and it remained to be seen whether they had survived war.[20]

However, British officials were already ill-disposed to a customs union by 1946. Spaak's views on economic co-operation had been heard in London during the war and in June 1945 Duff Cooper had proposed that Britain should try to build a framework for economic co-operation in Western Europe to strengthen the proposed Western bloc. (In a perceptive statement he warned that if Britain did not do this the continent might itself take steps towards greater economic unity.) But when on 25 July, just before the British election results, the Foreign Office, the Treasury and the Board of Trade discussed this idea, the economic departments raised three

powerful objections to close British co-operation with Western
Europe: British sovereignty and independence must be preserved;
economic ties to the Commonwealth must not be upset; and the
search for a global, multilateral trade system – not regional systems
– must continue or America would be offended. Thus America and
the Commonwealth were judged to be more vital than Europe to
British economic considerations, and a Western European customs
union was certainly ruled out. This was why, notwithstanding
Bevin's interest in the subject, the Western Department did not
discuss economic co-operation fully at the 13 August meeting.[21]
The Foreign Office confirmed the July 1945 decisions after looking
at the issues again in March 1946.[22] Following these precedents
Alphand's new scheme was rejected immediately in London. Instead, on 7 August, the Foreign Office and other government departments met and discussed the more mundane subject of France's
trade deficit. The meeting agreed this was a serious problem, but the
economic departments declared that Britain was helping France as
much as possible, and insisted that any concessions to her must be
bought by concessions to Britain in return.[23] The very same day
Massigli told Harvey his worries about the stagnation in Anglo-
French relations,[24] and the inter-departmental meeting certainly
seemed to justify the ambassador's concern at Britain's inability,
and sometimes unwillingness, to help France's economic recovery.
Fortunately, however, Bevin was about to stir his officials into
action, both on the short-term problem of French recovery and on
the larger issue of Western European economic unity.

On 8 August, almost a year after framing the 'grand design',
Bevin discussed Anglo-French economic relations with the Western
Department. Like Massigli he was deeply concerned with the
stagnation in relations and he announced that there must be
progress in the economic field to breathe life into the French relationship. Specifically, he wanted to pursue two lines of advance.
The first was by far the most dramatic: he wanted, he said, to study
a Western European customs union. At this his officials baulked,
pointing to the previous rejections of such ideas. But Bevin was
insistent, and was even prepared to present a Cabinet Paper to
initiate a study. Secondly, Bevin wanted to see a distinct improvement in short-term aid to France. Again his officials' response was
muted: they could only give an account of the inter-departmental
meeting of 7 August. At this Bevin was discouraged, but not undaunted. He had restated his faith in economic co-operation and he
was determined to move forward. He ordered his officials to act.[25]

On the customs union issue the Foreign Office prepared a
Cabinet Paper by early September, arguing that a study of this idea
should be made for two reasons: because Western Europe might
soon have to unite against Soviet expansionism; and because
alternatives to multilateralism should be explored in case such a
global system failed to emerge. The paper acknowledged that a
European customs union could affect Britain's economic ties with
the empire and the world: from the start no-one in Whitehall failed
to appreciate this.[26] The economic departments raised strong
objections to the whole idea, repeating all their arguments of July
1945 and pointing out that staff shortages made a study impossible.
But the Foreign Office would not be dissuaded: the staffing problem was overcome by handing the study over to a group of university economists. However, Bevin delayed the presentation of the
paper to the Cabinet until January, fearful that a Communist-
dominated government might yet emerge in Paris. The delay
did not make his opponents more amenable: the Treasury and the
Board of Trade continued to argue that the study was a waste of
time.[27]

However, these arguments were important for the future, not for
the difficult situation of August 1946. And events still seemed to
conspire to prevent Bevin improving Anglo-French economic relations in the short term. In late August the Foreign Office were
deeply offended by an appeal from Bidault, over Bevin's head, to
Attlee, calling for the co-ordination of the British and French
economies. Given Britain's previous failures to help France this was
understandable, but to Bevin it came as a snub, just as he was
prepared to act. Alphand, who was obviously the inspiration behind
Bidault's appeal, became a British pet-hate: Bevin himself soon told
Alphand that Britain wanted no Anglo-French 'five-year plans',
because in London a pragmatic approach to economics was taken.
(This accent on British pragmatism in European co-operation was
vital for the future.) However, Bevin was not diverted from his
basic aim: he told Attlee that Bidault's appeal agreed with his own
approach, and using the Paris embassy as a base (since he was
currently attending the Peace Conference) he prepared an important
new initiative in Anglo-French relations.[28]

On 5 September Bevin made his first move. He met Bidault,
declared that there must be closer Anglo-French economic co-
operation, and suggested that to achieve this a group of economic
experts from each country could meet periodically to discuss problems in trade. These experts, he said, could meet for the first time

within a few days. Bidault was delighted with this novel initiative, but Bevin had other moves to make.[29] The Chancellor of the Exchequer, Hugh Dalton, was due in France for financial conversations, and Bevin planned to use his visit to maximum effect. He had asked Dalton to delay any possible beneficial moves for France until now, and on 10 September, when the Chancellor arrived, he told him why. Anglo-French relations, Bevin said, had been stagnating, primarily because of the French (!), who had adopted an impossible Ruhr plan, refused to make a treaty and were infested by Communists. Now, however, there was a chance to breathe new life into the situation by economic concessions.[30]

During the next few days Dalton's talks and the first meeting of the Anglo-French experts group were held simultaneously, and ended in a twofold agreement. On the financial side a complex web of debts, stretching back years, which had been worrying the Treasury, was clarified, and the French were given a very low interest rate for the remaining repayments. On the commercial side the idea of periodic meetings of experts in an 'Economic Committee' was formally accepted, and a broad principle was adopted that unnecessary competition between the two economies should be reduced. This fell far short of Alphand's desire for full economic co-ordination, but it did go some way towards it, and everyone – Bevin, Bidault, Dalton and the French Finance Minister, Robert Schuman – came away highly pleased with the discussions. Schuman was especially happy that Dalton had agreed to take more French exports.[31]

In the September talks Bevin had taken a poor position, where officials said little could be done, and squeezed the maximum from it. The debts settlement and the promise of future meetings were hardly epic events, especially when compared to Alphand's ideas, but the British actions compared favourably with former disappointments. The principle of reducing unnecessary competition (over which the Foreign Office expected trouble with the Board of Trade[32]) showed a strong mutual commitment, although it could not be put into effect before each side had the details of their reconstruction plans ready (Jean Monnet was currently leading the work on a French recovery plan); and the Economic Committee (which met again in November) was a new, ongoing form of co-operation which Bevin later saw as the beginning of wider Western European co-operation. Taken together the decisions provided a fillip for Anglo-French relations which fully justified Bevin's faith in economic co-operation. They also showed that the German problem, the delays to a treaty and communist influence in Paris had not weakened Bevin's commitment to co-operation with France and Western Europe. He had now taken up two important lines of advance: the customs union, which was to grow in importance in 1947; and short-term economic improvements, which came only a month before new French elections and paved the way, at last, to an Anglo-French treaty.

5

The making of the Treaty of Dunkirk

October 1946 – March 1947

IN LATE 1946 the chances of making an Anglo-French treaty soon did not seem high. Although the problems created by de Gaulle's character, the Levant and economics had been resolved, those caused by Germany and French communism remained. And in mid-October Bidault expressed his concern to Bevin at what he sensed was a new and growing Anglo-French division because of East–West tensions: Britain (as seen in the 'bizone' union) was obviously 'pro-American' in outlook, while France (with her Communist ministers and attempts to co-operate with Moscow) was viewed by many as 'pro-Soviet'. To reverse this trend Bidault suggested a bold, new initiative: an Anglo-French treaty should be made, around which Europe could unite, independent of Moscow and Washington. This idea showed a recognition of common Anglo-French interests and, in many respects, resembled Whitehall's desire for a Western bloc. But then, when Bevin said that Britain would make a treaty at any time, Bidault backed away: a treaty, he said, must await the formation of a stable government in Paris following new elections. (Such elections were held in November, after the French people had approved a new constitution.)[1]

It is doubtful, anyway, whether Bevin would have supported Bidault's vision of European co-operation in full at this time. For although the Foreign Secretary supported the Western bloc he also still wanted to co-operate with Russia and, more especially, America. Many left-wing Labour M.P.s were currently, like Bidault, critical of Bevin's 'pro-Americanism' and some called for him to lead a European 'third force' which would stand apart from Soviet-American rivalry. Churchill and the Conservatives also wanted greater Western European co-operation. But Bevin, always realistic, refused to answer these appeals: he continued to seek closer links with the United States, knowing that only they had the resources to save the West from the economic and military dangers which threatened it. The winter of 1946–7 was to be a dreadful period for the Foreign Secretary: crises in Palestine (over Jewish immigration), India (over demands for independence) and Greece (where communist guerrillas threatened the government) were gathering, against a background of continuing economic problems in Britain, growing suspicion of Russia, and his own continuing ill-health. In such a situation it was impossible to abandon an alliance with America in favour of a 'third force' alongside the weak and confused Western Europeans. Nevertheless it was in this situation that an Anglo-French treaty was forged at last as the basis for British co-operation with Western Europe.[2]

British officials were unimpressed by Bidault's hints that an Anglo-French treaty might be possible after the November elections. Political instability was expected to reign in Paris for many weeks following the polls, and even then a government might emerge which did not favour a treaty.[3] In fact, in December an all-Socialist government emerged in Paris, but only as an interim administration until the President of the new Fourth Republic was chosen. The British still keenly desired a treaty, and on 21 December Sargent reaffirmed the need for an alliance, for three main reasons: as an anti-German security device; as a step to general Western European co-operation; and as a means of strengthening Britain's diplomatic position in the world. (Despite East–West tensions, therefore, the French treaty was seen very much as it was in 1944 – as an anti-German device.) Sargent felt Britain should prepare herself to discuss a treaty once a stable French government emerged, but Bevin, fearful of the Communists, wanted to see the make-up of such a government first. Nothing in London, therefore, pointed to an early treaty.[4]

However, a treaty soon became possible because of the French Socialists. They had an affinity with the Labour Party, the importance of which it is hard to measure. Bevin, of course, had talked in 1945 of being able to co-operate with France because 'left understands left' and there was no doubt that the Socialists, greatly impressed by Labour's election in Britain, were the most anglophile French party. Just as important, they favoured a mild policy towards Germany, rather than de Gaulle's thesis. (In April 1946, of course, their desire for a new German policy and a British alliance had led to Harvey's ill-fated mission.) Now, despite being an interim government, they aimed to put their policies into practice. A major revision of France's German policy was begun, and Leon Blum, the great Socialist leader, who was now both Prime Minister and Foreign Minister, was determined to improve Anglo-French relations. So too was his deputy at the Quai d'Orsay, Pierre-Olivier Lapie.[5]

The new government decided to make a new initiative in Anglo-French relations in the area of recent success – economics. The 'Monnet Plan' for French recovery was now ready (though it did not receive Cabinet approval until 14 January), and on 23 December Massigli took a proposal to Bevin, suggesting that special talks should now be held, along the lines discussed in September, for the integration of the British and French recovery plans. Monnet wanted to see this because (even more than Alphand) he was aware of France's need for external support and knew the value of international economic co-operation. In itself Monnet's plan, directed by his own small staff, could achieve much for France, but it had its problems – domestic inflation, a lack of foreign exchange, and shortages of coal, foodstuffs and labour – and co-ordination with Britain's much stronger economy could help enormously. But the French initiative, like Alphand's earlier schemes, did not get far, for several reasons: Bevin still wanted to await a stable French government before making any important new moves; the British believed they were doing enough for Anglo-French economic co-operation through the Economic Committee, the idea of a Customs Union Study (which France did not know about), and some new talks, which were just beginning between experts of both sides, to explain the nature of the Monnet Plan; and, finally, there was the simple fact that Britain had no recovery 'plan' comparable to Monnet's: it would be months before Britain could gather the statistics on her recovery together. Thus on 9 January, Massigli was asked to concentrate any economic talks in the Economic Committee.[6] Although Alphand continued to press ideas for economic integration (even returning to the scheme for a Western European economic unit), Britain continued to lack suitable machinery for talks on this well into 1947.[7]

However, while this initiative stalled, Duff Cooper seized the opportunity given by an anglophile government in Paris to begin his own moves towards a treaty. On 26 December (through the good offices of Lapie) the ambassador visited Blum and wasted little time before suggesting that the Socialists might make a formal alliance with Britain. Even Blum was taken aback at this, knowing that his government might not last long; but the idea of a treaty was tempting, and Lapie supported it. Certainly the Socialists' moderate views on Germany meant that that issue need not prevent negotiations. Therefore Blum said he was willing to talk, though in order to create the right psychological moment for a treaty (and to provide France with some much needed economic aid) he suggested that Britain might increase supplies of Ruhr coal to France. From this meeting a treaty was to spring, and Duff Cooper was to take much of the credit for it. But at the time even he was uncertain whether this new initiative would succeed. He had acted without instructions from London, and in reporting events to the Foreign Office he did not dare say that *he* had raised the treaty idea with Blum: instead he hinted the *Blum* had put the idea to him. The French too had their doubts about the situation and rightly suspected that Duff Cooper's approach to them was unofficial. Over the next few days the ambassador was very reticent about further discussing a treaty with the French, and he summed up 1946 as a bad year in his diary. The Foreign Office and French diplomats still believed a treaty was months away.[8]

Again the French Socialists had to take the initiative. After reviewing the situation, Lapie pressed an idea which proved to be decisive: there should be a meeting between Blum and Attlee. This would exploit the socialist link, arouse great public interest, and provide an excellent cover for talks on Anglo-French relations. Blum was still hesitant, but agreed to write to Attlee, expressing a desire to visit London and to see a treaty. But in his letter Blum also made much of the coal problem in France, and after years of disappointment, the Foreign Office could not believe that the way to a treaty was not barred by French conditions. There was some doubt in London about how to respond to Blum's approach but since he could not be snubbed, and since Attlee sent a very friendly reply to the French premier's letter, Bevin and the Foreign Office decided, on 16 January, that Blum had to be invited to visit London. Even if a treaty was not signed, officials argued, the French might be reassured in such talks about British policy in Germany (where some Frenchmen suspected that Britain, in league with America, wanted to revive the German economy). The British Cabinet approved the idea of a visit – though the Board of Trade had to be reassured that economic integration would not be discussed with Blum – and Attlee duly sent an invitation. But no-one could be certain what the results would be: Massigli (who was currently very worried by British links with America, and their policy in

Germany) was annoyed at Duff Cooper's behaviour in encouraging the talks; Duff Cooper himself frantically pressed the Foreign Office about the need to offer something positive to France.[9]

However, the Blum visit of 13–16 January went far better than anyone, even Duff Cooper and Lapie, expected. In official talks on 14–15 January old problems simply seemed to melt away. To Massigli's surprise Blum was quite satisfied when Bevin announced that Ruhr coal supplies to France could not be increased for some months, and that economic co-operation must be studied through existing lines for the time being. On Germany, Bevin said that there must be continuing Allied controls on, and exploitation of, the old enemy and he added that an Anglo-French treaty was one way to prevent future German aggression. He also expressed his intention to base British policy towards Europe on the French alliance and hinted that an Anglo-French entente should be possible on all the world's major issues. Massigli was very pleased with this positive attitude and Blum responded by making the vital concession: an Anglo-French treaty could be made *without* prior agreement on Germany. The French premier abandoned de Gaulle's policy of conditions for a treaty, in favour of making the treaty first and hoping that any problems could be solved later. Both sides, intoxicated by the atmosphere of socialist brotherhood and Anglo-French friendship, agreed to publicize their decision to make a treaty.[10]

Almost immediately, this breakthrough was followed by Blum's resignation and the formation of another tripartite government, with Bidault as foreign minister. For a time the Foreign Office feared a reversal of Blum's policy by Bidault. But events had already gone too far to be reversed easily, the Socialists were very strongly placed in the new government (holding the Presidency, with Vincent Auriol, and the premiership, with Ramadier) and, besides, Bidault had always claimed to want a treaty.[11] On 25 January, he told Duff Cooper that a treaty could be made and agreed with British suggestions that it should be negotiated by Massigli, in London. On 29 January Sargent and Massigli agreed to begin formal talks once their draft treaties were ready. They planned to sign a pact before the next C.F.M., which was due in Moscow in March.[12]

There were few major problems in the treaty negotiations but a long initial delay was caused by the British in devising a suitable draft. The Foreign Office had actually had draft Anglo-French treaties ready in 1945, based on the Anglo-Soviet Pact of 1942 against future German aggression. (They were keen to keep the

French and Soviet Pacts almost identical to avoid offending either of these countries by seeming to offer the other greater concessions.) And, as early as 3 February, the Office had drawn up a new draft which it considered suitable. Copies were sent to the Board of Trade, to Duff Cooper and to the Chiefs of Staff (C.O.S.), and it was the Board of Trade which caused the delays. After the previous disagreements on economic policy towards France, Bevin had particularly asked that the Board should see the draft treaty, because an economic clause within it promised the harmonization of Anglo-French reconstruction plans. (The Office had considered an alternative clause to this, simply promising the French consultation on economic policy, but had ruled this out on the grounds that Russia might insist on a similar clause being inserted into their treaty and thus gain an opening into British economic policy planning.) But the Board of Trade had no wish to become committed to helping French recovery, and they argued that a clause applying to short-term reconstruction plans was out of place in what was to be a fifty-year treaty. They got the Treasury to support these arguments, and it was days before a suitable compromise clause was found. This simply promised consultation and co-operation on economic issues of mutual interest. The Foregin Office was content that this wording limited the potential for Soviet interference in British policy, should they be given a similar agreement, but the vague formula and the long delay that had been caused were disappointing.[13]

Duff Cooper, in commenting on the draft, was critical of the influence Soviet considerations were having on the pact. He wanted to see an altogether different treaty, with promises of extensive co-operation on such issues as Germany and the colonies; and taking on the ideas for a 'third force' in the world, he argued that the British and French empires should be united to match the superpowers. The Foreign Office, he felt, were being far too cautious. But in London, officials were unmoved: they rejected Duff Cooper's 'instant' approach, in favour of the gradual development of co-operation. (This emphasis on gradualism was important for the future.[14]) The C.O.S., in their own way, were just as cautious: they approved the treaty as the way to make France 'the keystone of a strong Western region of defence...'; but they also said the treaty should not be made if it upset America, because America was 'the keystone on which our major strategy and planning are based.'[15]

On 13 February Bevin approved the draft treaty, despite some disappointment with the economic clause,[16] and the next day Sargent and Massigli exchanged drafts. The French, like Duff

Cooper, had considered the idea of a general entente on issues such as colonies and the Middle East, but then dropped the idea in favour of a simple draft based on the Franco-Soviet Pact of 1944 and therefore similar to the British one. There was a good deal of minor rewriting to marry the two drafts together over the next ten days, but only one major problem arose. This centred around the treaty's essential clause – the promise to act against German aggression. Whereas the British wished only to act in this against *direct* aggression, the French wanted a promise of action against any German *menace*. The British fear was that such a sweeping clause, if written into the Anglo-Soviet Pact as well, would undermine the value of an American commitment to European security: American isolationists and the Russians might argue that, since there was a powerful anti-German alliance in Europe, an American guarantee was unnecessary. The Foreign Office still hoped that the Byrnes Treaty (the four-power German demilitarization treaty, suggested by Byrnes in 1946) might be adopted and they had no wish to ruin this by clumsy wording in the French treaty. The French, understandably, were offended by this interest in America and it was several days before a clause emerged which satisfied both sides by promising consultation with America and Russia against a German 'policy of aggression'.

The treaty was provisionally agreed on 25 February and it was planned to sign it in London.[17] It was Bidault who suggested that Dunkirk would make a better venue for reasons of sentimentality and publicity: the Anglo-French alliance would be remade where it was broken in 1940. Bevin agreed enthusiastically.[18] On 28 February the British Cabinet approved the treaty;[19] and the French, despite some fear of Communist opposition in the Cabinet, followed the next day.[20] That same afternoon both parliaments were told of the treaty and gave it a warm response. In the French Assembly the announcement received a standing ovation; despite the delays, the desire for such an alliance had long outlived the Liberation.[21] Unfortunately, following this, the build-up to the signature was discouraging. To the dismay of Duff Cooper and the French, the Foreign Office (following complaints from Washington) insisted on a note to accompany the treaty, safeguarding any future four-power treaty. Fortunately Bidault, though offended by the continuing interest in American wishes, agreed.[22] Then, the day of the signature – 4 March – turned out to be cold and wet, and the ceremony had to be held in an uncomfortably small room because most of Dunkirk still lay in ruins. Finally, the car carrying the treaty copies broke

down and Bevin and Bidault had a long, embarrassing wait before
these could be recovered. The Dunkirkers, however, made a brave
attempt to welcome everyone, and after the signature the two
foreign ministers went on a symbolic walk along the famous
beaches.[23]

De Gaulle condemned the Treaty of Dunkirk, arguing that it gave
France nothing and tied her, indirectly, to the Americans.[24]
Certainly the alliance came without the firm agreements he and
Bidault had wanted to prove British goodwill. On Germany, Britain
and France were still divided, and Anglo-American ties showed
that, despite Bevin's protestations of faith in the French alliance,
America was still foremost in British minds. But Frenchmen such as
Blum, Lapie and Massigli took a view very different from de
Gaulle's: they did not feel that a treaty required firm, prior
agreements on difficult issues, but rather believed that a treaty could
pave the way to common understandings on other issues in an
atmosphere of friendship and self-respect.[25] The British shared this
hope: Duff Cooper had always wanted a full entente with France
and saw Dunkirk as a great personal achievement;[26] and the Foreign
Office (for all Duff Cooper's criticisms) had always remained true
to the basic aim of a treaty despite frequently exasperating French
behaviour. In March the Office prepared a paper, entitled 'Why it is
essential to co-operate with the French', which pointed to the
dangers for Britain brought by economic decline and growing
differences with Russia, and identified three great issues that must
be faced: Britain's economic survival, Germany's future, and the
development of Western European political and economic co-
operation as a way for Britain to safeguard its Great Power status.
France, it was said, was vital to the resolution of all these problems because she was so important as a democratic, colonial and
Western European state. As in August 1945, therefore, France – as
the key country in Western Europe – was judged to be vital to
British security.[27]

However, while both sides saw Dunkirk as a new beginning, its
actual form (in retrospect) marked the end of an era. An anti-
German treaty, it was soon said, came ten years too late; *Russia* was
rapidly emerging as the great threat to the West. Of course, some
Britons had wanted a Western bloc during the war as reinsurance
against Russia and later, after 1947, the Treaty of Dunkirk was seen
as the precursor of anti-Soviet security arrangements. But in actual
form the treaty was the product of a distinct era lasting from 1944 to
1947, an era in which it had been hoped to build world peace on the

Big Three and the U.N., with security measures directed against Germany. In March 1947 it was possible to see Dunkirk as completing a triangular Anglo-Franco-Soviet system in Europe directed against Germany.[28] The period 1944–7 had been a frustrating one for everyone: the U.N. had proved ineffective; the Big Three argued among themselves; and the world still faced economic and political upheaval. For Anglo-French relations too it had been a time of disappointment. Both countries had recognized new dangers and problems, and men on both sides wanted an alliance between them; but the dangers were not yet great enough to prevent old disagreements reappearing in the Levant and Germany, and the new problems in the world – especially economic difficulties and the rise of the communists – brought their own troubles. Both countries had shown that a treaty was not as vital to them as other considerations: the French had insisted on putting agreements on the Levant and Germany before a treaty, and the British had shown wariness, always fearing to upset America and Russia. Eventually, when the treaty was signed, it was only because of a short-lived anglophile ascendancy in Paris. It was merely coincidence that this occurred just as the immediate post-war era was coming to an end, and the Big Three collapsed, creating a situation in which the great problems of March 1947 – the future of Germany, Western European survival, and British and French decline – had to be resolved against the background of a growing Soviet menace. In this desperate situation, however, the Anglo-French alliance was to be given new life and importance.

Part II

THE MAKING OF 'THE WEST'

The Anglo-French alliance from Dunkirk to 'Western Union'
March 1947 – July 1948

6

The Moscow C.F.M. and its aftermath

March–June 1947

IN JANUARY 1947 Bevin was still able to declare that Germany was a greater danger to peace than the Soviet Union,[1] and it was anti-German thinking which dominated preparations for the Treaty of Dunkirk. Furthermore, in looking forward to the long-awaited discussions on a German peace treaty at the Moscow Conference of Foreign Ministers, the British were still, as in 1945, unwilling to put at risk the formation of an anti-German alliance among the Great Powers by pursuing a Western bloc. Of course it had always been intended that an Anglo-French treaty would form the basis of a Western bloc and, inevitably, the Belgian foreign minister Spaak was encouraged to believe that Dunkirk might be followed by other British alliances in Western Europe. On 10 February Baron Gruben, head of Belgium's foreign ministry, after learning of the Anglo-French treaty negotiations, had hinted to Oliver Harvey that an Anglo-Belgian treaty might now be made – a suggestion which Harvey felt was premature, but which Orme Sargent was very pleased about.[2] The Dutch (always cautious in international affairs) were less keen about making a treaty, but had already expressed an interest in forming an Anglo-Dutch Economic Committee similar to that formed by Britain and France in late 1946.[3] So, in mid-February, Bevin decided to adopt the approach to Belgium and Holland that had proved successful with France: he would form Economic Committees with them and later, when the time was ripe, move on to formal alliances.[4] Spaak was somewhat disappointed with this gradual approach but on 3 March the Foreign Office decided that, at least, an Anglo-Belgian treaty could not be made until *after* the Moscow C.F.M. The main reason for this (apart from Bevin's absence from London) was that the Office did not want to upset the prospects of a four-power anti-German arrangement: they feared (as they had feared with the French treaty) that a strong European alliance system would fuel the arguments from American isolationists and the Russians that an American guarantee of European security was unnecessary. Bevin himself almost upset this decision when, after the Dunkirk signature, he passed through Brussels (en route to Moscow) and talked of making an Anglo-Belgian treaty. But on arriving in Moscow he confirmed the Office's approach. The French too had been approached by Spaak about a treaty but decided to delay any talks. For the moment, although it seemed that an eventual Western bloc had been brought nearer by Dunkirk, the four-power relationship remained predominant in British thinking.[5]

However, there were growing signs that four-power co-operation and the emphasis on the German threat would not last much longer. Since Bevin came to power there had been friction with the Russians, who had seized most of Eastern Europe before the war ended and who, the British feared, would try to penetrate into other areas such as Western Europe and the Middle East. The Americans (who were not very close to Britain in late 1945, despite the wartime alliance) had tried to keep the peace with Russia at the Moscow C.F.M. of December 1945, but 1946 had seen increasing tensions: a crisis over Russian designs on Iran, and Churchill's talk of an 'iron curtain' around Eastern Europe (in his famous Fulton speech) had been followed by the bitter arguments in Paris over the future of Germany. The two sides had still managed to agree on treaties with Italy and the Balkan States, but the great hopes of 1945 for a post-war Big Three alliance had largely faded, and Britain and America had drawn together (most visibly in the 'bizone') against their wartime ally. This situation, of course, had had its ill-effect on British relations with France, since Paris still tried to co-operate with Moscow. As the Moscow C.F.M. opened there was an important new sign of friction when President Truman inaugurated the 'Truman Doctrine', declaring that the communist advance must be 'contained' wherever it threatened.

Against such a background deadlock soon set in in Moscow on the German treaty. The Russians demanded heavy reparations, a share in controlling the vital Ruhr, and a centralized German state; the Anglo-Americans opposed all these. The French largely adhered to their old thesis although, partly thanks to the influence of Blum's government (and especially the efforts of Lapie) some changes to French policy had been made. Most importantly, Bidault now proposed only four-power control of the Ruhr, having realized that political separation was virtually impossible. However, France's ambiguous position in Germany remained: like Russia she wanted high reparations from Germany and international control of the Ruhr; unlike Russia she favoured a decentralized constitution and the Byrnes Treaty.[6] The inevitable result in the long meetings was that progress became impossible: on 28 March Bevin and Bidault both agreed that the conference had lost direction; by mid-April Bevin was hoping that the C.F.M. would come to an early end.[7]

Yet, beneath the confusion and arguments, Moscow was surprisingly positive for Anglo-French relations, for it was here that Bidault first noticeably began to draw away from a neutral position to the Anglo-American camp. Before the meeting such a shift had certainly seemed unlikely: General Catroux (now Ambassador to Moscow) had offered to concert Franco-Soviet actions, on certain issues, at the C.F.M. with Molotov; France's new President, Vincent Auriol, was very reluctant to join in the East–West arguments; and Paris was very concerned (as seen in the Dunkirk talks) that the Anglo-Americans might seek to revive the Western German economy. Massigli was still worried about Anglo-French differences over the Ruhr, the centralization of German government and the 'bizone'.[8] But two issues in particular changed this situation in Moscow. The first was the Saar, which France wished to see tied into her own economy (mainly because of its value as a coal-producing area). It has already been seen that the Anglo-Americans were sympathetic to this aim – it was the one part of de Gaulle's German thesis to which they were sympathetic – and they had allowed France to erect a customs barrier around the area in December 1946. Now, in Moscow, Bidault hoped to get four-power agreement on French plans for the Saar, and he raised the question in early April. To Bidault's extreme annoyance, however, Molotov simply refused to discuss the issue. Molotov's motives can only be guessed at, perhaps he was annoyed that Bidault did not support Russian claims in other areas, perhaps it was just another example of Soviet contempt for France after the debacle of 1940. But the result was a great deal of personal animosity between Bidault and the Russians, who openly began to insult each other at the many Moscow banquets. After years of trying to steer a middle course between East and West, the emotional Bidault felt a keen sense of betrayal at Molotov's unexpected action.[9]

The second issue which drew Bidault to the West was coal. In January Bevin had been unable to offer more coal supplies to Blum, and French needs had only worsened since then, as Europe was

struck by a terrible winter. General George Marshall, America's
new Secretary of State, had visited Paris before the Moscow C.F.M.
and learnt that coal was probably the most important international
issue for France at the time. Marshall, a far more forceful and
competent character than his predecessor Byrnes, had assured the
French that he would try to improve their coal situation.[10] Bevin,
too, recognized that Bidault was 'likely to measure everything at the
moment by coal.'[11] During the C.F.M. Bidault even threatened to
block all other discussions unless Ruhr coal exports were discussed
and, finally, the French approached the British delegation pleading
for a resolution of the problem behind the scenes. The Anglo-
Americans were reluctant to make a four-power agreement on coal
(because of Russia's unco-operative attitude on Germany) but they
did agree to help the French. The result, after talks between experts,
was a sliding-scale for coal exports adjusted according to the level of
Ruhr coal production. The French were grudging in their acceptance of this, but since France already virtually controlled the Saar
coal mines it marked a reasonable settlement. Furthermore, it was
the only important agreement made at the Moscow conference.[12]

Moscow did not end in complete despondency: Bevin was
surprisingly positive in his report to the Cabinet.[13] But the problems between East and West seemed enormous and, in retrospect,
some saw the conference as the start of the Cold War.[14] Bidault
especially was disappointed, saying that all he gained in the talks
was 'un peu de charbon'. Everyone now wanted to know whose
'side' France was on.[15] If the world continued to divide it was
probably always inevitable that France, as a democratic, colonial,
Western European state, would veer westwards. But it was only in
Moscow that this really became clear. The Anglo-Americans had
shown that while no-one agreed with France's thesis on Germany,
they could offer far more than Russia: they favoured France's Saar
claim, they wanted a decentralized German government and, most
important, they controlled the Ruhr coal supplies. The Moscow
C.F.M. was in fact the first major event between March 1947 and
July 1948 which was to widen the gap between East and West, drive
France closer to Britain and America, and thus help to build a
closer, more constructive relationship between Britain and France
on the foundation of Dunkirk.[16]

Even before Bidault reported the Moscow events to his Cabinet a
second event occurred which shifted France westwards: on 5 May
premier Ramadier expelled the Communists from his Cabinet.
Friction had been growing between them and the other parties for

some time, over colonial policies and co-operation with Russia, and finally they had voted against the government in a vote in the Assembly. The Communists later claimed that U.S. influence in Paris had led to their expulsion, but although certain ministers favoured closer American friendship, it is doubtful if the Americans could have 'ordered' Ramadier to expel the communists, especially since President Auriol and others were still keen to co-operate with Moscow. By voting against the government in the Assembly the Communists actually sealed their own fate.[17] The Foreign Office had been watching the growing tensions in Paris for some time. After the problems they had caused for Anglo-French co-operation in 1946 the Communists' departure was certainly welcomed in London.[18] Unfortunately, however, the expulsion only worsened France's other great political problem – instability. The moderate Socialists and M.R.P. now faced two extremes: the Communists, supported by more than a fifth of French voters; and a new movement, with neofascist elements, begun by General de Gaulle, the Rassemblement du Peuple Français (R.P.F.). Within six months both these extremist groups would begin to fuel support for each other, and pose a serious threat to the Fourth Republic's survival.

The Moscow C.F.M. had a great effect on everyone's thinking about European security. Russia had again rejected the four-power Byrnes Treaty (which now seemed unlikely to emerge) and the era of the Big Three alliance appeared to be ending. Furthermore, ideas for stronger treaty links between East and West European states took a mighty blow at Moscow. A proposed revision of the Anglo-Soviet Pact at the time came to nothing, and the French and Belgians became very doubtful about treaties, which they had wanted since the war, with Eastern European states such as Poland and Czechoslovakia. (Paris and Brussels had hoped for such treaties to maintain traditional links to Eastern Europe, to extend the anti-German security arrangements in Europe, and to please their own powerful communist parties.) The British and Americans doubted the use of such treaties anyway – the British feared they would have little practical value, and would dilute the value of the proposed Western bloc – and the Moscow deadlock almost killed them off.[19] Both Bidault and the Belgians now remarked that Eastern European treaties were unnecessary because there was no longer any need to pander to the wishes of the Communists.[20] Even the Dutch were affected by East–West division: the British ambassador felt that they now feared Russia more than Germany.[21]

Most important, however, was the effect of the Moscow C.F.M. on the Western bloc. Spaak quickly renewed his attempts to achieve an Anglo-Belgian treaty when the conference ended, adapting his approach to the new situation of friction with Russia, and he declared that the Americans might now support the Western bloc. In the Foreign Office there was some support for the view that since the Byrnes Treaty and co-operation with Russia were now seriously threatened, the Western bloc could prove a very useful insurance policy for British security.[22] As a result Bevin held a meeting on 7 May where he remarked that since the Americans were predominant in the Western hemisphere and the Russians in Eastern Europe, Britain ought to look to her own security and begin to organize Western Europe with determination. Bevin had always supported the Western bloc, but since 1945 he had put the Big Three relationship, and the 'global' approach of the U.N., formost in his considerations. But he was now willing to consider a 'regional' approach to security, regardless of Russian and American attitudes. Though he did not rule out saving Big Three co-operation he was now determined to see treaties with Belgium and (if possible) Holland.[23] The French were also willing to pursue such treaties, it emerged,[24] and in reporting the Moscow C.F.M.'s failure to the Commons, on 15 May, Bevin gave special prominence to the Treaty of Dunkirk. Certainly, at this time, the idea of greater Western European co-operation had a great appeal in the Commons: Eden and other Conservatives went so far as to call for a European economic unit at this time and were very disappointed at Bevin's failure to form a Western bloc.[25]

By early June the Foreign Office were hoping to make an Anglo-Belgian treaty soon,[26] and the military's Joint Planning Staff reported that such a treaty would be an excellent way to give Britain defence-in-depth in Europe against what was termed 'a major power from the East'.[27] The Foreign Office were still surprisingly traditional in their outlook, however: the Belgian treaty draft which they devised was an anti-German alliance, based on Dunkirk, and still providing for a possible Byrnes Treaty.[28] And Bevin seems to have had some doubts in June about whether his decisions of 7 May were the right ones: not only were the Foreign Office unwilling to abandon the anti-German, four-power outlook they had held since 1945, they also became very slow with their preparations for a treaty. (Only on 30 June did Sargent inform the Belgians that the British Cabinet was about to look at the treaty proposal.)[29]

Meanwhile the Belgians had also been holding discussions with the French and Dutch, and on 8 June Spaak and Bidault met secretly to discuss Franco-Belgian co-operation. Here Bidault revealed that after trying to co-operate with Russia for years, he had finally given up and now wanted to tie France to the Anglo-Americans.[36] But it was at this very moment, when the stage seemed set for a Western European alliance, that events became dominated by a new initiative from America. On 5 June General Marshall had publicly offered American aid to restore the European economy, in a major speech at Harvard. This proposal was to reshape the future of the continent.

7

The Marshall Plan

June–September 1947

GENERAL MARSHALL's offer to underwrite a European recovery plan was itself partly a result of the Moscow breakdown. This had left the Americans fearful that Russia meant to exploit Europe's grave weaknesses and, like Bevin, they resolved to act despite the risk of offending the Soviets. European recovery had undergone a major setback in early 1947 with a terrible winter that cut industrial production, destroyed crops and decimated trade, at a time when the dislocation and destruction left by the war were still immense. Governments found their hopes of minimizing inflation and unemployment (to prevent a recurrence of inter-war economic problems) severely undermined: Britain introduced greater austerity measures; France had even greater need of coal and wheat imports. Although 1947 was actually to see rising wages, food consumption and production levels in Europe the winter's psychological effect could not be erased. It was a breeding ground for discontent and communism. With Britain and Russia strained by war, only America could help this difficult situation. America was so wealthy that her strength itself was a major problem for Europeans, who needed coal, wheat, metals and machinery for their recovery plans, but were quite unable to earn dollars in sufficient quantities to pay for all these. The situation was known as the 'dollar gap'. In 1945–6 America had tried to help the Europeans with bilateral loans, like those to Britain and France, while looking forward to a multilateral world economic system, but in early 1947 a multilateral system seemed no nearer and the bilateral loans (as well as Europe's gold and currency reserves) were being used up. Fortunately, however, the Americans had two very good reasons for helping European recovery. First, they did not want their European export market to collapse, for this could have led to a recession in North America. Second, they wished to forestall any further communist advance in Europe. Therefore on returning from Moscow, General Marshall had begun studies for an aid plan: the result was his speech of 5 June, at Harvard University.

The reaction to Marshall's generous offer was swift. The French had been considering an appeal for American aid anyway,[1] and although the speech was deliberately low-key (to prevent premature Congressional criticism of any increased American spending) and preceded by no official contacts, the British had some warning of what was about to occur. Bevin and the French were quick to take up the offer. For Anglo-French relations the vital point was Bevin's determination to base the European response to Marshall on joint action with Bidault, on the lines of the 'grand design': such a policy would help Anglo-French friendship, mark a major step towards co-operation with the continent, and allow a genuine 'European' reaction to the Marshall Plan. Duff Cooper told Bidault of Bevin's intentions on 10 June, and three days later British ministers decided that Bevin should visit Paris to co-ordinate Anglo-French actions.[2]

At this point, however, certain differences with France began to appear.[3] Most important, in replying to Britain's idea of a meeting Bidault insisted that Russia must also be consulted. For although Bidault was increasingly anti-Soviet, the French Cabinet remained fearful of East–West divisions, especially since these led to growing divisions within France itself because of the strong communist party. Somewhat surprisingly Washington shared the French approach: while seeing the Marshall Plan as a way to forestall communist growth, Americans did not want to seem to be dividing the world, and they wanted Russia to have the opportunity to join the plan (though they expected her to reject it).[4] Hitherto Britain had not considered an approach to Moscow, because of East–West tension and Soviet press criticisms of the Harvard speech, but now, somewhat reluctantly, Bevin agreed to involve her. On visiting Paris on 17–18 June, however, he received an assurance from Bidault that if Russia rejected the plan, France would still join it.

Another Anglo-French difference arose over procedure. Initially the French felt the Marshall Plan should be handled by the U.N.'s Economic Commission for Europe (a result of the wartime ideas for a European body under the U.N.), which was about to be established in Geneva. But it was further evidence of changes in British thinking on the world since 1944 that Bevin wanted to exclude the U.N. The U.N.'s central bodies had proved divided, slow and cumbersome – and they included Russia. Bevin preferred a few European countries to take the lead on the Marshall Plan to ensure speed and efficiency (and to preserve Britain's leading role). After some discussion, Bidault agreed. A third difference arose over an old trouble-spot, Germany: France did not want to see Europe's economic recovery lead to a parallel strengthening of Germany, but Britain had already been forced to restore the Ruhr economy somewhat and the Ruhr was the obvious industrial area to stimulate as a powerhouse for the continent's general economic revival. For the moment this argument did not need to be resolved: it would become more important as the Marshall Plan progressed.

Bevin returned from the Paris meeting disappointed with Anglo-French differences, but with a wide area of agreement to work on: Bidault had acknowledged the need for swift action; an agenda for a meeting with Russia had been prepared and an invitation sent to Molotov; and it was hoped to have some planning machinery in being on 5 July, with the aim of putting a comprehensive scheme to Washington in September. Over the next few months this Anglo-French agreement was to prove vital in turning Marshall's proposal into a successful recovery plan, and fully justified Bevin's faith in co-operation with Paris.[5]

On 27 June Anglo-Franco-Soviet talks began in Paris on the Marshall offer, and immediately the Russians objected to the American wish that the new recovery effort should be a *comprehensive* plan. Molotov criticized this as an attempt to undermine the sovereignty of European states. He wanted each state to present its own needs to Washington, thus maintaining a *bilateral* approach to economic problems. Bidault made determined efforts to show that America did not want to abrogate the sovereignty of other states, but merely to collect figures together and make Europe's total recovery needs clear. But Molotov was unimpressed and finally, on 2 July, left the meeting.[6] The next day Bevin and Bidault alone invited other European states to a conference to draw up a detailed plan.[7] Whether Molotov ever intended to join the Marshall Plan is impossible to say. Perhaps he only came to Paris in the hope of sabotaging the American initiative in some way, possibly by dividing Britain and France. If so, he was sorely disappointed. For although Bidault made great efforts to satisfy Molotov about the plan, the French government remained loyal to it in principle. The British made little effort to bring in Russia: the general view was that the Paris talks were a waste of time and an opportunity for Molotov to cause discord. Bevin sent gloomy reports to London throughout the discussions and told the Cabinet later that they were 'doomed from the start'.[8] The French noted this negative British approach with disappointment, but ultimately Bevin seemed completely justified: Russia's refusal to co-operate with the Western powers was made clear to all the world.[9]

Molotov's departure from Paris made the division between East and West, in economics at least, clearer than ever: Moscow ensured that no Eastern European state joined the Marshall Plan, which thereby became an American–Western European scheme. Anglo-French co-operation had, however, received a great boost. Bevin returned to London expressing unprecedented confidence in the French: 'I cannot speak too highly of ... M.Bidault' he told the Cabinet. Within months of Dunkirk, Anglo-French leadership of Western Europe was in being. But already events had greatly altered the framework in which Dunkirk had been made. Whereas Dunkirk could be seen as completing an Anglo-Franco-Soviet security 'triangle', Molotov's walk-out left the Anglo-French alliance as the most meaningful security link in Europe. The wartime ideas of a four-power anti-German system had taken a decisive blow, but it was a blow from which Anglo-French relations could only gain.[10] Paradoxically, however, this new co-operation in economics ended ideas of a military Western bloc for the time being. In early July the Foreign Office was still keen to pursue an Anglo-Belgian treaty (Harvey now talked of this as a way to check the Belgian communists) but Bevin felt that it was right to concentrate on economic co-operation because of the Marshall Plan. Fortunately Spaak was not disappointed with this turn of events – he too was very impressed by Marshall's offer.[11] In early July the old security order based on the U.N., four-power co-operation and anti-German treaties was being pushed aside. The main features of the new order were Western European co-operation, Anglo-French leadership and American support.

The West Europeans met in Paris on 12 July and, with Bevin as chairman and a determination to act swiftly, the ministerial level of work was soon completed. By 16 July a Committee of European Economic Co-operation (C.E.E.C.) of officials from the member states had been established and begun work on a detailed recovery plan. This was to take a little over two months to complete, a remarkable feat considering the diversity of the European states, their various needs, and the lack of previous planning, and was an important step towards the greater unity of the continent. Throughout, Britain and France remained predominant: British civil servants were vital in providing expertise; the French had the prestige of hosting the conference. But American influence was also important: the Under-Secretary of State, Will Clayton, was especially keen to press greater co-operation on the Europeans, to make them help themselves (and so ensure that Washington's money was well spent). Clayton and others hoped the Europeans would work towards a freer, larger and more competitive European economy, on American lines, and they particularly wanted to see greater trade within Europe itself and the creation of a permanent organization to direct the recovery plan. In early September Clayton became so critical of the Europeans for failing to do enough on these lines that the whole plan seemed in danger, but eventually an agreed report was finalized on the 22nd.[12]

Two major problems endangered Anglo-French co-operation during this period. The first, predictably, was Germany. On 7 July Bidault told Duff Cooper that the revitalization of Germany would fuel communist propaganda and divide Britain and France. But Bevin was adamant that Germany's economic potential had to be considered in planning European reconstruction.[13] The British were still desperate to minimize costs in the zone in Germany, and by mid-1947 they relied heavily on American support there. The Americans, however, wanted to keep their own costs in Germany down and, even before the Harvard speech, had pressed Britain to increase industrial production in the Ruhr to make Germany pay for herself. The British were somewhat reluctant to do this: they feared reviving the German menace, breaking previous (four-power) agreements, and upsetting the French.[14] But now the need to revive the European economy in general strengthened the arguments for reviving Germany, and in Paris most Europeans agreed that her economic potential must be used in the Marshall Plan. Even the French agreed with this as a general principle: they had never objected to milking Germany for coal and reparations to help the recovery of her neighbours. But what the French would not accept was that Germany should be revived without safeguards. So a second principle was accepted by the C.E.E.C.: that Germany's revival must be strictly controlled to prevent it becoming a danger to peace. How this two-sided agreement would work in practice was unclear, but it succeeded in avoiding arguments in Paris.

At the same time Anglo-Franco-American talks were held to discuss West Germany's economy, and to ease Bidault's fears about American intentions. These talks achieved little in substance – industrial production in the bizone was increased anyway – but they did succeed in placating Bidault: the announcement of the new production increases was delayed until August; Bidault was assured that Germany would be prevented from manufacturing armaments; and coal exports to France were again increased. Indeed these concessions upset some Americans, led by General Lucius Clay, governor of the American zone, who declared that 'we cannot have a common German policy with the French'. Certainly great differences between France and the Anglo-Americans had always existed in Germany, but now that the Marshall Plan was under way, some resolution of these differences had to be found for the sake of Western unity. Washington was now willing to treat French fears of German revival seriously, and the Marshall Plan, by introducing the idea that Germany could be revitalized only under strict controls and within a wider Western scheme, was a great step forward.[15]

The other divisive subject for Britain and France was the old issue of economic integration. The Americans, in their determination to see European revival, gave new impetus to this issue by stating that the creation of a single, competitive market (like America's) in Western Europe would improve the region's economic strength. Interest in greater European unity had grown in America in early 1947, as Americans looked for ways to end the continent's weakness, and State Department preparations for the Marshall Plan had included hopes for greater European economic union. (This contrasted with earlier American fears that European unity would damage U.S. economic interests.)[16] In Britain, meanwhile, Bevin remained favourable to customs unions in principle and told Duff Cooper in June that a European customs union and a common currency were desirable.[17] In late June, when Clayton visited London, many ministers were upset to find that the Americans discussed Britain simply as 'part of Europe', but Bevin again said that a customs union must be considered.[18] The Board of Trade, as usual, were opposed to Bevin's ideas. Although they could no longer claim that customs unions would upset Washington's multilateral schemes, Board officials continued to argue that a union would disturb Commonwealth co-operation, present massive practical problems, and demand painful economic readjustments in Europe. They also pointed out that Europe's economies were *competitive* not complementary: they could not, together, form a balanced economy able to stand on its own. Furthermore, they strengthened their case by presenting an alternative policy to a customs union, in three parts: the gradual reduction of trade barriers in Europe; the extension of the principle (already agreed between Britain and France) of removing unnecessary competition between countries; and – most interesting – support for limited,

continental customs unions which, the Board conceded, might be
viable. A Franco-German-Benelux union was specifically mentioned.[19]

In the Paris talks a customs union became an issue because of the
American interest in it, and its appeal to some continental countries.
On 15 July Italy's Count Sforza spoke in favour of a customs union.
But the French really started movement on the idea in August.
British observers believed the main French motive was to impress
the Americans, but French feeling was much more genuine than
that: the ideal of European economic co-operation was already
deeply implanted in Paris (as seen in Alphand's ideas) and, of
course, it had its practical side for the French economy – Bidault
told the Cabinet that a Franco-Italian-Benelux customs union
(which seemed possible) would bring Italian labour and Belgian
industry to France's aid.[20] Some British officials, including Duff
Cooper and Edmund Hall-Patch (the Foreign Office's leading
economic expert), urged Bevin to take up the customs union idea,[21]
but the economic ministries maintained their opposition: on 17
August, Harold Wilson (then Secretary of Overseas Trade) told
Clayton that Britain could not join a customs union because Europe
took only a quarter of British trade, and the Commonwealth had to
be preserved.[22] A fundamental Anglo-French difference seemed to
be emerging: on 13 September Alphand announced that France
would join any other state which was willing in a customs union;
but the British were still arguing among themselves on the subject.

A deep Anglo-French division over customs unions was avoided,
however. Most members of the C.E.E.C. felt the French were
moving too quickly on the issue: only Italy took up Alphand's offer
of 13 September; and the Benelux States still preferred to be led by
Britain, not France. To resolve the arguments it was decided to
establish a Customs Union Study Group (C.U.S.G.). This would
carry out a full study of the proposal (which everyone agreed was
necessary before a customs union could be made), but it meant no
ultimate commitment to join a customs union by anyone. Indeed,
Britain framed the resolutiuon which led the C.U.S.G. to be established.[23] A mere study of customs unions also helped the British
ministries to remain united. By mid-September the doubts in
Whitehall about the whole idea were increasing. The Colonial
Office had now looked at ideas for a colonial customs union and
concluded that any advantages would be outweighed by the loss of
revenue from tariffs, radical changes in trade patterns, and colonial
opposition to any central political direction; and there was a grow-

ing feeling in London that since a customs union would affect the whole economy, it would probably necessitate a *full economic union*, with results that were hard to estimate.[24] But Bevin was still keen to look at a customs union, not only with Europe but also with the Commonwealth and the empire; he told the T.U.C. so, on 3 September.[25]

Although the study by British university economists, established back in January, had finally reported against a customs union, Bevin pushed it aside, arguing that the situation had radically changed since it was set up. And on 25 September, the Cabinet decided to establish their own, new study group of officials in response to Bevin's wishes.[26] This satisfied both Bevin, who wanted to see the facts before rejecting a customs union, and the economic ministries, who were certain that a full study would reveal the problems with the proposal. (Meanwhile plans were made to discuss the question of customs union with Commonwealth countries.[27])

The C.E.E.C. may have emphasized Anglo-French differences on Germany and European economic integration, but on both issues bitter arguments had been avoided. The overall effect of the Marshall Plan was very positive for Anglo-French relations. The two countries, unmoved by Russian opposition, had successfully led concerted Western European action on a reconstruction plan. It was a great turnabout from the days early in June when Western Europe was in confusion following the Moscow C.F.M. and when the best initiative Bevin could find was an Anglo-Belgian treaty. The full positive effect of the Marshall Plan was seen when Bevin and Ramadier met to discuss Anglo-French co-operation as the C.E.E.C. conference ended.

8

The Bevin-Ramadier Talks

September–November 1947

IN THE six months since March, Anglo-French relations had been transformed by the Dunkirk Treaty, the Moscow Conference and the Marshall Plan, and on 22 September Bevin met the French premier, Ramadier, in a completely friendly atmosphere to discuss further co-operation. As in the January talks with Blum old arguments faded away and Bevin again spoke of Europe as the most vital area of British foreign policy. Although France was now committed to the Western camp, Ramadier was concerned about the possible effect on his country if the East–West rift widened further, and he returned to the now well-established idea of an Anglo-French 'front' which could act as a peacemaker between Russia and America. In replying to Ramadier on this point, Bevin went further than ever before in expressing his desire for Western European co-operation, suggesting that Britain and France (with their colonies) could indeed match the two superpowers and that peace with Russia might be possible at the next Conference of Foreign Ministers. He particularly hoped for Anglo-French economic co-operation to be extended, following the Marshall Plan, by improving tourism, fostering colonial economic improvements, and even giving British support to the Franco-Italian talks on a customs union (which were just beginning). On leaving the meeting Bevin declared, 'We've made the union of Britain and France this morning'. Ramadier, and Duff Cooper, hoped this was true; René Massigli was impressed, but knew that British reliance on America would be hard to break.[1]

Bevin's bold statements to Ramadier were in line with the 'grand design' of August 1945 and, if carried out, would have extended the policy of co-operation with Western Europe, and especially France, seen in the Dunkirk Treaty and Marshall Plan. Hitherto the Levant and German problems, the need to placate America and Russia, and the reticence of the economic ministries had hindered progress, but now Bevin seemed determined to advance and even to try to erect a third 'superpower' on Anglo-French co-operation. Unfortunately the aftermath of the Bevin–Ramadier conversation was to prove once again that bold words on Western European co-operation were very hard to fulfil.

Bevin had promised most progress to Ramadier in the field of economics. This was the Foreign Secretary's favourite area for action, and on 26 September he met Foreign Office officials, brushed aside any problems they put forward, and said that British and France must create vested interests in each other's economies, a policy he hoped to extend throughout Western Europe later. (The similarity to the August 1946 talks, when Bevin stimulated economic co-operation, was remarkable.)[2] On 2 October the French were promised that new proposals for economic co-operation would soon be coming from Whitehall. Meanwhile the French became very excited by the Bevin–Ramadier talks: the Quai d'Orsay hoped for co-operation on colonies, the Middle East and defence; Massigli talked of creating a self-sufficient Anglo-French unit; and Bidault inspired an article in the *l'Aube* praising the Anglo-French union idea of 1940. But this unguarded enthusiasm only fuelled official reticence in Whitehall about Bevin's ideas. Even the francophile Oliver Harvey declared that 'hasty' action must be avoided. The old division between the 'gradual' approach of Whitehall to Western European co-operation and the 'instant' approach of others, like Duff Cooper, reappeared.[3]

On 8 October representatives of the Foreign Office, Treasury, Board of Trade and other departments met to discuss Bevin's latest scheme. The meeting began briskly enough, with Oliver Harvey outlining the proposal to form a powerful economic group based on Britain, France and their colonies. But the ensuing discussion only revealed the unpopularity of such an idea in Whitehall. A third of the time was spent debating whether Eire could join such a union, before deciding that that was too confusing. Then all the usual arguments against an Anglo-French union were produced: Britain lacked the resources to help France; a customs union was impractical; the Commonwealth would be upset. The Foreign Office representatives showed little more determination to act than other ministries. On short-term issues, too, officials felt little could be done: it was agreed to maximize Anglo-French trade but not to treat France as a trading priority; financial problems still dogged the revival of tourism; and France was criticized for her large trade deficit with Britain.[4] Duff Cooper was thoroughly disgruntled when he heard reports on this meeting. He wrote bitterly to Bevin on 16 October, asking him to order action by the civil servants. Although Bevin asked for an optimistic reply to this letter the Foreign Office did not send one until 27 November. There were certainly enormous problems for the British officials to face: the franc was overvalued, the French economy had little to offer Britain, and Britain was in desperate financial difficulties and quite unable to give 'charity' to others. But it was the negative *attitude*, rather than the actual problems raised by officials, which Duff Cooper disliked, and which was to damage Britain's standing in Europe over the next few years.[5]

Hopes for colonial co-operation after the Bevin–Ramadier talks were similarly disappointed, mainly because of the vastly different colonial philosophies of the two countries (already seen in the Levant). In Asia co-operation was almost impossible because, while Britain gave independence to India and other areas from 1947, hoping to develop a new, free association with them, the French became involved in a bitter colonial war in Indochina, with which Britain (whilst supporting the regime of Bao Dai which the French eventually established there) did not want to be associated.[6] In the Middle East co-operation was also almost impossible because, of course, the French had left the area in 1946. By 1947 the British were deeply embroiled there in the struggle between the Jews and Arabs over Palestine, and this caused some Anglo-French differences. The French felt some satisfaction at seeing their old Middle East rival in such a predicament. Furthermore French leaders were generally pro-Zionist and disliked Bevin's attempts to restrict Jewish immigration into Palestine. Great friction with the French Socialists was generated by the 'Exodus' incident in 1947, though fortunately this did not harm wider Anglo-French co-operation.[7]

Real scope for colonial co-operation was confined to sub-Saharan Africa, where nationalism was not yet a potent force. By 1947 the idea of harnessing Africa's resources to help strengthen Europe was widely canvassed. The Foreign Office had considered such an idea during the war, alongside the Western bloc, and in 1944 the French had suggested Anglo-French co-operation in West Africa. But the Colonial Office – like the Treasury and Board of Trade in economics – was not keen on the idea of co-operation[8] and although Anglo-French talks were held in November 1945 they were strictly limited to exchanges of information on such issues as disease and education. In 1946 co-operation remained on a technical level.[9] In May 1946 Bevin mentioned the possibility of utilizing Africa's resources to

Bidault,[10] but when Duff Cooper pressed for colonial co-operation as part of the Treaty of Dunkirk his idea was rejected.[11] In 1947 a form of colonial Western bloc actually emerged when, in May, Anglo-Franco-Belgian discussions were held about Africa, but again the subjects discussed were purely technical.[12] After the Bevin–Ramadier talks Alphand (typically) went so far as to suggest a West African customs union, but the Foreign Office, convinced of the benefits of 'gradual' progress, put no real pressure on the Colonial Office to act.[13] In February 1948 more Anglo-French talks were held which concentrated on issues such as marketing and communications.[14] Individual attempts to inspire progress continued: George Rendel, ambassador to Brussels, pressed for Anglo-Belgian co-operation, and President Auriol continued to hope for European co-operation in Africa. But, as one French colonial governor later commented, Western co-operation in Africa after 1945 'was limited to subjects which did not call for ... a concerted political position'. Differences of colonial philosophy, bureaucratic reticence and a lack of genuine political initiative, for which both sides were responsible, prevented real action.[15]

In the short term too, Anglo-French military co-operation remained limited. Since the war Britain had been trying to rebuild France as a military force (the main reason for rebuilding France at all, of course, was to make her the cornerstone of Western European defences). In 1945 the new Labour government had agreed to equip the French air force and allowed the French to manufacture British types of aircraft; they also gave France several ships – including an aircraft carrier – on loan or at bargain prices, and rebuilt the French naval air arm. The traditionally anglophobe French navy became well disposed to Britain. But the French air force and navy remained weak,[16] and, more important, their army was very unimpressive. The 1940 defeat, fratricidal conflicts in 1940–4, and Indo-China, all reduced the army's efficiency and status. Duff Cooper's first post-war report on the army had said that it was unlikely to become a strategic force in Europe soon: it had low morale, old equipment, poor training and too many commitments (in Germany and the empire). Since then the situation had not improved: in January 1948 a report by General Revers, the French Chief of Staff, pointed to exactly the same problems.[17]

In late 1947 France's military weakness was closely associated with her political and economic problems, which were worsening at the time. Marshall Aid would not begin to flow for some time and, in the meantime, inflation and food shortages continued. The

French Communists, completely alienated from the government by October, and under the direction of Moscow, placed themselves at the head of a growing strike movement with the intention of ruining the economy. De Gaulle's R.P.F. experienced a dramatic rise, drawing half-a-million people to a rally in Vincennes in early October. The extremists began to generate support for each other, and the moderate parties, sandwiched in between, recognized that a kind of 'cold war' was growing inside France: thus they named themselves the 'third force'. In November the strikes brought down Ramadier's government, and the Foreign Office believed that de Gaulle might soon gain power. There was terror in France at the prospect of a simultaneous civil war and Third World War, which would destroy the country.[18]

France's reaction to her military, economic and political weakness was twofold. First she hoped to stop the East–West rift widening further – hence the hopes for an international 'third force' to act as a moderating force in the world. Internally this was matched by a mild policy towards the strikes; in December a new government formed under the M.R.P.'s Robert Schuman who promised that there would be no retribution against the strikers. This moderation, helped by the break-up of the main (communist-led) trades union, the C.G.T., succeeded in pacifying the country and created a good impression in London. The second, and somewhat paradoxical, French response to the world situation, however, was to seek an alliance with America and Britain.[19] As early as 11 June Bidault told the U.S. ambassador that France would feel safer with American atomic bombers based on the Elbe.[20] Even de Gaulle wanted an American alliance now[21] and, following the Bevin–Ramadier talks, French military chiefs hoped for staff talks with the Anglo-Americans. In October Chauvel visited London and, in contrast to France's former anti-German outlook, requested that military preparations be made to defend Western Europe from Russia. But although the British feared Russia and were even considering proposing a tripartite (Anglo-Franco-American) Byrnes Treaty, they rejected Chauvel's ideas for several reasons: they wanted to give four-power co-operation one last chance to succeed, at the next Conference of Foreign Ministers (due in London in November); the C.O.S. were wary of talking to the French, partly because communists were still believed to be entrenched in the French civil service, and partly because of the character of the French Chief of Staff, Revers, who was politically naïve (he had talked to a Spanish general about forming an anti-Soviet alliance);

and finally, most surprisingly, they did not want talks because Britain's own assessment of the West's military situation was so pessimistic that it would only demoralize the French! This refusal to talk, however, brought more complaints from Duff Cooper, and Bevin himself was upset by what he called the 'anti-attitude' of some officials. The Foreign Secretary agreed that military talks were premature but he got his officials to promise the French that, if the London C.F.M. failed, military talks could begin.[22]

The French desire for staff talks seemed contradictory to their policy of preventing East–West division. In fact, inside the French Cabinet, there was a split between the anti-Soviet Bidault and a moderate group (led by President Auriol) about how to balance the search for world peace against the need to take precautions against Russia. Ironically, after trying to mediate between East and West since 1944, some elements in Paris now seemed to want a Western alliance more than London and Washington did: with their internal weaknesses, their recent experience of conquest and occupation, and their exposed position on the continent the French were far more terrified of a Russian attack than Britain or America, and far more divided on what policy to adopt in the face of the Soviet menace.

The staff talks proposal was Duff Cooper's last chance to condemn Whitehall's reticent policy towards co-operation with France. In December he left Paris, having been ambassador (initially in Algiers) since 1943. Bevin had faced pressure to remove the former Conservative minister for some time, but Duff Cooper was still shocked at being replaced. Though he had seen an Anglo-French treaty made he was very disappointed at the failure to extend co-operation further. He kept a flat in Paris after leaving the embassy and remained very attached to France until his sudden death in 1954.[23] His successor was Oliver Harvey, an efficient career diplomat, who had served in Paris before and was, of course, very familiar with Bevin's French policy. The only major criticism of him as ambassador was that he ended the glittering social entertainments of the Duff Coopers. Some felt a plainer style was well suited to the Fourth Republic, but by the mid-1960s the embassy had become something of a social backwater, and the then Foreign Secretary, George Brown, had to encourage it to return to a more extrovert outlook.[24]

From the results of the Bevin–Ramadier talks Duff Cooper was justified in feeling disappointed about progress on Anglo-French co-operation. But the French themselves made no complaints about the lack of British action. Britain's promise to hold staff talks if the London C.F.M. failed, Bevin's positive approach to France, and the beneficial effects of the Marshall Plan still made relations seem close. Just as important, there were signs of growing co-operation on the usually divisive German problem.

At the Moscow C.F.M. it had become clear that the French thesis on Germany had no chance of being adopted. To have tried to maintain it would have isolated France while Britain, America and Russia revitalized their zones.[25] Therefore, in the months after Moscow, Bidault had gradually turned towards a new policy, co-operation with the Anglo-Americans (with whom he was increasingly having to co-operate in the wider world), in the hope of inducing them to keep some strict controls on Germany. (This new policy was first seen during the Marshall Plan talks, and the tripartite talks on Germany's 'level of industry' in July–August.) In October Bidault tried to develop this policy by suggesting tripartite talks on Germany before the London C.F.M. He hoped to gain some concessions to French wishes in Germany, in return for forming a tripartite 'front' at the C.F.M. and he was even willing, now, to accept economic controls on the Ruhr – as Britain had always wanted – rather than its political independence. Despite some Foreign Office doubts, Bevin was delighted with Bidault's new attitude and the result was a visit by Chauvel to London in October. Here, as with the staff talks proposal, the British were unwilling to start full discussions before seeing the outcome of the London C.F.M. – Bevin was still keen to keep the peace with Russia if at all possible – but the British did agree to hold three-power discussions, at which a list of desiderata shared by the Western states was drawn up, for use at the London C.F.M. These desiderata included the Byrnes Treaty, a decentralized German government, and so on.[26] Thus although Bevin still claimed to want agreement with Russia, and although President Auriol was concerned at the worsening East–West tension, tripartite Western co-operation on Germany was very much in being *before* the London C.F.M. Indeed, these talks on Germany, together with the other Anglo-French discussions on military security and Western European co-operation following the Bevin–Ramadier meeting, were very much the forerunners of a new policy of Western co-operation that was to emerge after the London C.F.M. – the policy of 'Western Union'.

9

The London C.F.M., Brussels Pact and 'Western Union'

November 1947–March 1948

ALTHOUGH, in the talks with France on Germany and military security, Bevin had insisted on giving four-power agreement one last chance to succeed, he showed little hope that the London Conference of Foreign Ministers would achieve anything positive. On 25 November he told the Cabinet that Russia was bent on dominating Europe, and he promised a major review of foreign policy if the C.F.M. failed. The same day he told Bidault that Britain and France must co-operate no matter what occurred in London. Bidault too, to Auriol's disappointment, had little hope for the C.F.M.[1] and when the London meetings began there was deadlock. Both East and West accused each other of seeking to dominate Germany, the Anglo-Americans rejected Soviet demands for high reparations, and the Russians again blocked discussion of the Byrnes Treaty. On 15 December the C.F.M. adjourned and thereafter no-one even pretended that there was four-power co-operation in the world.

Everyone agreed that this failure made British opposition to Russia unmistakably clear.[2] After London the last vestiges of early post-war security thinking were to disappear: a Western alliance, regional co-operation in Western Europe and Germany's quite rapid revival replaced four-power co-operation, the U.N. ideal and controls on the wartime enemy. Talks which led to this new system began immediately after the C.F.M. Bevin and Bidault met on 17 December and Bidault, fearful of Russia, was keener than ever to see Anglo-Franco-American talks on Germany. This Bevin was now ready to concede: he proposed talks on all the major issues in Germany, including the formation of a West German government, with which Bidault did not disagree. But Bevin did not want to discuss only Germany. He had two other important ideas on

Western co-operation. First, he wanted to see greater European unity against communism, even the formation of what he called a 'federation'. This was yet another in a long line of enthusiastic declarations on Western European co-operation from Bevin, and he was rather vague on its details. He would develop it later. For now, his second proposal was more clearly defined: he wanted to begin Anglo-French military talks, and even to get an American security commitment to Europe. Bidault, though somewhat exasperated by Bevin's long exposé, fully agreed that greater Western European co-operation and an American alliance were needed, and even offered to take British advice on an approach to Washington.[3]

The position in December 1947 was certainly difficult. Bevin and Bidault expected Soviet subversion of a pathetically weak Western Europe, which seemed more exposed than in the 1930s: Bidault believed the Russians would soon repeat the Nazi coup of ten years before, in Czechoslovakia (the one Eastern European state where democracy still survived). But there were two hopeful factors. First, Bevin was willing to co-operate with France as a partner and draw all Western Europe together, so that Hitler's piecemeal victory of 1940 would not be repeated. Second, there seemed to be time to act: the British believed that Russia was still too exhausted by the last war to launch an immediate invasion of Western Europe. So far, having defeated Germany, the Russians had avoided the use of armed force in seeking to expand their influence, and even Churchill, in his rabidly anti-Soviet Fulton speech, had declared, 'I do not believe that ... Russia desires war'. But the danger was that Moscow would use *other* means, short of war, to advance the communist cause: in Western Europe they could use political discontent and communist supporters to subvert governments from within. Faced with this situation Bevin wanted to strengthen Western Europe's ability to resist communism, while building up the continent's long term military security. To do this he aimed to combine two old British aims: an American alliance (for only America had the military and economic potential to resist Russia) and Western European co-operation (to give the continent faith in itself and in democracy). In the long term his vision was of a strong, independent Western Europe, able to stand alone without American support, and which would force Russia to give up all hopes of conquest.[4] This hope for a united West, overcoming the present crisis and building a lasting peace, was soon shared by others. Bidault certainly seemed to have grasped it, since he told the French Cabinet on 19 December that peace could only be achieved now in alliance with America, Britain and the rest of Western Europe.[5] It was, as one Canadian said, a 'time of fear and hope'. But the execution of Bevin's vision would require great effort. He had spoken great words before about a Western bloc, a customs union and Anglo-French co-operation, and failed to live up to them. Now the necessity for genuine action was greater than ever, but the room for problems was immense.

Bevin also saw Marshall after the C.F.M., and outlined to him his hopes for tripartite discussions on Germany, a 'spiritual confederation' of Western Europe, and American action on security. On the last point Marshall made an important suggestion (based on the tactics used in the Marshall Plan) that Western Europe ought to draw together in an alliance first, and then ask America to make up any military deficiencies. This would impress the American people (by proving that Western Europe wanted to resist communism) and give time to win Congress over to a commitment to European security. This basic concept was to guide Western military preparations over the next eighteen months. On Germany, meanwhile, it was agreed to begin tripartite discussions soon.[6] Early in January Bevin presented his new policy to the Cabinet: pointing to the Soviet menace he called for 'some form of union in Western Europe... backed by the Americas [sic] and the Dominions' to be created. This fused the three main areas of British interests in the post-war world into one comprehensive policy but at the time Europe was the central concern to Bevin, who hoped to draw all free European states together, from Portugal to Greece. He admitted his vision seemed 'somewhat fanciful' and was still vague about how it should be formed – speaking of common ideals, rather than common institutions as the uniting element – but his commitment to some form of Western European unity was unquestionable. The later claim by historians that Western European cooperation was nothing more than an attempt by Bevin to induce American support for Europe was ridiculous.[7]

Just how far the Foreign Office supported European unity at this time was seen in a remarkable discussion among officials on a Western European customs union. On 6 November the British study group on this issue, established in September, had produced an interim report pointing to the advantages of a customs union (such as expanding markets) and its disadvantages (such as short term economic disruption), and recommending that Britain should continue its studies. Bevin was somewhat upset by this unimaginative paper[8] but, since the C.U.S.G. (the study group established by the C.E.E.C.) was only beginning its studies – it held its first meeting in mid-November – the British indecision did not yet affect international discussions. Also in November, it became clear that Commonwealth countries had grave doubts about British membership of a European customs union, and this fuelled the criticism of the idea from the economic ministries. (The British actually raised the Commonwealth doubts with Alphand, but he viewed this as just another 'excuse' from London to avoid closer European integration.)[9] However, after the London C.F.M. broke down and Bevin became more determined to progress with European co-operation, the Foreign Office began to state the political case for a European customs union more forcefully than ever. R.B.Stevens began the debate by arguing that a union (while, perhaps, threatening Commonwealth unity) would weld Europe together, strengthen weak continental regimes, encourage American support, deter a Russian attack, and even solve the German problem (by making Germany merely part of a European union). A customs union could, it seemed, fulfil all Britain's important political aims in Europe. Other officials, notably Gladwyn Jebb and Hoyer-Millar, reacted enthusiastically to Stevens' arguments. Jebb even proposed that a full politico-economic union might be pursued. This discussion led to a special Foreign Office meeting in late January, which decided to try again to stimulate action on a customs union throughout Whitehall. To do this the Foreign Office planned a Cabinet Paper which would establish yet another British study group, on a politico-economic union. Never had British officials come closer to endorsing real European unification.[10]

Meanwhile moves had begun on the military staff talks which Bevin had promised the French. On 17 December Marshall had agreed with Bevin's proposal for such talks but both men realized there could be grave problems: Bevin feared that personal relations between Anglo-French military leaders could never be close, and was concerned with France's lack of confidence in herself; Marshall was more worried about her lack of military equipment.[11] Bevin's first fear soon seemed to be justified. Although Montgomery (now Chief of the Imperial General Staff) reacted well to the idea of a Western European alliance and Anglo-French staff talks, the C.O.S., meeting on 23 December, raised the same arguments they had put against such staff talks before the London C.F.M.: the dangers of leaks to French Communists, Britain's embarrassing military position, and so on. All that they were willing to let Montgomery discuss with France's General Revers was army reorganization.[12] Fortunately – as with customs unions – the Foreign Office were now unwilling to be dissuaded. They had promised talks with France and they pressed the C.O.S. to agree to them, even if it did mean giving Revers a realistic appraisal of the military situation. On 7 January the C.O.S., whom Bevin bluntly accused of being 'backward' on the question, agreed to the Foreign Office wishes[13] and the Revers visit duly occurred late in January. Revers returned from it quite satisfied – among other things Montgomery had said the Rhine must be held in another war – but he noted a distinctly reticent attitude from the War Office, contrasting with Foreign Office enthusiasm.[14] The experience showed that, while Bevin might be determined to progress, opposition within Whitehall to close Western European co-operation remained.

Bevin had given Ivone Kirkpatrick the task of making a blueprint for progress on a Western European military alliance. But it was Bidault who, on 23 December, proposed that Britain and France might now pursue the long-considered Belgian treaty. This coincided with yet another Belgian approach for security arrangements, and it soon formed a major part of Kirkpatrick's considerations. There were signs that Holland might favour a treaty now, and on 9 January Kirkpatrick's initial ideas appeared, proposing the formation of a 'core' arrangement with Belgium and Holland, based on bilateral treaties similar to Dunkirk, which could be extended later to the rest of Europe. This would be done by Britain and France in unison, and America would be kept fully informed – two principles which Bevin personally underlined. Western Europe had already overcome great problems in the economic field with the Marshall Plan, and Bevin now wanted to repeat the formula of Anglo-French leadership, backed by America. But in June 1947 America had been publicly committed to action by the Harvard Speech. In early 1948 Western Europe was more aware of being alone. Exactly how to get a U.S. military commitment was still undecided, although the British considered two ideas: one was a regional security pact such as the U.N. Charter allowed; but most popular remained an Anglo-Franco-U.S. version of the anti-German Byrnes Treaty.[15]

Bevin soon informed Bidault and Marshall of the proposal to make a treaty with the Benelux states which, in order not to offend Russia openly, would be based on the anti-German Treaty of Dunkirk. Bidault, who was very pleased to be closely involved in Bevin's ideas, agreed,[16] but the State Department questioned the suitability of the Dunkirk model because, obviously, Germany was not the enemy at present. American officials felt the recently signed Pan-American 'Rio Pact' would be a better model. This, like the Foreign Office's alternative to the Byrnes Treaty, was a multilateral arrangement, based on the U.N. Charter's sanction for regional pacts.[17] The next person to be told of Bevin's plans was Spaak. Then Bevin was ready to announce his new policy to the world.

Bevin's 'Western Union speech', delivered to the House of Commons on 22 January, described the growth of the Russian threat and called for a 'Western Union' to resist it. It specifically proposed a treaty with the Benelux countries, tripartite talks on Germany, colonial co-operation and (on a popular level, typical of Bevin) improvements in tourism. But the long-term vision remained vague: Bevin spoke of European 'consolidation' but ruled out 'ambitious schemes' in favour of 'a practical programme'. Bevin's pragmatism, dislike of idealism, and faith in Britain's unwritten constitution shone through; his hope was that various forms of co-operation – economic, military, colonial – would knit together, and evolve somehow into a genuine unity, which would simultaneously preserve Britain's links to the Commonwealth.[18] René Massigli was one of the few people to grasp these points from the start.[19] But this deliberately vague policy had three obvious problems: continental governments, used to written constitutions and precise arrangements, would inevitably find it difficult to understand; it was not definite enough to resist the bureaucratic opposition in Whitehall (even when the speech was being drafted several government departments expressed worries over the commitments it might lead to);[20] and it would need very careful execution. Bevin had many ideas about *what* to try to seek in Western Europe – military strength, sound finances, a strong industrial base – but he had few ideas on exactly *how* to get these, beyond forming a military alliance.[21] His vision was at once grandiose and gradualistic, and over the next few years the tension between his massive ideal and his practical approach would prove difficult to control.

Bevin's immediate aim, a Benelux treaty, soon bore fruit, but not without difficulties. Bidault welcomed the Western Union speech,[22] and on 31 January Benelux foreign ministers met and agreed to pursue a treaty. But the Benelux countries also asserted their independence by arguing (probably due to American influence) that a multilateral, regional pact was more suitable than a Dunkirk-style treaty. Bevin, keen to proceed quickly, sent his Minister of State, Hector McNeil, to clarify these Benelux proposals in early February. It was clear that Spaak was very much the Benelux leader and that he had powerful arguments for proposing a regional pact: it would make more sense than an anti-German treaty, would please America, and could easily be extended later. McNeil suggested that a conference of the five negotiating powers was the best way to decide these issues quickly. But another point McNeil noted was that the Benelux leaders disliked France's joint leadership of the new alliance.[23] This soon became a vital problem because the French now insisted that bilateral treaties based on Dunkirk must remain the model for the new security arrangement. The British found themselves having to balance the strong wishes of their French and Benelux allies, reluctant to displease either for fear of ruining the nascent alliance. There were certainly arguments against a regional treaty: it would be outrightly anti-Soviet while making no material improvement in Europe's defences. Chauvel wanted Britain and France to submit a Dunkirk-style treaty to the Benelux countries for discussion, and he rejected McNeil's idea of a conference (fearful that France would be isolated in five-power talks).[24] This deadlock continued for some time until Bevin, keen to progress, proposed a compromise: a Dunkirk-style treaty would be formally put to the Benelux countries, but France must be prepared to hold a conference and to consider other types of treaty. The French reluctantly agreed, and on 19 February the Benelux states were approached. But, although Britain pressed them to respect the French attitudes, the situation still seemed difficult. The Benelux states soon replied that they would still prefer a Rio-style Pact, and the Foreign Office was increasingly impressed by the arguments in favour of this course.[25]

The situation was saved by the Russians who in late February shocked the world by sponsoring a communist takeover in Czechoslovakia. At the London C.F.M. Bevin and Bidault had predicted such communist advances in the spring, but since then the Russian threat had become less apparent, which probably contributed to the recent delays on the Benelux treaty. Now the menace had returned. In France there was renewed fear of war, and Russia was completely discredited. Furthermore, the crisis led France to agree to a multilateral treaty: there was little point in refusing to upset Russia by such a move now. The British responded by drawing up a second version of their multilateral pact, which included some anti-German clauses so as to please France. Then attempts began to marry the British and French drafts.[26]

On 4 March a five-power conference met in Brussels and, thanks to the Czech coup, agreement was reached on a treaty in only ten days. Britain and France concerted their approach in meetings between

Chauvel and the Foreign Office in London. Only two major problems arose in the talks. First, Britain and France pressed the idea of anti-German clauses, because the French still genuinely feared Germany and wanted to limit criticism from the Russians and French Communists. But the Benelux countries disliked the idea: they now believed that it was time to bring Germany back into the comity of nations. This problem was overcome remarkably easily, however, because Germany's status was now being discussed in separate talks between the Western powers (which will be covered in the next chapter). As a result the Brussels Pact, as the treaty became known, did not specify any enemy: it simply promised mutual defence against an aggressor. The second problem was pressure from Spaak for a commitment to far-reaching economic co-operation as part of the treaty. Economic co-operation in Western Europe had always been a vital complement to Spaak's vision of a political Western bloc, but the British and French opposed his idea, arguing that other Europeans would be upset if an 'inner five' emerged in the Marshall Plan and that Marshall Plan co-operation should remain quite distinct from political-military moves, for practical reasons. But, as in the Dunkirk Treaty, there was a clause on general economic co-operation. There were also clauses on cultural and social co-operation, and the establishment of a 'Consultative Council'. The exact form of this Council was uncertain, but it was seen by Bevin as a vehicle to build up Western Union. The pact, for Bevin, was therefore far more than a military arrangement – it was a first step towards his vision of general Western European co-operation.[27]

The British Cabinet approved the new treaty on 15 March,[28] and two days later it was signed by the foreign ministers in Brussels. It came a year after the Dunkirk Treaty, to which it was directly related in being part of the old British plan to build a Western bloc around an Anglo-French alliance. But in the Brussels Pact the original perception of the Western bloc had changed: as Spaak acknowledged, 'the measure we had seen as a move to protect us from Germany was in fact turned against the Soviet Union'.[29] Furthermore, whereas in the Dunkirk talks the French had resented American influence on British thinking, by early 1948 Bidault was as keen as Bevin to receive American military support. The pact was also specifically designed to lead to more extensive co-operation on non-military issues than Dunkirk had done. All these developments had one common influence – the growing perception of a Russian threat to Europe, and, on a higher plane, of communism to democracy.

But on 17. March 1948, Europe was still far from safety: Western Union had still to receive an effective organization, an American security guarantee was needed, and the German problem remained. Anglo-French relations were intimately tied into the resolution of all these questions. Despite the growth of multilateral arrangements between the Western powers – in the Marshall Plan and the Brussels Pact – the bilateral relations of the two most important Western European states were vitally important. In the Marshall Plan and Brussels Pact negotiations Bevin had made Bidault his partner in the leadership of Western Europe, fulfilling the 'grand design' which he had outlined in August 1945. Bevin had done this despite France's continuing weaknesses (military, political and economic), the delays she had caused to an alliance in 1945–7, and the fact that other European countries disliked the idea of French leadership. But the French preserved their determination to be more than Britain's 'junior partner' in Europe, and over the next months the issues of Western organization, the American alliance and Germany's future were to show that Britain and France had widely varying interests, despite the new, common framework they now operated in.

10

The 'Western Union' in operation

March–July 1948

EVEN AS the Brussels Pact was signed the five members began work on its organization. Bevin was determined to make the pact the vehicle of Western Union – still an indefinite vision – by building up military, financial, social and cultural co-operation. (Economic co-operation would be handled by the Marshall Plan.) Initially Bidault seemed to agree with Bevin on the pact's organization: on 17 March the two met and agreed that military and financial co-operation should be covered by the pact, that moves must be made against communist infiltration (the British believed this was rife in continental governments), and that the Consultative Council made up of foreign ministers should meet regularly to provide continuing co-operation. With this Anglo-French agreement secured Bevin successfully pressed these points at a meeting of all five foreign ministers later in the day.[1] Over the next month, however, two differences arose about the details of this new organization, and showed that the desire for greater Western European unity could not yet overcome the search for national status. The first problem arose because the French refused to accept a British plan (supported by Benelux) to centralize the Brussels Pact machinery in London. The French wanted instead to scatter the machinery through the member capitals, and to rotate meetings of the Consultative Council around these capitals, so as to give a greater sense of 'unity' in the pact (though with some loss of efficiency). By 30 March a possible Anglo-French compromise had been reached among officials, for the Council meetings to rotate while all permanent bodies in the pact were based in London, but Bidault had refused to accept this. Meanwhile the second problem had arisen when Britain, France and Belgium each put forward their own candidate for the key post of Secretary-General of the pact machinery.[2]

In April these Brussels Pact problems became inextricably tied into difficulties surrounding the Marshall Plan. It will be recalled that in September 1947 the Americans wanted a permanent body to be established in Europe, to handle Marshall Aid efficiently. Since then pressure in Congress for a visible sign of European co-operation had continued, and in January 1948 the British contacted the French about it. Maintaining their joint leadership of the Europeans in the Marshall Plan, London and Paris decided to send a joint team, formed from a Foreign Office representative, Eric Berthoud, and one of Monnet's aides, Philip Marjolin (a great exponent of Anglo-French co-operation), around the European capitals to sound out members on the general idea of a permanent body.[3] The team found, however, that many countries, such as Switzerland, Turkey and Sweden, had little wish to submit their economic policies to any international body such as Washington wanted to create, and Berthoud concluded that a permanent organization could only have quite general powers, such as the broad supervision of the aid programme, and the writing of progress reports.[4]

Berthoud's views coincided with those of the British government's London Committee, which had been established to handle Marshall Aid issues. The London Committee recognized the need for genuine European co-operation in the Marshall Plan, and were willing to accept some restrictions on British freedom to fulfil this aim. But they also wanted to preserve Britain's ultimate economic independence and were not interested in European co-operation for its own sake. The main aim of the new permanent organization in the London Committee's eyes was to remove the 'dollar gap' with America, which was so damaging to British and European economic prospects. The full force of the dollar problem had been brought home to the British in the summer of 1947 when, at American insistence, they had tried to make sterling convertible into dollars, only to face such a massive run on the pound that the experiment had to be halted within weeks. Thus the London Committee was willing to move a long way towards European co-operation, and especially to reduce intra-European barriers as a way of creating a European system that could operate with the minimum use of dollars. But officials had little wish to go beyond this. Treasury and Board of Trade representatives had never liked the prospect of upsetting the Commonwealth, or the danger of surrendering control of their own economy through over-close European co-operation. So they wanted the new permanent body to work on an *inter-governmental* basis through national delegations; they certainly did not want an independent, executive body that could 'dictate' actions to member nations. Bevin, though more eager to co-operate with Europe than the economic ministries, also believed in the value of inter-governmental co-operation as the most practical approach to European unity. (His attitude will be discussed more fully in later chapters.) In early March the Cabinet approved this line.[5]

These ideas, however, were far from what the Americans and French wanted. In Washington the hope was for a powerful permanent body to be established that could prepare investment, production and import programmes for members;[6] and the French felt that only a strong independent secretariat could lead the new organization and direct the European recovery plan efficiently.[7] (These arguments were an important extension of earlier Anglo-French differences about economic integration.) For the present, however, the British view won through. By now it had been decided to call a new C.E.E.C. meeting on 16–18 March in Paris to discuss a permanent organization. This was preceded by Anglo-French talks, among officials led by Hall-Patch and Alphand, who were soon locked in argument about the form of the new permanent body. On 14 March Bevin and Attlee discussed the problem and confirmed the London Committee's policy. But they also reaffirmed their commitment to Western European co-operation – Bevin genuinely believed that an independent secretariat would not be as effective as inter-governmental meetings. This British commitment to European co-operation, her position as the accepted 'leader' of Western Europe, the doubts of so many other countries about a strong permanent body, and the fact that Britain and France agreed on most other aspects of the Marshall Plan problem, meant that the pressure was put on Paris, rather than London, to give way on the permanent body. Just as important, the Americans failed to support the French with determination at the time: the State Department had no wish to engage in bitter arguments with Britain, since she was considered the most 'reliable' state in Europe. As a result, on 18 March, after five days of talks, the French finally gave way and agreed to the British ideas.[8]

The C.E.E.C. meeting, meanwhile, established a working party to draw up the details of the new continuing organization. The working party was to report to another C.E.E.C. session in mid-April. The American Congress, content with this evidence of European co-operation, approved the Marshall Aid programme in early April and established an Economic Co-operation Administration (E.C.A.), under Paul Hoffmann (an industrialist and an exponent of European economic unity) to work with the Europeans on the plan. As with the Brussels Pact, however, there were arguments between Britain, France and Belgium over who should fill the leading posts in the new organization and where it should be based. In April the argument over both bodies became entangled. The Belgians wanted the Secretary-Generalship of at least one of the two bodies; Bidault continued his pressure over the siting of the Brussels Pact machinery as a tactical move to ensure that Paris remained the seat of the Marshall Plan; and the Benelux states proposed that a five-power meeting to resolve the arguments on the Brussels Pact ought to be convened during the C.E.E.C.'s mid-April session.[9]

Fortunately this mid-April meeting resolved all the problems. For Marshall Aid an Organization for European Economic Co-operation (O.E.E.C.) was established under an all-powerful inter-governmental Council, whose decisions required unanimity (though it was given quite extensive supervisory powers over the joint recovery plan). The Council was helped by two permanent bodies – an executive committee and a secretariat. The chairmanship of these three bodies was given to Britain, France and Belgium respectively, and Paris remained the seat of the organization, but Bidault was very resentful of the Benelux tactics and feared that joint Anglo-French leadership of European co-operation was being undermined by Spaak. On the Brussels Pact the compromise suggested in March, for rotating Council meetings, while the permanent bodies met in London, was now accepted, and Bevin specifically tried to reassure Bidault about France's importance to him: the permanent bodies created included a Military Committee to build up military co-operation (something Bidault had particularly wanted) and, once again, Bevin and Bidault met to concert their tactics before the five foreign ministers met. Bevin used this five-power meeting to reaffirm his belief in a pragmatic, 'evolutionary' approach to Western European co-operation.[10]

Over the next months the Brussels machinery was put into effect with mixed success. There was, for example, an attempt on a five-power basis, to resolve France's problem of an unrealistic exchange rate. This problem had been growing worse in 1948, especially from London's point of view, though Anglo-French economic relations had never, of course, been particularly good. In November 1947 when the Anglo-French Economic Committee met for one of its now regular meetings, things seemed to be improving: Alphand (whom the British still disliked) had ceased to represent France on this body; the French were now satisfied with the level of Ruhr coal supplies; and Paris promised to control its trade deficit with Britain. But the volume of French luxury exports, a temporary accumulation of sterling in Paris, and France's general economic performance worried Whitehall.[11] Then on 25 January 1948 the long-overvalued franc was finally devalued (as Britain wanted) but by differing amounts against sterling and the dollar. The British (and the I.M.F.) had tried desperately to prevent this French action, because it threatened to upset Britain's dollar position, but once it was carried out Whitehall decided to accept the situation without further protest: ministers and officials did not want to upset France's delicate trading position.[12] By March, however, the situation was rapidly worsening as France's excess of sterling disappeared and an enormous deficit grew. In April London decided to seek talks about this in the Brussels Pact. The main reason for this was that Belgium, by a fortunate combination of circumstances, had emerged from the war with relatively strong financial reserves, and was one of the few European countries able to help the French problems.[13] A meeting of the pact's finance ministers was duly held on 28–29 April, with moderate success. A system of British and Belgian credits for Paris was arranged, and the short-term crisis was overcome.[14] Unfortunately, as the British recognized, the sterling-franc problem was 'only the most acute example of the present disequilibrium in Western Europe' with regard to finances.[15]

Financial weakness in Britain and Western Europe undermined military co-operation in the Brussels Pact. Although the British were important suppliers of military aid to Western Europe, and wished to build a Western European alliance, it has already been seen that the C.O.S. were reluctant to co-operate too closely with the continentals. Even in early 1948 Attlee and the air and navy chiefs were reluctant to commit British land forces to Europe's defence because of the financial burden and the risk of another Dunkirk. Bevin and Montgomery objected to this attitude, arguing that the whole purpose of Western Union was to boost the morale of Western Europe and give it self-confidence, in the knowledge that an actual Russian attack was unlikely. But only in May was it agreed in principle to use British forces on the continent in a war. That same month Brussels defence ministers met and agreed to pool resources and standardize their equipment, and the new Military Committee began to prepare an inventory of resources, but the actual morale and equipment of the continental forces (especially the French) remained poor, and Western Europe's financial problems made matters worse: in June, Stafford Cripps, Dalton's successor as Chancellor of the Exchequer, had to agree to supply military materials to France without immediate payment. In this situation Montgomery recommended advances in an area where material resources were irrelevant: he pressed for a Western Union military command to be formed. The other chiefs, still doubtful about such 'political gestures', only agreed to this idea in July.[16]

The financial and military weakness of Western Europe only underlined the need for American support: in May the Brussels Pact adopted a strategy based on holding back any Russian assault until American forces arrived. But discussions about an actual American security commitment went slowly, despite appeals to Washington from Bevin and Bidault (supported by the other Brussels powers) throughout the first half of 1948.[17] The Americans preferred to press the Western Europeans into beginning their own military preparations while themselves debating what form of guarantee to give the continent. Some Americans, including the State Department's experts on Russia, George Kennan and Charles Bohlen, feared antagonizing Russia unnecessarily by a military alliance and wanted to build up Europe's economic and spiritual defences against communism, rather than to 'militarize' Western co-operation. But Truman, Marshall and others wanted to give solid support to Europe and in June the Vandenberg Resolution was passed through the Senate favouring a U.S. commitment to regional security systems. Despite its vague formula, this marked a major step for a country which hitherto had shunned peacetime alliances. And it paved the way to talks on Atlantic Security between America, Canada and the Brussels powers in Washington, early in July.[18]

Importantly, however, highly secret talks had *already* occurred in March–April between only three of these powers: America, Britain and Canada. These talks had discussed Atlantic security and had ended in a proposal for talks with the other Brussels powers. In themselves they were very tentative discussions, somewhat disappointing for the British, which were followed by long American delays on a pact, but they showed, once again, that Bevin's desire for Western European co-operation could be outweighed by Britain's historical links to America, and by short-term practicalities. The French were excluded from the talks, partly because of American fears that France would demand immediate

military supplies from Washington, and partly because of the old
British fear that many French officials were communist
sympathizers. (This latter argument was very ironic, since one of
the British negotiators, Donald Maclean, was a Soviet spy.) Thus
while Bevin claimed to be treating Bidault as a partner, and even
made joint appeals with him to Washington for an American
alliance, the British were secretly paving the way to such an alliance
behind the French backs.[19]

Talks on Germany had been under way throughout the first half
of 1948. An initial Anglo-French argument was caused in January
when the British and American governors publicly announced their
intention to create a bizonal German government. This led to an
immediate and vigorous French protest: Paris was not yet ready to
see her recent conquerors regain their national self-government.
But, personally, Bidault recognized that France could now do little
to prevent Germany's gradual revival, and he played down the
importance of the Anglo-American action in Cabinet. He intended
to develop the policy he had begun in 1947: to co-operate with
London and Washington and hope that they would give concessions to French views.[20] In the Assembly in February he spoke of
this new policy and even expressed the hope that France and
Germany might learn to co-operate in the new Western European
framework which was developing: Germany, he hoped, could become an integral part of a greater European whole.[21] Meanwhile, in
early January Bevin told his Cabinet that a stable, peaceful and
democratic Germany must be built up to resist Russian pressure.
This was very much part of Bevin's general policy of strengthening
the West and he was determined to work with France upon it. So
long as the French agreed with the general line of British policy in
Germany he was willing to make concessions to them to guarantee
their security from a German military threat.[22] The conciliatory
attitudes of Bevin and Bidault seemed to point the way towards
Anglo-French agreement at the three-power meetings on Germany,
promised after the London C.F.M., which began in London in
February and lasted until July. (To reinforce Western European
co-operation Benelux representatives were included in most of these
discussions.)

In the first session of this London conference (23 February–6
March) the French pressed their old aims in Germany in a diluted
form: they now wanted an International Control Agency in the
Ruhr (to control its steel and coal production, and guarantee coal
exports), a three-power Byrnes Treaty, a long occupation of the

Ruhr-Rhineland, the continuation of reparations, and a de-centralized government. Although the Anglo-Americans proved unwilling to discuss a Byrnes Treaty (because it was involved in the whole question of an American guarantee to Europe) and insisted that reparations deliveries must be reduced, they did agree to French wishes on decentralization and a Ruhr authority, and Bidault made much of these 'concessions' in the French Cabinet.[23] But not all his Cabinet colleagues liked Bidault's new policy. Germany remained a very emotive issue in France and many ministers, especially President Auriol and the Socialists, were terrified that the London conference would revive the German menace and provoke Russia into war. On 22 April Socialist ministers wrote to premier Schuman, protesting against Bidault's actions and demanding that France should work for peace in the world. Auriol even contacted Bevin and Harvey with a view to forming an Anglo-French 'front' for peace which would seek a meeting with Russia. But this idea, another variation on the 'third force' had no appeal for Bevin.[24]

In the second London session (20 April–7 June) Bidault won more concessions: it was agreed to establish a Ruhr Control Authority, to keep a long occupation of Germany and to set up a Military Security Board to supervise Germany's long-term dis-armament. But most important were discussions on Germany's political structure, where French officials retreated further from their old thesis than on any other issue, by agreeing to the early formation of a West German government (though one which was federal in structure). Bidault knew that, for his critics, such a policy was doubly worrying: it would both recreate a German state and deeply antagonize Moscow. But by minimizing his retreats and emphasizing Anglo-American concessions he retained Cabinet support on it into May. Then, however, he had second thoughts: he pressed the Anglo-Americans to grant more con-cessions to French wishes, so as to satisfy his Socialist colleagues. The Anglo-Americans, however, were now determined to push on with their policy and offered Bidault nothing more than a slight delay in the establishment of a German government. Bidault still believed that the London decisions must be accepted: the alternative, he knew, was that the Anglo-Americans would establish a German government anyway, that France would be-come isolated, and that all Western co-operation would be threatened. But in the Cabinet on 26 May even his M.R.P. colleagues expressed doubts about his policy, and a fateful decision was made to put the London Agreements to the Assembly for approval.[25]

This decision created a grave situation for Western co-operation in early June. The Anglo-Americans began to prepare bizonal policies, with Bidault's knowledge, in case the French rejected the London Accords; Bevin deliberately rushed approval of the Accords through Cabinet to put pressure on France to agree to them; and in Paris Bidault faced criticism from his fellow ministers over his tactics in London. But the crucial element in the situation was now the Assembly. Assembly members had expected *some* retreat from France's old demands in Germany, but they were totally unprepared for the scale of this retreat. The details of the London meetings had remained secret until early June, when suddenly the deputies found that high reparations, firm international control of the Ruhr, and many other old French demands were not going to be granted; the stark truth was that Germany was to have a government again. Communists and right-wingers opposed the new policy, and there were enough doubters elsewhere to put the government in jeopardy. Bidault frantically pressed the Anglo-Americans for some changes to the London Accords to please the Assembly but the response was negative, partly because such changes could have threatened the whole London policy and partly because of confusion at Bidault's attitudes: as late as 1 June Bidault had been content with the Accords and was confident of their approval. The French government became so uncertain about winning the vote that they refused to make it one of confidence and Bidault, shaken, was uninspiring in defending his policy before the Assembly. French officials and ministers – and even representatives from the British embassy and Labour Party – desperately lobbied deputies to support the London Accords, however, and a communist-inspired strike at the time, at Clermont-Ferrand, probably helped muster government support. Finally the Accords were passed, by only eight votes. The Western allies breathed a sigh of relief.[26]

Surprisingly, in contrast to 1945–7 these events in Germany did not gravely harm Anglo-French relations. Instead, the approval of the London Accords, though difficult, was another sign (alongside the Marshall Plan and Brussels Pact) of how far France had moved towards co-operation with Britain and America since March 1947. Even those like Auriol, who questioned Bidault's recent policy, favoured Western co-operation: what they disliked was the *degree* to which France had become anti-Russian, pro-American and associated with Germany's revival, not the broad lines of Bidault's policy. The arguments over the London Accords were not so much between France and the Anglo-Americans, as between Bidault and his critics. And it was Bidault who paid the price for the Accords. Though still respected as a former Resistance leader, he had alienated too many ministers and deputies to survive as foreign minister: in July he departed from the Quai, to be succeeded by the former premier, Robert Schuman, who quickly reassured the British that he would maintain established policies of Western co-operation on Germany's revival. Indeed, Schuman, who came from Luxembourg and was educated at German universities, hoped to bring about a Franco-German rapprochement, if that were possible. A tall, thin man, well-educated and with a grave but charming manner Schuman seemed the very antithesis of the bulky, jovial, ex-worker Bevin but the two men were to strike up a far closer relationship than Bevin and Bidault ever did.[27]

Schuman's arrival at the Quai d'Orsay, the London Accords, the opening of the Washington talks, and a new French proposal (to be discussed fully below) that the time had come to create a European parliament, signalled the beginning of a new phase in Anglo-French relations in mid–1948. Their co-operation had advanced a long way since the difficult years of 1945–6 when it seemed that an alliance between them would never emerge. Against the background of Russian expansion, four lines of Anglo-French co-operation had emerged: economic co-operation in the Marshall Plan; the development of the concept of Western Union; the search for an American alliance; and the controlled revival of Germany. During the next eighteen months co-operation in the four areas was developed but the period was also to see an increasing Anglo-French division on the precise form of Western European co-operation which should be pursued. During this period it will be easier to examine the Atlantic Alliance, European co-operation and Germany separately, whilst remembering that, frequently, important events in all these areas occurred simultaneously.

Part III

THE DEMISE OF
'WESTERN UNION'

Anglo-French relations and the shape of Western co-operation
July 1948 – February 1950

11

The creation of NATO

FROM mid–1948 until May 1949 the Russian blockade of Berlin dominated East–West relations and highlighted the need for Western unity. The blockade began when the Western powers introduced a new currency into their zones, an action which portended the creation of a West German state. For Vincent Auriol the blockade represented the inevitable (and potentially fatal) result of the London Accords, which he had always opposed, and he now became keener than ever to reopen talks with Moscow. In contrast, America's General Clay was willing to risk war in order to stay in Berlin. Auriol and Clay represented two extreme answers to the question of how to preserve Western security while avoiding a new global conflict and both were rejected when, in a remarkable feat of ingenuity, the West found that Berlin could be supplied by air. The blockade generated enormous fear – like the Czech crisis in February 1948, it was compared to Hitler's aggressive actions in the 1930s – but it succeeded in uniting the West more than ever: Britain, France and America concerted their approaches to Moscow over the blockade; the West German government was founded; and an Atlantic Alliance was formed. Eventually Stalin had to end the blockade and turn to the more subtle tactic of a 'peace offensive' to weaken Western resolve.

The formation of an Atlantic Alliance took far longer than its exponents had hoped. Mainly because of the American presidential election in 1948 (which made Washington unwilling to pursue controversial policies) a treaty was not signed until April 1949. Anglo-French relations were strained by two major problems during the negotiations: in July–September 1948 they argued about how to get a U.S. commitment to defend Europe; then they differed on the pact's membership and extent. But the eventual signature emphasized their co-operation as leaders of the West.

The first period of the Washington talks, between the Americans and the ambassadors of the other powers, was intended merely to be exploratory and the Foreign Office hoped it would see a wide degree of agreement. The Office suggested that the Brussels powers should have a common directive to guide their ambassadors in the talks, based on securing a firm American commitment to join a regional pact, before moving on to its details. But when the Brussels foreign ministers discussed this in mid-July they agreed only on a vague 'statement of principles'.[1] The reason for this failure was that Paris and Washington had differed fundamentally on how to make an American commitment to Europe. The French, having been excluded from the Anglo-American-Canadian talks in March, had little idea of American thinking on a pact, and had developed their own firm views on how to proceed. Basically the French sought to strengthen Europe's defences as soon as possible and to do this they wanted America (and Canada) to associate with the Brussels Pact, and American military aid to be sent to Europe, to be centred on the Brussels powers, not spread thinly over the continent. But the Americans differed from this approach in three important respects. Firstly, Congress, in approving the 'Vandenberg Resolution', had emphasized that any treaty must preserve Congress's right to make war, so that America could not simply join the Brussels Pact, with its *automatic* promise to go to war against an aggressor. Secondly, the Americans wanted the new treaty to cover as much of Europe as possible, partly to secure military bases in war, and partly to form a 'trip-wire' over which the Russians could not step without bringing conflict. From the first the Americans and French (the latter supported by Belgium) talked past each other in the Washington meetings because of these fundamentally different approaches. Thirdly, although the Americans did take some action to help Europe's defences (U.S. and Canadian observers joined the Brussels' Military Committee and Truman began work on a military aid programme for Europe), it was constitutionally impossible for the President to answer French demands for arms and equipment immediately.[2]

As in the Brussels Pact negotiations, the British found themselves having to mediate between the (rather traditionalist) French and the new alliance members, this time the Americans. Again, this mediation amounted to persuading the French that their views would have to change. In mid-July Gladwyn Jebb saw Bidault and Chauvel about this but failed to change their attitude (though Bidault conceded that Scandinavian and Mediterranean 'wings' might be added to the new alliance later).[3] Bevin got no further when the Brussels foreign ministers met a few days later,[4] and Robert Schuman's arrival at the Quai d'Orsay did not change French policy.[5] By mid-August the situation, still deadlocked, was becoming dangerous: the Americans were exasperated with the French attitude, and especially by the undiplomatic tactics of France's ambassador, Henri Bonnet, who had even told Marshall that American military supplies were the 'price' that must be paid for France to join an Atlantic Pact. Some U.S. advisers now talked of abandoning the alliance idea altogether, and this led London to redouble its pressure on the French.[6] At last, on 23 August, during another visit by Jebb, Schuman and Chauvel agreed that American views on the need for a new pact were reasonable, and that French demands for immediate aid would cease.[7]

The unbending attitude in Paris may have been caused by the political impasse there following the disintegration of the Schuman government (partly because of the London Accords) in July. There were two vain attempts to form a stable government after Schuman's fall before Henri Queuille emerged with what was to be a lasting administration on 10 September. Even for the Fourth Republic this was an extraordinary political crisis which, French ministers and officials realized, did nothing for the country's international status. All the governments during the crisis were variations on the same 'third force' theme, and the Foreign Office was confident that the crisis would not affect France's pro-Western outlook, but the Washington talks probably suffered from the inability of the French government to change its policies rapidly during such a period of instability.[8] Even after Schuman agreed to the American view of the pact it took some days before the Cabinet approved his decision.[9]

In early September the Americans and Canadians themselves approached the Quai about the Washington deadlock, only to find that the British pressure had already changed the French attitude: new instructions were about to be sent to Bonnet.[10] On 9 September Jebb reported that 'the incredibly stupid behaviour of the French' had indeed ended. The next day the first stage of the Washington talks closed with an agreed statement declaring the need for an Atlantic Pact with American membership and outlining some of its possible provisions (discussions on which had been under way throughout the talks). Each country now had to say whether it wished to make such a pact.[11] The British could be pleased that they had done the most to overcome the Franco-American differences and pave the way to an American security guarantee.

On 25–26 October, the Brussels foreign ministers met and jointly agreed to pursue an Atlantic treaty. But now differences on the extent of the pact moved to the fore. Whereas the British wanted to extend the new guarantee to countries such as Norway, Denmark and Portugal, the other Brussels powers still feared that such action would dissipate the West's defence resources. At most Schuman was willing to consider the idea (already considered by Bidault and the Anglo-Americans) for separate Scandinavian and Mediterranean pacts. In October the Brussels powers all agreed, however, to exclude Italy from the new alliance.[12] Britain and the others had many reasons for excluding her: she was large, economically weak, and exposed to communist pressure from within and without, and could easily become a huge drain on resources; she might press for changes to her Peace Treaty as the price of joining the pact; she was not in the U.N.; and her inclusion might seem to isolate other pro-Western Mediterranean states, such as Greece and Turkey, who were not to be included. The Brussels Military Committee had considered Italian membership of the Brussels Pact and firmly rejected it.[13]

In early November Truman was re-elected as President and the prospects for an early treaty seemed good. At this time, however, Jebb visited Paris to discuss the pact and, though he was very impressed with a French draft treaty, he found that an important change of opinion had occurred in Paris: France now wanted Italy in the Atlantic treaty.[14] This became the main Anglo-French disagreement in the rest of the Washington talks. The French had various reasons for supporting Italian membership: as part of the policy of friendship with Italy begun by de Gaulle; to offset the effect of problems in Franco-Italian relations, such as the restriction of Italian immigrants into France; or to please those elements in the State Department who favoured Italian membership. But most important to the French were their own defence interests. The French military were already very upset that, in Brussels defence preparations, the British wanted any retreat before a Russion invasion to be directed towards the Channel (presumably for a re-run of 1940). Now they feared that if, as America and Britain wanted, most of Scandinavia was included in the new pact it would have a distinct *northward* orientation in its defence preparations. The inclusion of Italy was a way to counter this by forcing defence arrangements to have a central balance, with France at the heart.[15] Although the British argued that Italian security, along with that of Greece and Turkey, could be covered by a declaration of their importance to Atlantic security, France disagreed. As a result the Brussels powers again failed to agree on a common directive for the next session of the Washington talks, held on 10–24 December.[16]

The December talks managed to agree on almost all points except the pact's extent, and on this issue there was great confusion. On one extreme the Benelux states disliked any extension of the pact; on the other America wanted to guarantee as wide an area as possible. The French disliked the idea of extending the pact but, realizing this would probably have to be done because of American pressure, were determined to have Italy included. Not only this, they said that French North Africa should also be covered (further shifting the treaty's centre southwards). The British, however, were in the least logical position: they wanted to extend the pact in principle, and even agreed to include North Africa (partly to please France, partly with the hope of covering Libya as well), but they were absolutely opposed to Italian membership. Inevitably British support for North Africa's inclusion while still excluding Italy was criticized. The Americans, fearful of becoming associated with French colonial rule, were absolutely opposed to defending North Africa. The Belgians declared that if French colonies were covered by the pact, the Belgian Congo should be too.[17] Over Christmas the British quickly decided not only to abandon their support of North Africa's inclusion, but to press the French to do the same. In fact the French did retreat somewhat: they now only wanted to cover Algeria, which constitutionally was part of France. But as 1949 began the French line hardened on covering both Italy and Algeria, while the British now opposed the inclusion of either.[18]

The final stage of the Washington talks began on 10 January. Initially a delay was caused because a new Secretary of State, Dean Acheson, had to familiarize himself with the situation. But since Acheson already had experience in the State Department, and was a great believer both in firm opposition to communism and in support for Western Europe, the future of the Atlantic Alliance was assured. Italy now formally requested to join the new pact and America (which up to now had been doubtful about Italian membership) marshalled an impressive set of arguments in favour of her inclusion: Italy was strategically vital to Southern Europe; Western forces were inadequate for Europe's defence whether she joined or not; and the Atlantic Pact was intended to deter aggression against all Western Europe, not just to defend only those who could be defended.[19] In mid-January, when Schuman and Bevin discussed Italian membership in London, the French position was unchanged,[20] and later in the month the British, faced by this French and American pressure, retreated: Bevin agreed, alongside other Brussels foreign ministers, that Italian membership was

acceptable, though only *if* American insistence continued.[21] In
February the Algerian issue also became easier, when the Americans
proved willing to accept a general formula (such as 'Europe and
North America') to define the area within which aggression would
trigger the pact's mutual defence clause. After arguments over the
precise definition, a formula which covered Algeria was agreed on 1
March.[22]

After the apparent improvement in January, however, the Italian
problem worsened because of three events. First Britain and France
disagreed on their interpretation of the Brussels foreign ministers'
agreement: France said that Italian membership had been agreed;
Britain (correctly) that Italy should be included only if American
insistence continued. Then the Americans tried to wash their hands
of the issue by saying that the Brussels powers must decide whether
Italy should join or not.[23] Most important, however, was America's
insistence in February, following Russian diplomatic pressure on
Oslo, that Norway must join the Washington talks immediately.
This gave the French an excellent bargaining counter: they would
not let Norway in unless Italy joined the talks too.[24] The French, to
British despair, even threatened to leave the talks themselves, if Italy
were not included.[25] Fortunately the Americans remained conciliatory: they returned to their active support for Italian
membership, and suggested a compromise: Norway should join the
talks immediately; Italy and other new members should join when
the pact was signed. In response to this, Schuman moderated the
French position, and a compromise eventually emerged on the
American lines.[26] Two factors helped this final agreement. One was
the need for haste, because of the Russian threat (seen against
Norway) and the danger of press leaks (which might lead
opposition to the pact to gather, especially in France).[27] The second
was the fact that all other major issues were now settled. Bitter
arguments had occurred in February when Congressional pressure
led the State Department to want only a very weak mutual defence
guarantee in the treaty. Britain and France (and the other members)
were united in opposing this American suggestion, however, and a
suitable compromise formula was reached: an attack on any
member of the pact would be considered an attack on all, but, to
protect Congress's rights, each state would react to the attack
according to its own constitution.[28] On 7 March a final text was
agreed.[29] The French Cabinet, after a troublesome administrative
delay, approved the pact on 16 March,[30] and it was signed on 4 April
– a year after the Brussels Pact, and two years after the Dunkirk

Treaty, from which, through many changes, it could be said to have emerged.

Bevin, who had done more than anyone to steer the Western allies towards the Atlantic Pact, saw it as the pinnacle of his achievement. In the Commons he pointed to its dual importance: as a powerful security guarantee, and as a sign of Western co-operation, which would give confidence to Western Europe and defend democratic values.[31] As a security guarantee the pact was the culmination of British proposals in wartime for a Western bloc. Until 1947 the Western bloc was seen as a Western European, anti-German arrangement, and discussion of an American commitment to Europe centred on the four-power, anti-German Byrnes Treaty, but the Brussels Pact had implied a shift towards seeing Russia as 'the enemy' and looked forward to an American guarantee, as a way to restore Europe's shattered balance of power. Bevin's vision of Western Union in 1947 had recognized that a permanent American commitment to European security simply had to be made to save the continent from communism, because only America had the resources to do this. In addition, of course, the British had close personal and historical links to America.

For France, Britain's partner in developing Western European co-operation, there were not the same close links to America, however, and the pact raised more divisive issues. In the Assembly Communists and 'neutralists' questioned the need for a treaty.[32] And although French leaders believed in the need for an American guarantee, they would have preferred a genuine military build-up and a more automatic treaty to achieve this, as seen in their arguments of July–September 1948. Having experienced armed occupation once the French wanted real defences, not empty guarantees, to warn off the Russian menace, and as the pact was being negotiated the French Cabinet discussed the need for U.S. military aid more frequently than the pact itself.[33] The Americans were well aware of French fears but only in July 1949, after the Atlantic Pact had been ratified, could Truman ask Congress to approve a massive Mutual Assistance Programme. Congress eventually approved this in September 1949 (influenced by the explosion of Russia's first atomic bomb). Even then the French had their doubts about the pact: the Socialists especially feared that, by making an aid agreement with America, and by allowing American military bases to be established on her soil, France would lose her military independence. It was the supposedly 'nationalist' M.R.P. ministers, such as Bidault and Schuman, who insisted that such

American methods had to be accepted.[34] From the first, therefore, an American alliance was a practical, rather than an idealistic policy for the French – far removed from Bevin's vision of a close, living American-Western European relationship.

There was always a paradox in the Atlantic Pact with regard to a material military build-up. The Americans, supported by Britain, had deliberately extended the alliance over a wide area to prevent a Russian piecemeal victory in Europe, but by early 1950 material defence arrangements had advanced little: American military aid was still being negotiated, each member looked towards its own defence needs, and the organization behind the treaty amounted to no more than a basic institutional network, topped by an 'Atlantic Council' of foreign ministers. The Brussels Pact machinery (kept separate from the Atlantic Pact initially) also remained an empty shell. In October 1948 a paper strategy was accepted which aimed to defend Western Europe as far East as possible (something France insisted on), protect the Middle East and North Africa (British and French interests respectively), and retain control of air and sea. The plan foresaw a short-term retreat should the Red Army invade, but expected a successful counter-attack. But on the practical side all the Brussels powers planned to do was counter communist propaganda, redistribute surplus equipment, and await American reinforcements.[35]

The most important thing the Brussels machinery managed to do was to create a command structure. But even here there were problems. As with the Marshall Plan and Brussels Pact there were Anglo-French arguments over who should fill the leading posts in the new organization. Montgomery's choice as overall military commander was probably inevitable, but to compensate for this France filled the posts of army and navy commanders. The Royal Navy, however, insisted that only port facilities be included in the Navy section.[36] The French were then embarrassed because General Juin, their ablest commander, refused to accept the army commander's post and General Jean de Lattre had to be chosen instead.[37] He was an able general but a difficult character, who immediately argued with Montgomery. Placing a French commander under a British one was a recipe for arguments anyway, but Montgomery and de Lattre were natural foes, each strong-willed, successful and independent, and they soon differed on a whole range of issues, from the tactics of European defence to the accommodation of their headquarters.[38] In early 1950 the Western Europeans had their assurance of American support, but their actual defences remained appallingly inadequate, and the main hopeful sign was that Russia was still considered to be incapable of launching a war.

Despite the weaknesses of the Atlantic Pact and the Anglo-French differences over European defence, the Western military alliance was vital for showing that, as Western, democratic states, Britain and France were on the same side in a divided world: barring a dramatic change of regime in London or Paris an Anglo-French conflict was unthinkable. With American membership, the Atlantic Pact proved far more impressive than the Dunkirk or Brussels treaties, and ensured that, in a war, Britain and France would fight side by side. But the pact also revealed the inability of the two countries, not only to shape the post-war world, but to defend themselves. In 1939 Britain and France were seen, by some, to be the world's leading powers; ten years later they needed American support to survive. Moreover, there can be no doubt that by tying Britain and America closer together the Atlantic Pact did contribute to Anglo-French division. In 1949 there were some who hoped for increasing Atlantic unity, based on democracy and the ideals which inspired the U.N. Canada especially wanted this. Some Americans wanted a cohesive Atlantic structure, built on two pillars, one American, one European.[39] In 1948–9 Bevin rejected such schemes for greater Atlantic co-operation because at that time he wanted to concentrate on *European* co-operation.[40] But there could be no doubt that for Britain, unlike France, the pact was a sign of a close relationship with North America. And although, at first, Bevin saw the Atlantic Pact as a way to strengthen Western Europe, the success of the American Alliance, alongside other factors, was to lead him away from closer European unity after 1949 towards a new vision, which catered more for British links to America and the Commonwealth.

12

The Council of Europe

UNTIL mid-1948 Western Europeans concentrated on economic and military co-operation in the Marshall Plan and the Brussels Pact. But in July 1948, Georges Bidault produced a dramatic scheme for *political* unity which was to draw out deep Anglo-French divisions on the future of Europe.

For centuries philosophers and statesmen had toyed with the idea of a European political union, but it took the terrible experience of world war to bring the idea alive after 1919. The most important inter-war proposal had been the French foreign minister Aristide Briand's idea of a 'United States of Europe'. Similar schemes had, of course, appealed to Ernest Bevin at the time, but the troubles of the 1930s destroyed them, and it needed another devastating war to resurrect the belief that, in order to survive, Europe must unite. The Franco-British union proposal of 1940, Hitler's New Order, and the various ideas of the continental Resistance movements were all variations on the theme. But in 1945 hopes for peace again (as in 1919) centred on a world body, the U.N., and affairs were dominated by the Great Powers. Only in late 1946, with the breakdown of four-power co-operation, the emergence of the Soviet menace, and Europe's continuing weakness, did the pan-European movements really begin to gather force, led by such eminent figures as van Zeeland, Herriot and Churchill. At this same time, of course, the Labour left were pressing for a 'third force' in Europe and Bevin began to look at a customs union.

Churchill's support for European unity could be traced back to the 1940 union scheme and his wartime ideas of a regional 'Council of Europe'. In September 1946, he returned to such ideas with a speech in Zurich, calling for European unity to save the continent, but his proposals remained vague, and it was not clear whether he saw Britain as part of a European union or not.[1] Then in January 1947, he formed a British United Europe movement (including some Liberals and socialists). But the Labour Party and Foreign

Office disliked Churchill's ideas. Labour had always supported Socialist internationalism and were suspicious of any proposal from their great Conservative opponent. More important, both for Labour's National Executive Committee (N.E.C.) and for the Foreign Office, was the fact that Churchill's vision of Europe, though vague, was distinctly anti-Soviet and opposed to the policy of Big Three and U.N. co-operation which Bevin supported: Churchill wanted Europe to unite to save itself from the Russian threat. In early 1947 – around the time of the Dunkirk Treaty – such views were considered as undesirable and dangerous. The Foreign Office also raised two other points of long-term importance in opposition to a European federation: one was the fear that Germany would dominate any continental union if Britain was not a member; the other was 'it seems unlikely that, with her overseas commitments and her special relationship with America, the United Kingdom could ever merge her own in some European sovereignty'.[2]

The Marshall Plan, London C.F.M. and Bevin's Western Union speech changed the European situation so much that in early 1948, when the European unity movements decided to hold a grand Congress at the Hague, it seemed Britain might support the idea. In December 1947, of course, Bevin himself talked to Bidault of creating a European 'federation' to save the continent from communism. However, instead, early in 1948, Labour's N.E.C., still suspicious of Churchill, reaffirmed its opposition to European federalism, tried to prevent its members attending the Hague Congress, and stated that European co-operation on 'realistic' grounds, through the Marshall Plan, was the only way to proceed.[3] The Foreign Office adopted a similar position: they believed that Western Union should be a practical, gradual policy, built step by step on such bodies as the Marshall Plan and the Brussels Pact, not on grand 'instant' schemes for political unity. The most good that they expected from the Hague Congress was that it could stimulate public opinion in favour of general Western European co-operation.[4] Pragmatism and gradualism were the hallmarks of Bevin's foreign policy, of course. Though inspired by ideas for European unity between the wars, he was eminently realistic when executing his ideas, and his reaction to proposals for a political union in 1948 was one of horror: 'I don't like it. I don't like it. When you open that Pandora's Box you'll find it full of Trojan horses'.[5] His fellow ministers were even more sceptical: when Bevin suggested to a Cabinet Committee that the Hague Congress might be useful for mobilizing public opinion on Western Union he was heavily criticized.[6]

It was therefore inconvenient when, in early May, the Hague Congress proved successful. Hundreds of eminent figures attended, including Churchill, Spaak and many French leaders (Bidault, Schuman, Blum and others). It called for a European political and economic union, a European parliament and a Court of Human Rights. Many continental socialists attended, unable to understand, after the Western Union speech, why Labour disapproved of the Congress. There was clearly a fundamental divide between the pragmatic British and the more idealistic Europeans. The Foreign Office were unpleasantly surprised by the Congress.[7] Attlee and Bevin received a delegation (led by Churchill) to explain the Hague decisions, but showed no desire to take these up. Bevin pointed out that a European parliament would be used by communists for publicity. The government hoped the unity movement would fade away.[8]

On 15 July, however, Oliver Harvey was warned by Bidault that at the next Brussels Consultative Council of foreign ministers, he would propose the creation of a European parliament and economic union. He added that he knew these were unrealistic ideas but that premier Ramadier insisted on proposing them. The Foreign Office reaction was annoyed but optimistic: 'It is to be hoped that this item will not occupy too much time'.[9] The Office simply did not believe that Bidault could be serious. Although Harvey had recently re-ported that Jean Monnet now wanted an Anglo-French federation (a development of his 1940 proposals) and that there was a desire in France for more visible evidence of Western European unity, the Foreign Office believed that slow, careful progress was better than grandiose schemes which raised false hopes and created daunting practical problems. It is evident that Bidault too recognized some-thing of this. He probably only made his proposals as a last, desperate effort to remain at the Quai d'Orsay (by impressing Ramadier and others) and when he put his ideas to the Consultative Council they were so vague that Bevin easily managed to delay their consideration.[10]

Bidault had, however, moved the issue of a federation to the official level, and Paris had many reasons to keep it there. As the British realized, sponsorship of such ideas was a way to restore French prestige in Europe and provide her with opportunities of leadership: she was already identified with federal ideas because of Briand.[11] European union also fitted the French desire for a 'third force' to stand free of America and Russia, an idea especially appeal-ing to the Socialists. Just as important was the belief, raised by

Churchill (in his Zurich speech) and Bidault (in the Assembly in February) that closer European unity would act as a brake on German independence. This idea certainly appealed to the new foreign minister, Robert Schuman, who hoped, somehow, to end the historic enmity between Germany and France. In mid-1948, as seen with the London Accords, the French fear of German revival was as strong as ever, even though a Western alliance had begun to form and Germany was herself divided between East and West. But Schuman hoped that the development of European institutions could finally reassure France that Germany would never again become a menace.[12]

On 18 August the French Cabinet, dominated by Europeanists, decided to put a memorandum, drawn up by the federalist movement, to the Brussels Consultative Council. This memorandum proposed that a Preparatory Conference (of members chosen by parliaments) should meet to make recommendations on forming a European Assembly, initially with consultative, but later with executive, powers. The French publicized this decision, and tried to get Spaak's support for it, without first consulting Britain.[13] The new memorandum was far more detailed than Bidault's ideas, but British officials still disliked it. Oliver Harvey quickly recognized that the swift creation of a European parliament was very different from Bevin's vision of 'an association of fully sovereign states, bound together by intangible bonds of sympathy and common interest'. Gladwyn Jebb condemned the French ideas as naïve, and another official, Crosthwaite, suggested that British tactics should be to ask for a serious study of the French proposal, so as to reveal its impracticality (rather like the economic ministries' tactics against a customs union). Bevin agreed to Crosthwaite's idea. Officials were very upset at France's lack of consultation with Whitehall[14] but were encouraged by the fact that, as yet, America and Belgium seemed cautious about a European parliament.[15]

On 2 September Massigli, supported by Belgium, put the French proposal to the Brussels Permanent Commission in London, and was immediately faced by a British memorandum full of detailed questions such as: to whom would the new Assembly be responsible; to governments, member parliaments, or itself? what powers would it have? and what was the position of colonies within it?[16] With this barrage of inquiries the British hoped to shoot the French scheme down, and initially their questionnaire had some hope of success: Chauvel himself said that the French memorandum was hasty and ill-considered (the product of the same political crisis in July–September 1948 which upset French policy towards the nascent Atlantic Pact). On 10 September Bevin told the Cabinet that he wanted to state clearly Britain's positive and realistic policy on Europe, and on 15 September, in the Commons, he talked of building a European union, independent of America and Russia, but only by practical policies which maintained Britain's links to the Commonwealth. He condemned the idea of an immediate European constitution: 'I do not think it will work if we ... put the roof on before we have built the building'.[17] Meanwhile the French proved that they had not really fully considered their ideas, by taking a month to reply to the British questionnaire. When their reply was finally delivered at the Permanent Commission on 30 September, it was considered by the British to be both insulting (it accused London of failing to understand the Assembly proposal) and to justify their worst fears: the French said that the new Assembly would be a consultative, non-governmental institution, which would foster co-operation, but whose ideas could be rejected by governments. Kirkpatrick considered that such a body would be practically useless and would probably produce numerous embarrassing ideas. But he feared to be completely negative about the idea, since it was now attracting more and more European and American support.[18]

In September and October Bevin talked to Schuman, Ramadier (now Defence Minister), and Marshall about European co-operation, when the U.N. met in Paris. He pressed for 'realistic' progress and proposed a new idea: that high-level meetings of leading Brussels Pact ministers should be held periodically to show Western European co-operation to the public. Ramadier and Schuman were not impressed,[19] but the French were now on the defensive about their own proposals and willing to discuss other ideas. When the Brussels Consultative Council met late in October Schuman repeated his support for an Assembly because of its appeal to the public and the Americans, and because it might serve to tie Germany into a wider framework, but he was willing to discuss all the details of this scheme and said that if a suitable plan did not emerge after a fair study he would abandon the idea. Bevin, meanwhile, having realized that something had to be done to satisfy the French, had shifted from Britain's purely negative policy, and now wanted to create a body that caused minimum embarrassment. He formally put his new idea for periodic meetings of leading Brussels ministers to the Consultative Council, suggesting that the new body be called the Council of Europe. The Council decided to establish a Committee of Inquiry in Paris to look at the British and French ideas and report to their next meeting, in January.[20]

The next weeks were spent preparing for this Committee of Inquiry. Schuman hoped the committee would look at all possible ideas and therefore French delegates to the inquiry were not bound by any specific instructions.[21] Bevin, though now willing to create some type of new body, remained determined that this must be a 'practical' institution. On 4 November the Cabinet approved his idea for a council of ministers to fulfil this aim. Bevin told the Cabinet that the main reason for acting at all was because Britain could not humiliate the French, who were so vital to British policy in Western Europe. Thus the Foreign Secretary restated the need for co-operation with France but made it clear that he would not take this co-operation to the point of altering his own vision of how Europe should unite. One worry the British Cabinet had was that the French delegation to the Paris inquiry was largely a group of old, pro-European, ex-ministers, led be Edouard Herriot. The British, in contrast, sent a team of trusted men, including officials like Jebb, Inverchapel and Bridges, who were unlikely to oppose Bevin's 'practical' approach, led by a great opponent of European federalism, Hugh Dalton (now Chancellor of the Duchy of Lancaster).[22] On 17 November Bevin told Dalton that the Council of Europe must develop by 'trial and error' with no rigid constitution; it must not interfere with other areas of Western co-operation such as the O.E.E.C., it must not damage the Commonwealth, and it must be controlled by governments. But Bevin did intend that the Council could become a meaningful body: it might take charge of European economic co-operation when the Marshall Plan ended; it could be used to draw Germany into a Western European framework; and, most dramatically, it might eventually help to create a third world power, based on Western Europe and the Commonwealth. Thus Bevin was far from being anti-European; but he had his own vision of how to approach European unity, based on patient evolution and compatibility with Britain's other world interests.[23]

The Paris inquiry commenced on 24 November. Dalton immediately found the French to be 'unreal and escapist', but the meetings were friendly enough and Schuman assured the British that member governments would keep control of the new institution. A subcommittee was established to look at the British and French plans, and complex discussions resulted, on 16 December, in a compromise scheme for both a European Assembly, with consultative powers, and a smaller version of Bevin's Council of Ministers.[24] Given the strong views on both sides such a solution was probably inevitable, but, importantly, the agreement of the British delegation to this compromise was partly influenced by dissatisfaction in Whitehall with Bevin's ideas. When Bevin had first suggested his Council of Ministers scheme in September Attlee and others had been unimpressed by it. Ivone Kirkpatrick said it would not satisfy the French, or educate the public, or be very practical (it would mean a large number of ministers, speaking different languages). Kirkpatrick had suggested resurrecting Briand's scheme of 1930 for public meetings of government-appointed delegations. This would appeal to French vanity (being a French idea), educate the public, and yet preserve governmental control. Officials recognized a great weakness in Bevin's position: it failed to go far enough towards the French case for an Assembly to satisfy them. By mid-October, however, the critics were trying to polish up Bevin's scheme, rather than completely alter it.[25] Then, early in December, Jebb and Inverchapel both argued that the creation of both an Assembly and a Council of Ministers was the only solution: the main problem was how to make an Assembly that was neither too strong nor embarrassingly weak. But Bevin and Dalton remained cautious: in the Commons on 9 and 10 December, to criticism from Churchill, they both called for a practical approach to European unity and condemned 'precipitate federalism'.[26] Bevin decided to review the whole problem when the Paris meetings recessed for Christmas.[27]

On 29 December, in a Foreign Office meeting, Bevin finally agreed that his Council of Ministers must be supplemented by a form of Assembly to satisfy European opinion, and, in order to consult the Cabinet about this, he asked for a delay in restarting the Paris inquiry (due on 6 January).[28] On 12 January Bevin put a plan for both an Assembly and a 'Committee of Ministers' to the Cabinet. But he was determined to keep government control of the Assembly: it would be formed of government-appointed delegations, voting en bloc, and could only make 'recommendations' on issues put to it by the ministers. Bevin still saw this as an important step, chiefly to publicize Western European co-operation, but he was clearly determined to make it fit into his own European policy. Although Bevin now expected this Paris inquiry to make a divided report, the Cabinet approved his scheme, and also adopted an idea (originally from Jebb) that the Consultative Council be based in Strasbourg, a centrally placed town which was not a European capital.[29] Within a few days Schuman visited London, and discussed Bevin's latest ideas. Schuman was pleased with Bevin's professions of support of European unity and agreed that the Assembly must be carefully controlled, but he felt the British plan went too far on the latter point. The talks ended amicably, but with a profound Anglo-French division remaining.[30]

When the British put their plan to the Paris inquiry on 18 January no-one liked it. The continentals wanted much less government control, on lines suggested by the subcommittee in December, with individual delegates chosen by each national parliament, and with some freedom to discuss what they wanted. Even the British team found Bevin's plan disappointing, and, inevitably, the inquiry ended with a divided report.[31] Criticism of Britain gathered on the continent, and when the Brussels Consultative Council met on 27–28 January to discuss the Paris report, Bevin had to retreat further. Although the Assembly was still to be purely consultative, each member state would choose delegations by its own methods (thus the delegates need not be government nominees), and they would have some freedom of discussion, subject to a veto by the Committee of Ministers.[32] The Brussels Pact's Permanent Commission began to prepare a detailed plan on these lines in February, and members accepted the British idea of Strasbourg as the seat of the new Council of Europe, because of its central position and because it could become the symbol of a Franco-German rapprochement. In March the Permanent Commission completed its work and a conference opened with other powers who wished to join the new body. A treaty was initialled in London in May.[33]

The creation of an Assembly in any form was a great retreat from Bevin's position in mid-1948. Ultimately even the British delegation to the new body (though chosen by the government) included opposition M.P.s, able to vote individually. But the Council of Europe was an even greater disappointment for federalists. The Assembly's agenda was limited (it could not, for example, discuss economics and defence issues, since these were covered by the O.E.E.C. and NATO) and it had only consultative powers. When the Assembly held its first annual meeting in August the federalists were elated: some called for a European government to be established. The British Conservatives sent a strong group, under Churchill, which forced Labour (still suspicious of the whole federal idea) to send their own strong group under Herbert Morrison. Morrison, little known abroad, did particularly badly at his first international meeting: he soon considered the Assembly a 'talk-shop', he bickered with Churchill in public, and then left early. Churchill, in contrast, stole the limelight, and the Conservatives took a childish delight in having a forum in which they could defeat Labour in the divisions. It was, however, a hollow victory: the Conservatives became closely identified with the federal idea, although they did not really want Britain to become part of a European 'state', and they only confirmed Labour's view that the Assembly was embarrassing, practically useless, and dangerous. Continental members soon became disappointed at the Assembly's lack of real power, and there was an obvious division between 'federalists' (those who wanted a political union quickly) and 'functionalists' (who, like Bevin, wanted a gradual, practical approach).[34] After the Assembly Bevin condemned the federalist ideal in the Cabinet and reaffirmed his determination to keep the Assembly purely consultative. But in order to please the Americans, build up European confidence, and orientate the Germans towards Europe, he wanted to continue British support for the Council.[35] Hitherto West Germany had been unable to join the Assembly because her government was formed only in September. But in November the Council's Committee of Ministers (which met more frequently than the Assembly) agreed to the principle of West German membership.[36]

Although the Council of Europe served as a 'laboratory of ideas' for European co-operation, caused public debate, and led to the European Court of Human Rights, it never became the European parliament that the Hague Congress had wanted. Inevitably the British, who tried to limit the scheme from the start, were blamed for this failure. The appeal of the Assembly had forced Bevin to accept, first, that some action was needed, then that an Assembly must be created, and finally that it must have more powers than he liked. But ultimately, for Bevin, the Assembly was a 'safe' development, able to fit his own view of European co-operation. However, Bevin's success did not simply mark the defeat of a grand vision by the forces of tradition. The French themselves were partly responsible for the failure of the Assembly: originally, with an unstable government, they made dramatic proposals, without consulting the British and without, apparently, much careful thought; then they took many weeks to produce a more detailed but weak scheme; and finally they allowed Bevin to dilute this, and accepted strong government controls upon it. French vagueness, as well as British negativeness, produced the weak Council of Europe.

Nevertheless, ultimately, Schuman got the Consultative Assembly which he originally wanted, and he made France the champion of European unity. Spaak had been very suspicious of France up to mid-1948. This was seen in Franco-Belgian rivalry during the Brussels Pact negotiations[37], and by the fact that in October 1948 Spaak had talked of joining the British Commonwealth.[38] By mid-1949, however, the genuinely 'European' policy, and the calm but consistent approach of Schuman had made Spaak willing to accept French leadership.[39]

It is an unfair exaggeration to condemn Bevin's policy as 'anti-European'. He had a European vision, but it was founded on an evolutionary, unwritten approach, based on the development of the British Constitution. An Assembly, he believed, would raise false hopes of easy progress towards a European union; more preferable were practical steps such as the O.E.E.C. and the Brussels Pact. However, the continentals could be forgiven for expecting more from Bevin, after the Western Union speech: they were unused to talking in terms of unwritten constitutions and preferred clear, formal arrangements; their recent occupation made them better disposed to a genuine European union; and they faced pressure from large federalist movements. The events of 1948–9 had shown the strength of Anglo-French co-operation in one sense: Bevin agreed to act on the Assembly idea to avoid humiliating the French, and Schuman compromised on the idea in order to retain British co-operation. But the same events also showed fundamentally different traditions and interests and these differences were strengthened at the same time by events surrounding the economic integration of Europe.

13

The economic unification
of Europe

IN JANUARY 1948 support for a European customs union had been stronger in the Foreign Office than ever; but only two years later the British were as opposed to a European economic union as they were to a political federation. Naturally there were common reasons for rejecting both political and economic schemes in this period but, arguably, the economic decisions were more vital since they resulted in a precise definition of how far Britain could go towards Western European unification.

Support for a customs union decayed among Foreign Office officials from the moment, in January 1948, they decided to present a Cabinet Paper proposing a study group on the political and economic union of Europe. Though two drafts were prepared, this paper itself never emerged, because within a matter of weeks it seemed unnecessary: the O.E.E.C. initiated long-term European economic co-operation and the C.U.S.G. kept up its work. There was simply little else for a new study group to look at.[1] But another reason for abandoning the paper, apparently, was growing doubt among officials on the value of a customs union, which was fuelled by Commonwealth attitudes. In talks during December–February, Commonwealth representatives stated clearly that the onus was on London to ensure that any European customs union did not damage Commonwealth unity.[2] Norman Robertson, the Canadian High Commissioner, suggested that to preserve Commonwealth trade preferences Britain should approach European co-operation empirically, and seek to reduce tariffs with the continent gradually, rather than through a customs union. This idea instantly appealed to the pragmatic Bevin. Although R.B.Stevens, who had sparked off consideration of a political-economic union in December 1947, remained committed to his original ideas, his colleagues now accused him of being on a 'monorail', and by late February the Foreign Office was turning towards a pragmatic, gradual approach to European economic unity similar to the attitude it took to the Council of Europe.[3]

By March 1948 the Foreign Office and the Treasury were in fact drawing much closer together on economic integration with Europe. As the Foreign Office retreated from its radical ideas the Treasury advanced from its old, negative outlook. In December–January, after the successful beginning of the Marshall Plan, there was much talk in the Treasury of satisfying the pressure for European economic unity by pursuing policies short of a customs union. Gradual trade liberalization, a permanent Marshall Aid organization (which was, of course, eventually formed in the O.E.E.C.) and other, limited forms of economic co-ordination were suggested. These would still require hard work, they might not satisfy American desires, and they could still upset Britain's trade links with the Commonwealth, but they were far more preferable, for the economic ministries, than a customs union.[4] In the Treasury, as in the Foreign Office, a positive but pragmatic approach to economic co-operation in Europe was popular in the spring of 1948, although a definite difference in emphasis continued between the two departments for many months.

In March the C.U.S.G. held its third meeting, which decided to make a study among member-states of the effect of abolishing European tariffs. The aim was to gather enough information to decide whether a customs union was really possible. However, even this study was a huge challenge and a final report was not expected until early 1949. The British agreed with this decision although their reticent attitude remained obvious to the continentals and the French again discussed the possibility of a more limited customs union with Italy and the Benelux countries. Actually a quite positive attitude to customs unions remained in the Foreign Office: officials were willing to contemplate a customs union in the long term, and the financial problems of the Brussels Pact made Bevin favourable to a Western European currency union. But the British were already planning their likely excuse should they decide to leave the C.U.S.G.: they would argue, as the Treasury wanted, that O.E.E.C. co-operation was the only type of economic co-operation that Europe needed.[5]

In May the Foreign Office recommended in a paper for the Cabinet's all-important Economic Policy Committee (E.P.C.) that Britain should gather all possible information, so as to decide her position on customs unions just before the C.U.S.G. made its report. At the same time Britain's own study group, established in September 1947, rejected the ideas for a Commonwealth or colonial customs union because these would be of little practical use and would cause economic, financial and political difficulties.[6] Sir Stafford Cripps, supported by the Board of Trade, tried to take advantage of the growing doubts about a customs union to kill the whole idea off quickly: he recommended to the E.P.C. that Britain should make her final decision on whether to join a union in July, much earlier than the Foreign Office wanted. The C.U.S.G. was using up staff, the economic departments feared becoming implicitly committed to a union if they remained in it much longer, and Cripps restated, in the E.P.C., the Treasury's belief that O.E.E.C. co-operation was all that Europe now needed.[7] The E.P.C. meeting (held on 15 June) reached a compromise on the Foreign Office and Treasury views: Bevin conceded that, on balance, a customs union was now unlikely to prove desirable; the economic departments acknowledged that if Britain did leave the C.U.S.G. early it would offend the Americans, French and others; and it was decided that Britain would remain in the C.U.S.G. while trying to slow down its work.[8]

During the next months British reticence on a customs union was hardened by the experience over the European Assembly. In late June Jean Monnet suggested that an Anglo-French federation could now be formed. Monnet had recently visited Britain and was very impressed by her national discipline and relative economic success, and he believed an Anglo-French economic union would help both countries: Britain would obtain larger markets, the French recovery plan would be helped, and the union would be able to stand independent of America or Russia. But, farsightedly, Monnet recognized that France's internal weakness undermined her value to Britain, and that London might well turn instead to the Commonwealth and America for support. In April, dissatisfied with the extent of European economic co-operation, he had written to both Schuman and Bidault declaring that a Western European federation, led by Britain and France, was the only way to economic salvation. But during the next months the experience with the European Assembly showed that the British disliked the idea of a federation.[9]

In August the British study group produced a paper which judged that the gradual liberalization of European trade was preferable to a customs union. The Foreign Office were still uncertain that sufficient study had been done, but in September they put a paper to the E.P.C. which outlined the advantages and disadvantages of a customs union and suggested an alternative policy: first, to pursue more limited integration in the O.E.E.C. and second, to support limited customs unions on the continent (which again showed that, while rejecting a customs union for herself, Whitehall never rejected them for the continent). In the E.P.C. Bevin went rather beyond this paper, declaring that, for him, a customs union was now an impossible idea. How far this was influenced by his dislike of the European Assembly is impossible to say, but he did take the opportunity to condemn French weakness and instability. Bevin had finally abandoned any interest in a customs union, and the proposal now had little chance of being adopted by Britain.[10]

By October some officials, including Richard Clarke at the Treasury, were turning towards a new vision of 'Atlantic Union'. They still believed in a commitment to the O.E.E.C., but they wanted to concentrate on other areas of co-operation, with America and the Commonwealth.[11] In October the Foreign Office, the Treasury and the Commonwealth Relations Office produced a paper on the meaning of Western Union which showed the direction of British thinking. Western Union, it said, was designed to strengthen Europe's economy, counter the communist threat, and to answer U.S. pressure for Western European unity. It was also intended to interlock Western Europe, America and the Commonwealth into one system; and, although there was pressure to go as far as a European federation, Britain had to preserve her national sovereignty and the Commonwealth, and must work via a gradual, pragmatic policy.[12] Such views were similar to those found in Labour Party policy papers,[13] and in the Commons government spokesmen continually spoke of 'practical' economic co-operation in Europe, via the O.E.E.C., rather than sudden, spectacular advances.[14]

In November the British emphasis on O.E.E.C. co-operation became even firmer when officials began to press for the C.U.S.G.'s work to be transferred to the main O.E.E.C. body and on 14 November a special ministerial committee decided that, at the next C.U.S.G. meeting (due in December) Britain could not even suggest that she might be willing to join a union.[15] When the C.U.S.G. meeting took place, however, Britain was not criticized for her reticent attitude. Many other members were becoming despondent about the work, and it was generally recognized that tariff abolition alone (the main purpose of a customs union) would not only be hard work, it would also be almost useless unless all other European trade restrictions, quantitative and financial, were also removed. A general policy of trade liberalization, such as the British economic ministries wanted, was now preferred by most C.U.S.G. members, and even the French agreed that this policy was best handled by the O.E.E.C. The Treasury were very pleased by this breakthrough: all their doubts seemed to be proved correct.[16]

Just how far Britain's attitude had evolved in the year since a political-economic union was suggested in the Foreign Office was seen in January 1949, when the O.E.E.C. was preparing a long-term programme to ensure European recovery by 1952. Britain now had to define how far she would go towards European co-operation in this recovery effort, and on 26 January Bevin and Cripps put a joint paper on this to the E.P.C. On one side this paper argued that to ensure Europe's economic (and, therefore, political and military) strength Britain must take the lead in making sacrifices for European co-operation. But it also stated that if Europe collapsed, Britain must be able to survive, and rebuild herself with American and Commonwealth support. Thus Britain could not commit herself to Europe so far that she lost her independent viability.[17] In future every proposal for economic co-operation would be examined on its merits to see if it fulfilled this criterion.[18] On 24 February Cripps outlined these principles to the full Cabinet and stated how they would affect actual O.E.E.C. co-operation. On the positive side Britain would allow the O.E.E.C. to scrutinize her economic programmes, give technical assistance to others, and reduce trade restrictions with the continent; but to preserve her own economic strength she would refuse to open up her colonies to European traders, or to end trade restrictions against strong currency countries (such as Belgium and Switzerland). The Cabinet approved these attitudes, although they were expected to bring European criticism.[19]

The E.P.C. meeting marked a most important definition of how far Britain would co-operate with Europe. It came after long considerations, in which the importance and the potential of European economic unity were not underestimated, and it marked the culmination of an evolution in both the Foreign Office, which favoured a European economic union in January 1948, and in the economic departments, who had been very suspicious of any close European co-operation in 1945–7, until a common policy emerged. It was also the result of careful consideration of Britain's position in Europe, taking in numerous factors: European and U.S. feelings, European weakness, the communist threat, the Commonwealth, and so on. The E.P.C. principles were certainly selfish in their reasons for keeping Britain at a distance from the continent, but they did retain an important commitment to Europe. Britain simply had to take account of more areas than Europe in its foreign policy: in late 1948 Bevin had told Schuman that 'if Western Union is to succeed it must be the pivotal point ... of the territories not only in Europe, but in all ... the middle of the planet right through to the Far East'.[20] Bevin's grand vision of Western Union had now become narrower through the experience of the customs union and European Assembly, and a precise limit had been placed on how far she would go towards European co-operation.

In 1949 Britain and France began to divide more openly on European economic co-operation. On 11 February the French were told that British policy towards the O.E.E.C. was under review, and on 28 February–1 March, when the Anglo-French Economic Committee met, the British, replying to French pressure for greater economic co-operation, forcefully stated their belief in limited, practical co-operation. At this time Anglo-French trade still faced the problems of French luxury production, an unstable franc, and Britain's inability to take more French exports,[21] and these problems were discussed in talks between Cripps and Maurice Petsche, the French finance minister, in Paris. Jean Monnet intervened again during these talks with his ideas for an Anglo-French economic merger. He told Sir Edwin Plowden (chairman of Britain's Economic Planning Board) that such a merger was the only way to assert Western Europe's independence of Russia and America, and he proposed holding informal Anglo-French talks on the idea. To this Cripps and Petsche, without endorsing Monnet's ideas, agreed.

But the talks which followed only revealed Britain's reticent attitude to economic co-operation. In Whitehall the French were considered to be the ones who hindered Anglo-French economic co-operation, by their luxury industries, weak currency and political instability, and the Foreign Office and the Treasury never considered changing British policy in response to Monnet's ideas. Instead Plowden saw the talks with Monnet as an opportunity to convince a friendly French official that Britain's 'realistic' policies were the only way to proceed. Bevin supported this approach, and before the talks began Plowden was given a full exposé by the Foreign Office of the view that, although France was of vital importance to Western security, Britain could not possibly co-operate with her to the extent of endangering her independence. During the Monnet–Plowden talks (which were held in April at Monnet's

house at Houjarray) the British were quite prepared to discuss their
economic objectives and how they might aid the French economy,
but showed little understanding of Monnet's ideas for economic
union and tried to steer the talks towards more 'practical' schemes,
in particular a suggestion that the British might supply France with
coal in return for agricultural products. Since this proposal involved
vital economic items for each country Monnet concluded that it
might be the best way to progress towards an eventual economic
union, and when the talks ended he believed that Plowden was well
disposed to the idea of an eventual economic union. In fact,
Plowden never fully grasped Monnet's intent. The technical nature
of the talks, Monnet's anglophile attitudes, and his failure to put his
remarkable vision across clearly, masked the full scale of his ideas.
Monnet failed to realize that, for the British, economic 'unity'
(which they favoured) and 'union' (which they did not) were two
very different things. In the next months the coal–food exchange
failed to emerge and Anglo-French talks returned to the un-
spectacular efforts to improve French exports.[22]

Later in 1949 Britain and France divided even further because of a
massive, and sudden, devaluation of sterling. Earlier in the year
Britain's economy seemed healthy, with output increasing and
limited inflation and unemployment. But the strong dollar was still
a problem and in mid-1949 a slight American depression had
suddenly worsened Britain's dollar deficit and put pressure on
sterling. In July a series of crisis Cabinets began. For help in this
situation Britain turned, inevitably, not to Western Europe, which
was itself economically weak, but to far wealthier America and
Canada. In September, after the Cabinet decided there must be a
devaluation, Cripps and Bevin went to Washington and reached an
agreement with the North Americans to help Britain's post-
devaluation problems.[23] The devaluation was announced on 18
September and was followed by bitter complaints from the French
and other Western Europeans.

The French had three main complaints about the British action.
First, the Washington talks underlined Britain's reliance on
America and the Commonwealth rather than European aid. To the
uninformed the devaluation seemed like an Anglo-Saxon 'conspiracy'. Second, the size of the devaluation, by almost a third –
from $4.03 to $2.80 – was huge, and it led, inevitably, to a string of
other devaluations on the continent because of sterling's central
importance. But most resented was the lack of consultation with
Europe: the devaluation itself was not very surprising, but its size

and timing were. Petsche himself was in Washington at the time but received only a few hours' warning from the British of what was about to occur. The psychological shock in Paris was enormous: the Cabinet hastily had to decide its own devaluation, knowing that this would spark off more inflation just when France's internal problems had seemed to be receding. And because the French devaluation was less than that decided by Britain, Anglo-French economic co-operation now became more difficult. The British made their excuses: Western Europe could not have helped their predicament; Petsche had been forewarned before any other European finance minister; and the Washington arrangements would strengthen Britain's contribution to the O.E.E.C. Foreign Office officials were deeply offended by accusations that Britain had now abandoned European co-operation. But Cripps himself admitted to the Cabinet later that Britain ought to have consulted the Europeans, and it was not so much Britain's *actions*, as her *attitude* in carrying them out, which offended continentals. While Bevin talked of making sacrifices for Western European unity, Britain took action which at least one Frenchman described as 'a kick in the backside'.[24]

After the devaluation Anglo-French relations passed through a difficult period. Henri Bonnet reported from Washington, with gross exaggeration, that the Anglo-Americans now wanted to exclude France from all important Western decisions.[25] The French even accused London, once more, of seeking to dominate Syria (because a pro-French general, Zaim, had taken power there, only to be quickly overthrown). British policy in rehabilitating Germany, and towards the Council of Europe, was again condemned and President Auriol talked of cancelling a visit to Britain planned for 1950.[26] On 7 October Massigli told Strang that if Britain really favoured European co-operation she should show it; and the Paris embassy became concerned that 'neutralism' might gain a new force in France because of the Anglo-American behaviour surrounding the devaluation. The British were largely unrepentant, however: the Foreign Office were upset by French 'faithlessness' in the western alliance; Bevin told Schuman that the continental criticism of Britain was 'incomprehensible'.[27] Fortunately in November the problems receded and both Bidault (now premier) and Schuman acknowledged that Britain had to take account of world-wide commitments.[28] But the negative side of British policy towards Europe had been fully revealed in the devaluation and would not be forgotten.

Staff changes in both the foreign ministries earlier in the year had probably made the commitment of Britain and France to each other less certain. In February 1949 William Strang had replaced Sargent as Permanent Under-Secretary. Whereas Sargent, like Cadogan before him, had been a great believer in the French alliance and the Western bloc, Strang had worked almost entirely on German affairs in 1945–9 and knew France more for her negative German policy. In 1949–51 he was to show little sympathy for French internal weaknesses. The same month the anglophile Chauvel was succeeded as head of the Quai d'Orsay by Alexandre Parodi, a wartime Gaullist and ex-minister who, though well disposed to Britain, was not as committed as Chauvel to the British alliance.

In late 1949 Anglo-French divisions on European economic union increased further. The Americans now felt that European economic co-operation was stagnating and on 31 October Hoffman, head of the E.C.A., made an important speech in Paris calling for 'nothing less than the integration of the Western European economy'. The speech's terminology was vague and did not, as some Americans wanted, press for European political unity, but it stimulated European thinking, led to new talks on the liberalization of trade, and was important for suggesting that economic integration by small groups of countries – not the whole O.E.E.C. – would be welcomed by Washington. This last suggestion reflected American awareness that Britain was unwilling to join an actual European union: on 19 October, Acheson had sent a report to America's Paris embassy which said that Britain, alongside America, could only act as a 'sponsor' of a European union. He added that 'France alone can take the decisive leadership in integrating Western Germany into Western Europe'. American representatives in Europe were less certain that a viable economic union could be created without Britain: some American officials, especially those involved in the O.E.E.C., wanted to pressure London into joining in European integration. But Acheson believed that British views had to be respected.[29]

The British knew that the Americans were rethinking their attitude to European co-operation. London was forewarned of the Hoffman speech,[30] and the Foreign Office were currently being pressed by Washington to appoint Spaak (who had lost office in Belguim) as a 'superman' over the O.E.E.C. (The British opposed this idea because of the dangers of creating an independent executive in the O.E.E.C.)[31] Then, just before the Hoffman speech, Douglas, the American ambassador, had tried to persuade Bevin to be more positive on European co-operation. Bevin, however, had simply taken the opportunity to tell Douglas that Britain was a world power, and could not compromise her independence and strength by integrating too closely with Europe.[32] The British had been developing their own views on Europe quite fully because of various meetings at this time in the O.E.E.C., the Brussels Pact and the Council of Europe. On 27 October, Bevin and Cripps put another joint paper to the Cabinet, recalling the E.P.C. decisions of January and arguing that the devaluation crisis had proved Britain's need to rely on countries outside Europe. Indeed, the paper declared that America and the Commonwealth 'take priority over our relations with Europe', a definite change from the original concept of Western Union. The paper still talked of doing all possible to help European economic co-operation, but a message was sent to Acheson to make the limits of Britain's European commitment clear.[33]

At this time Bevin circulated another important memorandum on Western co-operation (drawn up earlier in the year) which finally rejected the idea that Western Europe might eventually become a third world power. The strength of nationalist feeling in Europe, the probable need for U.S. economic and military support even in the long term, and Britain's own reluctance to commit herself to Europe too closely, all contributed to this judgment. The idea of building a Western European-Commonwealth union was also rejected as being too grandiose. Instead Bevin favoured a more general consolidation of Western Europe, the Commonwealth and America into a 'natural' unit – a proposal as imprecise as the original Western Union – although he did hope that Britain and Western Europe could act together within this unit to prevent American domination. The great advantage of this vision for Britain was that she would provide the vital link between the three constituent parts. This latest variation on Bevin's policy of Western co-operation was the precursor of the later policy of 'three circles' followed by Britain in the 1950s.[34]

For France, however, this same period saw a greater commitment to European union. The Franco-Italian customs union proposal of September 1947 had led to an agreement in March 1949 to create such a union which, however, came to nothing: the similarity of the two economies and the opposition of vested interests quickly destroyed it. But a new scheme, also first suggested in 1947, was taken up in the autumn of 1949 for a Franco-Italian-Benelux union, to be called Fritalux. Influenced by Alphand, this was not actually a full customs union but an attempt to liberalize trade between the member countries. The devaluation of sterling encouraged the French to pursue Fritalux as a riposte to the British action, though actually the Foreign Office's view of the new scheme was positive: Whitehall had always been favourable to continental customs unions so long as they did not damage British interests.[35] Fritalux proceeded slowly and only in late November did London receive a French memorandum outlining the scheme. A British subcommittee looked at this and decided that Fritalux could be encouraged.[36] In December the member states held a conference in Paris and emerged with proposals which were so limited in effect that Britain could almost have accepted them. This limited scope reflected practical difficulties with European economic co-operation, which the British had always said existed. As with the European parliament the continentals had proved unable to carry through a dramatic scheme for a union.[37]

In 1950 Fritalux was simply overtaken by other events: trade liberalization in the O.E.E.C. and later the Schuman Plan. The British continued to take a lukewarm, but far from negative, attitude towards the scheme. Jean Monnet, too, was impressed by it.[38] But for all its failings, Fritalux highlighted the differences between Britain and France on European economic unity. The French had maintained their radical, if ill-considered, approach to the question, eager to escape their own economic weakness and insecurity. They would have preferred British co-operation in this, but proved willing to move without them, especially after the devaluation crisis. The British, meanwhile, had defined the limits to which their co-operation with Europe could go. Many Europeans (especially the Dutch and Scandinavians) still hoped for British leadership, and the British wanted to co-operate with Europe to a large extent, but Bevin's policy had already caused division with France and others. The great question in early 1950 was whether the continentals would finally agree with Britain on the 'impracticality' of European union, or if they would manage to create a viable scheme for economic union which openly divided Britain and France.

14

French instability and the German problem

FRANCE's political instability and her fear of Germany had harmed Anglo-French relations since Bevin came to power, and in 1948–50 both problems continued unabated, despite increased French security, through NATO, and economic improvements, brought about by the Marshall Plan. The two problems undermined the value of the French alliance to Britain and deeply affected the debate about European unity: the British came to believe that the main French reason for supporting a European union was their own internal weakness; the French looked to European union as a way to control Germany.

Bevin's great hope in early 1948 had been that Western Union would gradually strengthen Western Europe's self-confidence and, perhaps, even lead to a third world power being created. But two years later, France seemed no nearer to filling the strong, central role in Western defence that the Foreign Office and the C.O.S. had long wanted of her. The long government crisis of July–September 1948 which, it will be recalled, affected the Atlantic Treaty talks, was only the worst example of French political instability during this period. In 1948 there were also more (openly political) communist-led strikes, while de Gaulle's R.P.F. continued to draw massive support. The Foreign Office recognized that a 'cold war' was developing inside France, parallel to international tensions.[1] The moderate 'third force' governments themselves, despite the strong reasons for holding together, found so many tensions at work that they usually survived for only a matter of months. The fragmentation of political parties, their selfish desire for office and the complexity of France's problems all created division. The Socialists especially found it difficult to co-operate with other parties in the coalitions: the direct cause of the mid-1948 crisis, for example, was a clash between the Socialists and other parties over the military budget. Such political instability, when added to international tension, colonial problems, the psychological effect of the war, and economic difficulties (especially inflation) severely undermined French self-confidence and prestige. The Fourth Republic soon looked as weak as the Third Republic of the 1930s. There were some positive elements at work: the Socialists did generally support the government; there was a steady, if slow, economic recovery; and political continuity was provided by the civil service and the frequent return of the same ministers to office (from 1944 to 1954, except for Blum's short government, Bidault and Schuman were the only foreign ministers). But the general picture remained one of mediocrity. In October 1948 came a civil servants' strike and another devaluation; in November there were R.P.F. advances in elections to the upper house.

The British reaction to French weakness was paradoxical: frustration and criticism were balanced by the continuing need to build France up since the facts of geography and history still made her vital to Western European stability and security. In October 1948 the Foreign Office considered France 'the weakest link in the Western chain' and feared that de Gaulle was on the brink of regaining power, and even in the French Cabinet the effect of French weakness on Anglo-American opinion caused concern.[2] In November Harvey and Britain's O.E.E.C. representative, Hall-Patch, pressed the Foreign Office for more help for France for the sake of Western Union and the O.E.E.C., but both men conceded that she was an unreliable ally. Talks were currently under way for fulfilling the January 1947 agreement to co-ordinate Anglo-French recovery, to prevent unnecessary competition, and it was suggested that, before proceeding with this, Britain should get a 'declaration of intent' from France that she would carry out certain internal economic reforms. Hall-Patch specifically wanted France's notorious fiscal system (riddled by tax evasion, but popular with the electorate) to be reformed, and he feared that the French government would avoid such necessary reforms for as long as possible. Although Harvey was more confident about the French willingness to reform themselves, the Economic Policy Committee decided to do as Hall-Patch asked, and to press for such fiscal reforms.[3] Five days later the Foreign Office held a high-level meeting to decide what help it could give to the 'third force' governments in Paris, but practically, as in former years, found that it could do very little. Direct involvement in French politics, or economic 'bribery' (to

stimulate reform in France by offering economic aid) were unthinkable; all Britain could do was to maintain the Western Union policy
and try to persuade France to introduce reforms.[4] In December Bevin
assured Massigli (in a rather condescending fashion) that Britain
would continue to build up French power, but Massigli was only too
aware that France's internal weaknesses made the British despair.[5]

In 1949 the Monnet Plan, the Marshall Plan, and natural post-war
recovery brought more stable prices and an end to major shortages in
France. But her foreign trade remained cramped and later in the year
the devaluation of sterling was, of course, a hard blow. To British
satisfaction the moderate parties performed well in the March can-
tonal elections, and the R.P.F. began to decline (a violent riot in St
Etienne alienated their supporters). But de Gaulle remained a powerful figure – the Foreign Office expected 'an exceedingly bad time' if
he took office – and the communists, though no longer expanding,
were a strong force.[6] In October divisions between the 'third force'
again appeared, when Queuille's government collapsed, to be
followed by another long crisis before Georges Bidault returned to
the premiership. Fortunately he proved a surprisingly successful
leader: he clung on to power until June 1950. However, concern at
France's continuing weakness had led William Strang, the Permanent
Under-Secretary, to ask for studies on the subject in mid-1949. The
main result was a paper on France's world role which pointed to her
main problems – muddled politics, a weak economy, poor armed
forces – and her insecurity, and judged that, in herself, she was 'not
much' use to Britain. But since she was of central importance in
Western Europe the paper felt that she would keep her inflated
importance in the Western alliance and recommended that Britain
must continue to strengthen her where possible.[7] By now, of course,
France's failure to recover her former greatness was leading Bevin to
look towards more 'reliable' areas outside Western Europe for
British security. Strang, no lover of France, would return to his
criticisms of her in the spring of 1950.

In Germany, following the London Accords of June 1948, any
hopes of swiftly establishing a West German government were soon
dashed. As with the Atlantic Pact and the Council of Europe, the
complex issues involved could not be settled until the spring of 1949.
The Germans themselves had to devise a constitution within Allied
guidelines; the Allies had to draw up an Occupation Statute to define
their own powers vis-à-vis the new government; and the International Ruhr Authority (the main concession to France at the
London Conference) had to be created.

After the narrow approval of the London Accords in June the French remained very reticent about Allied policy in Germany. In July these doubts seemed to be justified by the German leaders themselves: the Minister-Presidents of the West German provinces proved reluctant to set up their own 'constitution' because this meant formally dividing Germany between East and West. General Koenig, governor of the French zone, would gladly have accepted this refusal to set up a West German government but the Anglo-Americans were determined to press on, and a compromise was reached: the Germans would be given self-government but without an explicit suggestion that a West German 'state' was being established; instead of a constitution written by a Constituent Assembly, there would be a 'Basic Law' written by a 'Parliamentary Council', which began its work in Bonn in September. The French accepted this solution in Schuman's first Cabinet as foreign minister.[8]

In late 1948 three areas of difficulty emerged in Germany which affected Anglo-French relations. The first was the old issue of the Ruhr. The French hoped to discuss this question soon after the London Accords, but not until November did a conference meet to draft the statute of the International Ruhr Authority. Furthermore, just before this conference the French were deeply offended when the British and American governors promulgated Law 75, which decreed that the Germans themselves could decide the future ownership of the Ruhr industries. This was to resolve an Anglo-American argument over whether these industries should be nationalized or left in private hands. It did not rule out stiff controls on industrial production, but it did rule out French hopes that the Ruhr industries could be internationally owned to ensure that they did not again become the basis of German aggression. France was officially forewarned of the proposal but, incredibly, the Quai d'Orsay failed to inform Cabinet ministers of what was about to occur. Inevitably, there was a strong reaction: the old fear that America wanted to rebuild Germany as Europe's economic bastion seemed to be being fulfilled. French complaints continued throughout the conference on the Ruhr authority (with some sympathy from British Conservatives). During the conference the French pressed both for firm controls on the Ruhr (to prevent the return of the former cartels and pro-Nazi industrialists, for example) and for international management (which, it was hoped, could act as a check on any future German owners). To save three-power co-operation and preserve French self-confidence, the Anglo-Americans proved willing to compromise: although Law 75 remained, France was allowed on to the bizonal 'Essen Groups' which supervised the steel industry, and her demands for stiff controls, including international management, were accepted. The Ruhr Authority was given powers to allocate coal and steel production between domestic consumption and exports, taking foreign needs into consideration. Thus the ideas of 1945 for milking the Ruhr, helping the recovery plans of the Allied states and preventing Germany's industrial resurgence were continued. The French Cabinet were more than satisfied with this and congratulated Schuman on the results he had achieved.[9]

The second problem involved another old French worry, the centralization of German government. To answer French demands here the Allies informed the Germans' Parliamentary Council, in November, that the 'Basic Law' must be of a decentralized, federal nature. Meanwhile, in talks between the Allied governors on an Occupation Statute, Koenig pressed for extensive Allied powers and decentralization at every step: he especially wanted powers of taxation to be controlled by the German provinces, not the central government. So negative and repetitive did he become that General Clay, an old opponent of French policy in Germany, complained to Washington that Koenig seemed to be opposed to the London Accords. But the State Department and Foreign Office refused to pressure France over Koenig's behaviour and in January the governors' talks broke down. The issue was taken up by an intergovernmental committee in London where the arguments continued.[10]

The third problem in late 1948 centred on reparations and other industrial limitations on Germany. Reparations deliveries, largely from the British zone, were still under way at this time, potential war industries (such as armaments, synthetic oil and chemicals) were either forbidden or controlled, and there was a ceiling on steel production which effectively limited output in the whole German economy. The French wanted to maintain these limitations, but the American Congress was pressing to reduce them to help Germany contribute to Western strength. Bevin stood between the two sides, recognizing the need to revive Germany as part of the West, but fearing to move too quickly and revive the German menace. Although, in the Cabinet, Lord Pakenham argued that the time had come to treat Germany as an ally, Bevin only agreed to an American investigation into reparations, with a view to reducing deliveries, with great reluctance. And when, in December, this investigation reported that 167 out of 381 industrial plants, earmarked for reparations, should not now become reparations, Bevin was no happier: he feared a violent French reaction, and believed that Germany was being rehabilitated too quickly.[11]

At the end of 1948 three factors stood out in Germany: the complexity of the issues left by the London Accords; continuing French reticence about Allied policy; and the determination of the Western powers to remain united. A Cabinet Paper by Bevin at the time outlined the progress made since the London Conference and stated that Britain must now balance the need to please the Americans and form a healthy, democratic, pro-Western Germany, against the need to satisfy France and guard against German independence and nationalism. The Cabinet did not object to this general view, but there were bitter differences among ministers on emphasis: some, like Pakenham, were now moderate towards Germany, believing Russia to be the great threat to peace; but others, like Hugh Dalton, remained very suspicious of her.[12]

Bevin's desire to steer a middle course in Germany was strengthened by the Foreign Office concern about French weakness at this time. Oliver Harvey recalled Anglo-French differences over Germany in the 1920s and hoped that, with British moderation, they need not be repeated. He pointed to positive elements in French policy such as their part in the London Accords and Schuman's hope for a Franco-German rapprochement, and believed that there could be Anglo-French agreement on the gradual rehabilitation of Germany. The Foreign Office had a less favourable view of France's reticent policy and believed that the French attitude was too close to obstruction to make an Anglo-French agreement easy. On 30 November the Office agreed to a suggestion from the Paris embassy that Schuman should visit London to discuss Germany.[13]

Schuman's visit took place in January 1949, and included discussions on the Atlantic Pact and the Council of Europe, as well as Germany. Harvey again pressed for a fuller co-operation with France before the talks, and Bevin seemed to answer his pleas when Schuman arrived, by expressing hopes for a common Anglo-French policy, condemning the American policy on reparations, and supporting the retention of controls on German industry. In reply, Schuman, who himself had to balance his own wish for a Franco-German rapprochement against the anti-German feelings of the French people, agreed that the London Accords must be fulfilled and hoped that Germany would fit into the new Western European framework that was developing. This meeting seemed to point towards the joint Anglo-French approach, which Harvey (and, before him, Duff Cooper) believed was possible. Since mid-1946 British policy had been closely linked to America and although Bevin had tried to make concessions to France (over the Saar and Ruhr coal supplies, for example), these had been more than outweighed by Germany's gradual revival. Now with France committed to the London Accords, and with his own fears about reviving the German menace, Bevin seemed more respectful of French wishes. However, practical problems still remained: Bevin and Schuman could not agree, for example, on the balance of tax powers between the German provinces and central government.[14] And in early 1949 the Foreign Office remained unimpressed by arguments that the French were now more positive about Germany's gradual revival.[15]

The main problems in establishing a West German government were not solved for another five months. In February 1949 Bevin successfully pressed the Americans to make a comprehensive settlement of the problems of reparations and industrial limitations. Tripartite talks on this ended in April, with an agreement to reduce the amount of reparations and ease other industrial restrictions, though by less than the Americans would have liked. The agreement suited the Anglo-French policy of gradual German rehabilitation.[16] Meanwhile, in Bonn the Germans had produced a democratic, federal Basic Law which the three Western governors found acceptable, except for certain points, the most important being central government powers over finance, the police and legislation.[17] Serious problems, however, had arisen over the Occupation Statute: the experts' meeting in London had produced a complex web of agreements (and disagreements) on this, which tried to embody all the safeguards the Allies wanted. The result looked restrictive and unworkable and was complicated by French demands that each Ally should have a veto power over future tripartite policies in Germany.

In April full agreement on West Germany's future became imperative when the Western powers agreed to hold another four-power C.F.M. to discuss Germany. The Western position had to be clear before this C.F.M. met in May and Bevin, Schuman and Acheson took the opportunity to discuss the problem at the time of signing the Atlantic Pact in April, an occasion which provided a favourable background for an agreement on Germany. The situation was solved by a novel and simple scheme to replace the complex draft Occupation Statute by a set of general principles, covering the powers the Allies should retain in the new Germany. There was also agreement on an American idea to replace Allied military government by three civilian High Commissioners which appealed to Bevin 'particularly since it means liquidating Generals Clay and Koenig'. The French even received certain veto powers (over, for example, amendments to the Basic Law). Such three-power meetings became quite regular when the Atlantic Pact nations met in future. They were resented by the smaller powers, but were a great boost to French pride: the impression grew that France, alongside Britain and America, was one of the 'Big Three' Western powers. It was an inflated position of strength that General de Gaulle would have loved.[18]

The final details of the Basic Law were settled by 12 May. This completed the preparations for a West German government and made an agreement with Russia at the C.F.M. in Paris, which opened some days later, very unlikely. Despite Auriol's renewed hopes for East–West agreement, French opinion was now very much pro-Western. A common three-power position was agreed before the C.F.M. and Alphand declared that any four-power agreement must be based on the principles of democracy and federalism which the West wanted. The Russians raised their old demands for high reparations and a share in the Ruhr and the C.F.M. made no progress. After its breakdown Western plans continued and in September, four years and four months after her defeat, Germany, or rather West Germany, had a government once more.[19]

The French acceptance of a German government was remarkable following the hard-line thesis de Gaulle had proposed in 1945, but almost immediately French patience was tried even further when the Germans pressed for even greater freedoms. The powers of the provinces (over education, the police and local government) and the High Commissioners (over foreign policy, disarmament and reparations) restricted the work of the Bonn government, and all Germans were offended by the continuation of reparations. The Americans and, to a lesser degree, Britain (which bore the brunt of criticisms against reparations) wanted further concessions to Germany and talks were held on this in November in Paris. The talks, though concentrated into a few days, were long and difficult: some of the most difficult that Ivone Kirkpatrick, for one, ever experienced. Schuman feared a series of attempts to 'outbid' Russia for German support was about to begin (Russia was currently conceding rights to the East Germans) and some French ministers, such as the socialist Jules Moch, wanted no more concessions to Germany. The talks, followed by contact with the new German

Chancellor, Konrad Adenauer, led to the Petersberg Agreements, which relaxed dismantling even further, gave Germany representation on the Ruhr authority, and allowed her to enter consular and commercial relations with other powers. But in return there were three important concessions to France: Germany had to recognize the separate existence of the Saar (all that remained of de Gaulle's thesis), to accept the powers of the Ruhr authority and, more positively, would be able to join the Council of Europe (which Schuman saw as a first step towards Franco-German co-operation in a European framework). Despite some grave worries in the French Cabinet on 22 November, these concessions were enough to win French acceptance.

The Petersberg Agreements continued the trend of French policy begun by Bidault in mid-1947: too weak to avoid concessions to the Anglo-Americans, the French gained enough concessions to accept German rehabilitation and de Gaulle's old thesis gradually disintegrated. The great breakthrough for this approach had been the approval of the London Accords: by late 1949 the policy was accepted and the Assembly passed the Petersberg Agreements with a majority of almost 80. The Germans themselves, faced with a separate Saar, the Ruhr authority, and various Allied controls, were actually less pleased than France with the agreements. For Anglo-French relations the agreements also continued a trend: Britain, less determinedly than America, pushed France along a course she was not disposed to take, but, in surprising contrast to 1945–7, this did not gravely upset Anglo-French relations in general. This was because factors other than British pressure were forcing the French to change (American opinion, the development of Western alliance, the Russian menace) and because of good personal relationships. Bevin's sympathetic view was vital in winning France over to the Petersberg Agreements.[20]

However, another factor in the French acceptance of Germany's revival was to divide Britain and France in the near future: the fear of Germany's apparently inevitable revival led France to seek a 'European' solution to the problem. It was clear that the remaining controls on Germany would gradually disappear, but since early 1948 the possibility of controlling West Germany in a Western European framework had grown in appeal. German participation in the O.E.E.C. and Council of Europe was very important to the French, and the Americans encouraged France along this line: Dean Acheson said that Schuman should be responsible for framing a positive Allied policy towards Germany.[21] The British were well aware of these developments. Churchill had done much to popularize the idea of a Franco-German rapprochement, and, for Bevin, the chance of bringing such a rapprochement offset his otherwise unfavourable view of European federalism. In October 1949 he told the Cabinet that if Britain was going to contract out of a more united Europe, then Germany must be brought into a Western European framework immediately 'so that the process of reconciliation of France and Germany... may be begun with our sponsorship.' In this statement Bevin encapsulated a rather contradictory British view of European union: on one side this was seen as an impractical idea, almost certain to fail, in which Britain could not participate; on the other it was recognized that a union would please America, strengthen French self-confidence, and help a Franco-German reconciliation.[22] At the beginning of 1950, however, German reconciliation with the rest of Western Europe still seemed years away: Frenchmen especially still felt a deep hatred and distrust of their historic enemy.

The events of mid-1948 to early 1950 showed that, despite the creation of the Atlantic Pact, the advance of European co-operation and the formation of a West German government, Bevin's original, imprecise vision of Western Union could not answer many of the problems which arose. Bevin's triumphant march towards Western security had led to a division with France and others who wanted a more far-reaching approach to European unity. Both Bevin's Western Union and the proposals for a federal Europe sprang from the same causes: European decline, the Soviet menace, and a belief that nation-states must learn to co-operate with each other. But France's vulnerability, her economic needs, her fear of Germany and her tradition of formal arrangements of co-operation drove her apart from Britain. Meanwhile, Bevin's own pragmatic approach was itself affected by the rapid changes in the world and had veered away from the original Western Union. Bevin had always tried to make France a partner in his European policy but he also wanted her to fulfil a certain role in doing this, and he resented her independent approach with regard to Europe. He was even more disappointed with her failure to overcome her internal weaknesses. By early 1950 Western Europe, with its deep economic and political troubles, its fear of Russia and its premature federalist ideal seemed, to the Foreign Office, to be an unreliable basis for British foreign policy. NATO, the devaluation crisis and the Commonwealth link had led Bevin to rely more on areas outside Europe in late 1949. Britain and France now faced a fundamental, but as yet unclear, division in their view of the world. In 1950–1 that division was to become obvious for all to see.

Part IV

DIVIDED
VISIONS

Anglo-French relations under Attlee's second administration
February 1950 – October 1951

15

Before the Schuman Plan

February–May 1950

IN FEBRUARY 1950 a general election was held in Britain which drastically cut Labour's parliamentary majority to six. Attlee then began a second term of office that was relatively insecure and, within months, the strain of attending Commons' votes began to tell on ministers. One main sufferer was Bevin – already gravely ill, and exhausted by ten years as a minister – whose foreign policy now lost most of its brilliance, especially towards France and Western Europe.

In surveying Anglo-French relations at the New Year Oliver Harvey felt that generally co-operation was good, but he was concerned at the recurring difficulties over Germany and European unity: the French, he said, were not convinced of Britain's commitment to the continent. Harvey underlined his worries to Kirkpatrick in mid-January, noting that although French leaders preferred Britain to share the leadership of Western Europe, they were willing to pursue Fritalux without her. Harvey (unaware of the Cabinet's definition of how far co-operation with Europe could go) rightly feared that economic considerations in Whitehall prevented close Anglo-European links; but he hoped these considerations could be overcome: he believed that only a Britain active in Europe could sponsor a Franco-German reconciliation, and thus end the bitterest of intra-European conflicts. However, Kirkpatrick (following Cabinet policy) replied that O.E.E.C. co-operation was sufficient for Europe. For Harvey it was an exasperating response: in Paris there was indeed hope that Britain would draw closer to Europe, especially to balance Germany's might; this was something which Schuman, Bidault and others all wanted, but during the next months the French showed that, as Harvey feared, they were capable of moving without Britain if she failed to act.[1]

During the election Harvey repeated his fears about Anglo-French differences on Europe,[2] but relations still seemed close. In March, President Auriol made a state visit to London (originally suggested in the autumn of 1948), which went remarkably well and was seen in retrospect as a high point of co-operation.[3] Harvey sent a report to London to mark the visit, declaring that 'fundamentally Anglo-French relations have probably never been better'; co-operation in Western security and on Germany had erased the memory of the lean years of 1945–7. But he could not resist mentioning the European problem again. The Foreign Office themselves had their worries about France, but not because of the European problem. Strang was primarily concerned with French weakness, internally and externally. In late 1949, of course, he had asked for papers on this subject, with little result, and now he pressed this idea again.[4] There were certainly reasons to be despondent about France. Recently Harvey had reported on French 'neutralism' – the continuation of old ideas that France could stay out of the Soviet-American struggle – which sprang from a mixture of demoralization, anti-Americanism and Communist influence. Although Harvey believed that most Frenchmen supported the Atlantic alliance, Foreign Office officials were dismayed at the neutralist phenomenon.[5] There were also reports on the continuing inadequacy of French armed forces: their air force was still useless, and their army, which Britain wanted to become the key continental fighting force, still suffered from a lack of finance, poor training and the demoralizing war in Indochina. The War Office were so disgusted with this that they joined Strang in asking for a full report on French weaknesses. Thus encouraged, Strang ordered a study to be begun on 15 March.[6]

The Foreign Office continued to give little attention to Harvey's fears about an independent French policy on Europe. It seemed impossible for France to devise a scheme which both maintained control of Germany and achieved a Franco-German rapprochement. These doubts were fuelled in March when Adenauer himself suggested a Franco-German union (possibly including Britain as well). The general French reaction to this was abject terror: such a union, they felt, would be dominated by Germany. General Robertson, in Bonn, considered Adenauer's idea a 'stunt' and although Harvey still insisted that France wanted Germany's integration into Europe the Foreign Office doubted this. Instead, officials like Gladwyn Jebb argued that an Atlantic framework was the way to ensure security from Germany.[7] In the Commons at this time Churchill again pressed for Britian to sponsor a Franco-German rapprochement, but he also wanted a 'practical' policy which preserved the Commonwealth link. Government spokesmen underlined the latter sentiments, and Bevin remarked that something more than Western European co-operation was needed to strengthen the West.[8] The British avoided official comment on Adenauer's ideas and aimed to maintain existing policies, while developing the 'Atlantic community'.[9]

These attitudes dominated British preparations for the next Atlantic Council in London in May, which was to be preceded by more tripartite talks. Bevin planned to use the London meetings to review the Petersberg policy in Germany, which was having mixed success: Germany had joined the Ruhr authority, but was reluctant to enter the Council of Europe because the Saar (now economically united with France) was to enter the Council independently. Bevin wanted to maintain the Petersberg policy while emphasizing its positive side: rebuilding the German economy, reducing Allied controls and developing a trusting relationship. On Atlantic co-operation Bevin now told the Cabinet plainly that Western Union had given way to the Atlantic community. This was the inevitable result of the tide of British thinking since mid-1948. Bevin was well aware that the Americans wanted British co-operation with Europe, but he also believed they wanted a strong, independent Britain. The Cabinet willingly approved Bevin's line and it was again said that an 'Atlantic' solution was the best way to answer French fears about German strength.[10]

Bevin's doubts about closer European unity were probably hardened in early 1950 by the remarkable success of the Commonwealth, following an initial post-war crisis. In January, at the Colombo Conference, British hopes for a living community of ex-colonial states seemed fully justified and, in retrospect, Indian independence (granted in 1947) seemed a major triumph (contrasting sharply with French policy in Indo-China). Bevin had assured the conference that European co-operation would not be allowed to undermine the Commonwealth relationship.[11] Meanwhile events surrounding the Council of Europe continued to cause concern. In early 1950 much thought was given to resolving the rift between the largely federalist Assembly and the inter-governmental Committee of Ministers, and it had been suggested that a supranational body be established to ensure that members 'followed up' Assembly proposals. Inevitably Bevin rejected this in favour of a more limited scheme: regular, informal meetings of Assembly and ministerial representatives to resolve any differences. The Committee of Ministers accepted Bevin's idea in its March–April meeting (again proving that more governments than Britain's disliked federalism),[12] but these continuing problems made Bevin determined to clarify

Britain's European policy once and for all. He decided to do so via a Labour Party pamphlet, which the N.E.C.'s International Subcommittee agreed to prepare on 20 April. Provisionally entitled 'European Unity and the Council of Europe' it was partly based on an analysis of Bevin's ideas by Ernest Davies. This laid down established precepts – that Britain must keep control of her own economy, that the Commonwealth and the sterling area must be preserved, and so on – and stated that though Britain could accept wide-ranging co-operation, 'we must always stop short at surrendering sovereignty to that degree which would restrict our freedom of action'. Thus the Council of Europe must adhere to limited aims such as encouraging cultural co-operation, tourism, respect for human rights, and so on, short of executive power. Denis Healey set to work on preparing the pamphlet, and in early May it was still being redrafted.[13]

Meanwhile, on 27 April, Harvey again asked the Foreign Office to state clearly Britain's commitment to Europe. He wanted Britain to *balance* her commitments to Europe, America and the Commonwealth (all areas of primary concern, he felt), not to *choose* between them, and he hoped Britain would be positive about new ideas on European co-operation regardless of their practicality: Harvey knew that Britain's negative attitude, rather than her actual policy, often upset the continentals. The Foreign Office, in fact, claimed to agree with Harvey's views: they wanted to balance British commitments, and knew their attitude to Europe could be improved. These points had already been written into the paper on French weaknesses, which was now in draft form. But whether the Office recognized the full force of Harvey's criticisms is doubtful: Britain was definitely veering away from the old Western Union.[14] In early May 1950, British policy towards Western Europe was being clarified as fully as in August 1945 and January 1948. In approaching the major issues of Western security, European unity and German revitalization Britain had defined her main aims: to co-operate with Europe, but preserve British independence; to free Germany from controls while 'containing' her in Western arrangements; and to put more faith in Atlantic co-operation to compensate for Europe's weakness. The exact position of France – the driving force behind 'federalist' schemes, the state most fearful of Germany, and the main source of continental weakness – was still under review. Little did Whitehall expect a major new French initiative, such as Harvey feared, and which upset everyone's calculations.

British expectations that France would maintain her existing policies in the spring of 1950 were not unreasonable. She was committed to the Petersberg policy; her leaders wanted to retain British co-operation; and former attempts at radical European co-operation (such as the European Parliament and Fritalux) had come to little. Furthermore, in April France too seemed to turn towards an Atlantic arrangement when Bidault proposed the formation of a High Council to co-ordinate wide-ranging Atlantic co-operation. But actually the High Council was Bidault's personal idea and it drew little support in France or America.[15] It was overtaken on 9 May, two days before the London meetings began, when Robert Schuman suddenly announced that France would join other European states in a supranational body to control coal and steel. This proposal, the Schuman Plan, profoundly altered the European situation.

The Schuman Plan was, unsurprisingly, the brainchild of Jean Monnet, and it sought to answer those same problems that British policy-makers faced, of European weakness, the Russian threat, and German revival, but which had always caused far more terror and insecurity in Paris than in London. The Atlantic community had a great inadequacy for France, in that it was not specifically designed to control her great rival, Germany (indeed, it had developed as an anti-Soviet move in parallel to Germany's revival). And, although they were not neutralists, French ministers were attracted to developing a framework for action removed from the Cold War.[16] (The French had never, of course, shared Britain's affinity with the Americans.) Thus as the London meetings approached, the French ideally wanted to see a new initiative which could forestall the revival of a strong, independent Germany on their own terms. Ideally too this initiative would involve a Franco-German rapprochement – Schuman's aim since he became foreign minister in 1948, and something which Britain and America also hoped to see.[17] But how to achieve all this had long been a problem. The attempt to free Germany of controls while limiting her independence in an international framework had so far proved inadequate since Germany's revival had continued. Meanwhile, although Schuman and Adenauer (both christian democrats from the Franco-German border) had struck up a cordial relationship, tension between the two countries continued, especially over the future of the Saar.[18]

In Monnet's mind in early 1950 was an old idea for easing Franco-German tension: that the Ruhr–Lorraine industrial area might be put under a single controlling agency. Such ideas were canvassed between the wars, and in 1926 industrialists in the area had formed a cartel. In 1870–1925 most of the region had actually been controlled first by Germany, then France, and this proved far better than dividing it among two countries. In 1943 an economic 'Lotharingia' was proposed by French officials in Algiers, and after 1945 various individuals and institutions, including the State Department and the Council of Europe, produced variations on the same theme. The potential of the basic idea was clear: a Ruhr–Lorraine union would curtail Germany's economic independence, form a powerful industrial unit, and forge such a strong bond between France and Germany that war between them would become impossible.[19] In 1949–50 this idea gained in importance not only because of Germany's continuing revival, but also because rising European steel production was leading to a steel glut. Since 1945 Western European nations had sought to increase their steel output as part of their recovery plans (by 1950 France, under the Monnet Plan, was producing more steel and coal than ever) but, despite attempts in the O.E.E.C., there was no co-ordination of these plans and, alongside Germany's revival, they now threatened overproduction. Steel producers seemed likely to solve the problem with a new cartel. In November 1949 the French Cabinet discussed these problems and felt a European industrial plan was needed.[20] European socialists, who had a special dislike of cartels, had also discussed these problems in March 1949 and March 1950, when French and Belgian representatives had suggested supranational control of European coal and steel industries.[21]

A Ruhr–Lorraine unit had two other appealing points with regard to Germany. First, it could be seen as continuing the attempts to milk the Ruhr for the good of France. Second, and very important, there were signs that German leaders would support it because, while restricting their economic independence, it offered peace and equality with their neighbours (and it would restore Germany's economic link with the Saar). In April 1949 Adenauer, who had favoured European unity for years, suggested a European coal-steel body, and then in March 1950 came his grandiose and premature scheme for a Franco-German-British union, which, coming from a German, terrified the French. The Quai d'Orsay's response to this was remarkably similar to Britain's: Franco-German reconciliation must be gradual, developing from existing co-operation in the O.E.E.C. and the Council of Europe. It took Monnet to break France away from these established policies.[22]

For Monnet the Ruhr–Lorraine union had one other great potential use, however: it could provide the first, realistic but dramatic
step towards a European political and economic federation. Since
1945 the French, especially Monnet and Alphand, had tried to build
up long-term economic co-operation in Europe but all their
schemes, from Anglo-French economic co-ordination, through an
O.E.E.C. customs union and the Houjarray talks, to Fritalux, had
failed. France had also attempted a bold political scheme for a
European parliament, and seen it diluted by the British. Monnet had
hoped for European economic co-operation for the sake of France's
own economy which relied heavily on supplies from abroad. Since
1945 she had especially needed Ruhr coal and American finance
(first in a loan, then in the Marshall Plan). But the days of
guaranteed Ruhr supplies were now numbered because of
Germany's recovery, and Marshall Aid was to end in 1952. The only
countries which showed an interest in a customs union were Italy
and the Benelux states but these countries together could not produce a balanced economy. Monnet had tried to persuade Britain,
with her industrial base, to join in an economic union, without
success. Only one other country could provide an industrial base
for a European union and that was West Germany.

After considering these problems, in early April Monnet wrote a
paper which rejected both neutralist and Cold War attitudes as
providing hope for the future, and recommended the creation of a
supranational authority over the Ruhr–Lorraine industries, to limit
German independence, allow German equality and begin a
European union. Monnet's great strength was a sense of timing and
he believed that his proposal would achieve maximum impact if it
were announced just before the London meetings. So, quickly and
secretly, helped by a few aides, he drew up a scheme for a 'High
Authority' to control the coal and steel industries. Although the
essential element was to unite France and Germany, Monnet decided to invite all Western European countries to join. The Authority was to 'make a breach in the ramparts of national sovereignty
…' by taking decisions binding on all members. Once the plan was
ready, Monnet had to find it a political sponsor. At first he
approached Bidault, but he was concentrating on his own High
Atlantic Council and took no interest. Instead it was Schuman who
sponsored the scheme. His reasons were simple: he was favourable
to European union, even more favourable to Franco-German reconciliation, and was desperate to take the initiative on these issues at
the London Conferences. Two other ministers, who had been in-

volved in the 1943 Algiers talks, René Pleven and René Mayer, were brought into the secret and, with their help, Schuman was easily able to obtain Cabinet approval for the plan on 9 May. Meanwhile Adenauer was also informed, since his agreement was vital for the scheme's success and he immediately accepted Monnet's ideas. The Quai d'Orsay had its doubts about the plan, but had little choice but to agree to it, and Schuman announced it to the world within hours of the Cabinet decision. It was all done hastily and secretly, almost like a conspiracy, but thereby it achieved what Monnet intended: maximum impact.[23]

Various interpretations could be put on the Schuman Plan. In one sense it continued French attempts to unite Europe, though with a limited, 'realistic' scheme rather than a grandiose federal institution. But it was also clearly aimed at resolving the German problem. Then again, it appeared to some as the basis for a 'third force' or as an economic move to co-ordinate the European economies. Actually the plan sprang from a consideration of all these problems, and its beauty was that it tackled them all. But it seems true to say that whereas for Monnet the plan was primarily a way to European union, utilizing the German problem, for Schuman it was a way to Franco-German rapprochement, utilizing European machinery. The basic idea of the plan had been seen before but it took Monnet's genius to devise a viable scheme and unleash it on the world. France, however, had had her plans for European union dashed before, and there was no guarantee this new move would succeed. Monnet knew on 9 May that, in one sense, the work was only beginning.[24]

One problem was the role of Britain, the main opponent of former 'federalist' schemes, whose plans in 1950 were moving along very different lines. Britain had not figured largely in Monnet's preparations. Previously French leaders, including Monnet, had always wanted to include her in European schemes, but she had proved reticent, and now Monnet had found a new source of economic strength for a European union, in Germany. In a way Britain's response to the new plan was irrelevant, since her agreement was not necessary for it to succeed, and since French security and Franco-German rapprochement were the vital considerations in Paris. French officials realized the plan would force a final British decision for or against federalism. Monnet's view was that if Britain did join in, it was all well and good; if not he could proceed without her and, once the plan had succeeded, she would probably want to join it anyway.[25] He certainly did not trouble himself to make British agreement easy: thus, although Bevin received only a few hours' warning of the plan's announcement, both Adenauer and Acheson were told before the French Cabinet. Acheson was told on 8 May because, coincidentally, he visited Paris before attending the London meetings. The French later argued that they could not avoid telling him without seeming to insult him, but it was also true that American support, which Acheson gave, was invaluable to Monnet. And the fact that Acheson and Adenauer were so forewarned showed that French thoughts were not turned towards London on 9 May. Instead, on that date, both Britain and France were looking to their own interests: one to the world and the Atlantic community, the other to the German problem and European unity. And these diverse interests could no longer be contained in a single framework of activity such as Western Union.[26]

16

Britain and the Schuman Plan

9 May–2 June 1950

BEVIN's initial reaction to the Schuman Plan was one of shock and betrayal. The plan was far removed from the twin policies of Atlantic co-operation and the Petersberg Agreement, and it broke the principle of Anglo-French partnership in Western Europe which Bevin had pursued in the O.E.E.C. and the Brussels Pact. While avoiding official comment when Massigli informed him of the plan on 9 May, the Foreign Secretary made his displeasure clear, and when he discovered that Acheson had been told beforehand he accused America of joining in a 'conspiracy'. Massigli himself was astonished by Monnet's treatment of Britain and tried to underline the plan's European aspect to Bevin; otherwise, Massigli believed, the British would assume they were meant to be excluded from what was essentially a Franco-German move.[1]

After the initial shock, however, Britain looked at the plan calmly. The British press, generally, was not negative about Schuman's announcement,[2] and Attlee requested that strategic, economic and political studies be made, so that Britain could establish a position on the plan. The main problem was that Whitehall had few details on Monnet's thinking: apart from Massigli's information, and a note from the Americans, officials relied on a report in *The Times*. Certain assumptions, based on common sense, could be made. Thus, on 10 May, R.B.Stevens wrote that the plan was a new way to control German industrial strength. But the fact that Stevens concentrated on the German problem and referred to 'inter-governmental' co-operation showed that the European and supranational sides of the plan were not fully appreciated in London.[3]

On 11 May a still angry Bevin tackled Schuman about the lack of consultation on the plan, in Achesons's presence. But Schuman pointed out the need for secrecy in preparing the plan, and the fact that its details were still to be negotiated; and Acheson, playing down 'procedural' problems, recalled that Britain had not warned

France about the devaluation of sterling in 1949, a reminder that
Britain had not always treated France as a partner. These arguments,
and an apology from Schuman, served to pacify Bevin.[4] In the
afternoon a special Cabinet committee discussed the three papers
Attlee had asked for. These had mixed conclusions. The C.O.S.,
looking at defence issues, liked the Schuman Plan because a Franco-
German rapprochement could only strengthen Europe's defences,
but the Ministry of Defence added a more negative note stating that
Britain could not bind herself so closely to Europe, by joining the
plan, that she could not survive the fall of the continent. On
economic issues, a paper drawn up by a committee under Sir Edwin
Plowden was also, unsurprisingly, negative: apart from practical
problems in devising a supranational authority, the French scheme
would form a powerful Ruhr–Lorraine combine that might threaten
Britain's steel industry, and it would upset the search for a global,
multilateral approach to economic problems (which the economic
departments still hoped for). The Foreign Office's paper on political
issues, prepared by Kirkpatrick, was more balanced. It rightly saw
the Schuman Plan as a way to control Germany while granting her
equality, but feared that the plan could lead to a 'neutralist' third
force in the long term, and that it portended a European federation,
which Britain could not join. The paper advised that the political
gains of the plan justified some economic sacrifice if Britain was able
to join it, and that, if she could not join, she must be positive
towards it. Therefore even with limited information Whitehall
grasped much of the plan's meaning. But the committee had little
choice but to postpone judgment until more information was available. A committee of experts was established to look at the plan's
economic effects on Britain as more details emerged. (The fact that
this committee was given the initials F.G., standing for Franco-
German, showed that the Schuman Plan's European nature was still
unclear in Whitehall.)[5] In the Commons, where Conservatives were
sympathetic to Schuman's idea, Attlee welcomed the plan, but
insisted on the need for study. Massigli was well pleased with this.[6]

Kirkpatrick's paper to the Cabinet committee reflected Foreign
Office objectives (Franco-German rapprochement), fears (neutralism and federalism), and lessons from the past (the need to be
positive towards French ideas). Among diplomats the old liking
for Western European co-operation brought some support for the
Schuman Plan: Gladwyn Jebb saw positive factors in it; Oliver
Harvey and his deputy, William Hayter, hoped Britain would encourage it; Kenneth Younger (Minister of State since February) was

well disposed to it. American and German reaction put pressure on Britain to join. But the Office was also determined to maintain its Atlantic outlook: Kirkpatrick's paper ruled out a 'third force'; Jebb wanted the French to agree that the Atlantic community was vital to Western co-operation; and Harvey supported the plan partly because it could strengthen France's role in the Atlantic framework.[7] At the London meetings, meanwhile, the Atlantic idea was strengthened: in the tripartite talks (11–13 May) Schuman himself argued that America and Canada should join the O.E.E.C., and the Atlantic Council (15–18 May) improved the alliance's defence machinery.[8]

On 14 May Monnet arrived in London to explain his plan to the British, but was somewhat upset at their request for detailed information: for him the basic idea and aims of the scheme were what was important. He underlined the European potential of the plan of Plowden, and so impressed Cripps on 15 May that the latter said Britain ought to join the plan immediately. Cripps' motive in saying this was that he wanted to 'steer' the nascent proposal in ways acceptable to Britain, but his enthusiasm startled Bevin and Plowden.[9] Meanwhile Monnet had still not given much actual detail on the plan. Only on 16 May did he admit to astonished British officials that Schuman's announcement of 9 May was the main document yet prepared, and that little thought had been given to problems such as pricing, sales and investment. But he did clarify some points: West Germany was the only state which had to be involved, but other states could join; members had to surrender control of their coal and steel industries to a supranational body; and, most important, all members had to accept the supranational principle as a *non-negotiable* basis for talks on the plan. Massigli was flabbergasted by this last point, but for Monnet the plan would be useless without supranationality since it could not then control Germany or 'breach the ramparts of sovereignty'.[10]

The 16 May meeting convinced Plowden of Cripps' point that only by joining the plan immediately could Britain hope to 'control' it, and he put this to the F.G. Committee on 17 May. But the Foreign Office were more cautious, because of the continuing lack of details and the fear that merely entering into talks could commit Britain too far to Monnet's ideas. The Office preferred to encourage Franco-German discussions at first, which Britain might join later. An interim report by Plowden's office at this time showed that the British recognized the plan's significance more fully: the plan was said to be beneficial for the German problem and it was desirable that Britain should join it or at least be positive towards it; but its lack of detail and its supranational principle were major problems and, the vital point, if the Cabinet rejected the supranational principle, Britain could not enter talks on the plan at all.[11] Thus supranationalism was identified as the key issue. Hitherto Britain had condemned grandiose, 'federal' schemes for Europe, and had steered the European Assembly to inoffensiveness (as Cripps now wanted to do with the Schuman Plan). But the Schuman Plan was not merely another idealistic French idea. It was an immensely practical, 'functional' scheme, which sought to build up European co-operation in a limited economic project. And Bevin and the Labour Party had always liked such a practical, gradual approach: the Western Union speech had spoken of building up co-operation in many areas and hinted, ultimately, at something akin to a European state. Although he had turned more towards an Atlantic outlook in 1949–50 Bevin was still committed to Western European co-operation as one of the three main spheres of British activity and even Hugh Dalton supported 'functional' co-operation with the continent.[12] Thus Whitehall was willing to consider the Schuman Plan seriously. But their experiences with Marshall Aid and the Council of Europe had already led the British to define the point at which co-operation with Europe must end: and that point was where Britain lost her ability to survive if Western Europe collapsed. The question was whether the Schuman Plan, and specifically its supranational element, broke the limit to co-operation which ministers had established. By 19 May, when Monnet left London, the question was unanswered, but Britain was still positive about the plan.

Within a few days Monnet visited Bonn and reached general agreement with Adenauer on the plan. Meanwhile the British kept collecting information about French ideas and Parodi hoped London would be able to join.[13] Only now, after the London meetings, was Bevin able to look at the Schuman Plan fully, but on 23 May the E.P.C. met and decided, as the Foreign Office wanted, that Franco-German talks should be encouraged initially. Ideally ministers wanted British association in these Franco-German talks, but full membership would need careful consideration and a working party was established to look at the safeguards Britain would want if she were to join the plan. Importantly, ministers did not rule out a loss of sovereignty under strict controls but, on the negative side, Bevin said that the working party could draw up a 'practical' plan that would help Britain direct Schuman's initiative along 'realistic' lines.[14] On 25 May, somewhat irked at the lack of momentum from Paris, the Foreign Office decided to propose to the French their idea for British association (on what basis was unclear) in Franco-German talks.[15]

Since France and Germany were the essential components of the Schuman Plan, and since Schuman (to Monnet's annoyance) had told pressmen that British 'association', short of full membership of the plan, was possible, there was some hope for the British proposal.[16] But again Whitehall underestimated the 'European' content in Monnet's thinking. By sheer coincidence the British proposal came exactly when the French proposed a European conference on the plan, at which the supranational principle would be a non-negotiable basis of discussion. Italy and the Benelux states were also invited and a draft communiqué, to announce the conference, was annexed to the proposal. (Meanwhile Monnet sent more information on the plan to Plowden.)[17] The British proposal (on Bevin's instructions) was still delivered to the Quai d'Orsay, but was immediately turned down. Given Britain's willingness to talk, Parodi was hopeful she would join the international conference, but Oliver Harvey doubted that London could accept the supranational principle as a basis for talks before gauging what its practical effect would be; the idea of association in Franco-German talks had been to avoid this. On 26 May Harvey's doubts were confirmed: Britain rejected the French procedure. Massigli too criticized his government's methods, pointing out that the pragmatically-minded British could not possibly accept supranationalism without considering its practical results.[18] The Dutch also had grave doubts about the French procedure, but eventually joined on the understanding that they could leave the plan later if they disliked the way it emerged. There was some feeling that Britain should enter on the same terms,[19] and Schuman's assistant, Bernard Clappier, gave assurances that Britain could leave the talks at any time, so long as supranationalism remained the basis of the talks. (Monnet was adamant that Britain must not be allowed to break the all-important supranational principle: he feared, with good reason, that the British would try to steer his plan towards merely inter-governmental co-operation.)[20]

On 28 May Massigli went to the Foreign Office to reaffirm that supranationalism was non-negotiable and to get an elucidation of Britain's attitude. Younger told him that Britain, though willing to enter talks, could not be committed to a loss of sovereignty without knowing its effect. To some extent the two sides were talking past each other: the French, with Cartesian logic, could conceive of a 'principle' of itself; the 'realistic' British had to talk of a principle's actual effect. But the Foreign Office was also concerned that, whatever the French said, the act of entering into talks based on supranationalism would be the start of a slide towards a European federation from which they could not easily escape.

The British also feared that if they joined the plan, and did try to leave later, they would be accused of 'sabotage'. Massigli believed such British doubts could be covered by verbal changes to the draft communiqué that would announce the European conference, but Younger said such changes would have to make it emphatically clear that Britain, by joining the conference, was not committed to accept the detailed plan which emerged.[21] The British, still anxious to be positive (not least because of American support for the plan), were encouraged by the Dutch position to believe that compromise was possible.[22]

After this meeting Massigli visited Paris, where Monnet was willing to proceed without Britain while Parodi was more cautious. On 23 May a memorandum was drawn up, with Massigli's help, which sought to satisfy Britain by saying that though the supranational principle was non-negotiable there would be no prior commitment to accept the plan in its final form. But for the British this was not emphatic enough: they wanted to state their doubts quite bluntly. The problem was how to find a formula which made British reservations clear but maintained the principle of equal treatment for all and kept other countries, especially Germany, committed to pooling their sovereignty (the central point of the plan). Given the choice Schuman finally confirmed that controlling Germany and beginning a European federation were more important than British membership of the plan: on 1 June he rejected the idea of a blunt statement of British reservations and instead gave Harvey a new version of the French communiqué of 25 May, accompanied by a deadline: there had to be a final decision by 8 p.m. the next day, 2 June. Although the new communiqué disposed of an obvious textual problem (saying that the negotiators hoped to create a supranational authority, not that they had decided to do so), Harvey believed it would be rejected.[23]

Schuman's deadline was arguably the only way to force a decision in a difficult situation. The French, having produced their dramatic plan, had already caught Germany (the essential victim) in their supranational net, and although they ideally wanted British membership, they could not afford to let Britain hole the net: once in the talks in a 'reserved' position Whitehall could have done just that. The British, though keen to see a Franco-German rapprochement and to be positive towards the plan, and though willing to accept a *limited* loss of sovereignty, had never been willing to make an unqualified surrender of sovereignty, or to become involved in moves whose effects they could not reasonably measure. They could not become part of a move towards European federation. But the deadline, which the British called an ultimatum, was another dubious diplomatic act by the French, like the original announcement of the plan. After dithering somewhat in mid-May Schuman now put a one-day limit on what he knew to be a complex decision. And he did so at a time when Attlee and Cripps (who, importantly, had both been positive on the Schuman Plan) were on holiday, and Bevin (increasingly ill) was in hospital. Younger and Plowden had to take the new proposal, when it arrived, to the deputy Prime Minister Herbert Morrison, who had little experience in foreign affairs and remarked on hearing the news, 'It's no good, we cannot do it, the Durham miners won't wear it', reflecting Labour fears of 'surrendering' the coal industry to international control. The next morning Morrison and Younger saw Bevin and put the latest considerations of the Foreign Office to him. These were that Britain was being asked to risk upsetting the Commonwealth, the Atlantic community and, perhaps, the British people and to make the close commitment to Europe which ministers had always rejected. There were still strong reasons to join the plan – to please America and Europe, and influence the plan in ways Britain wanted – and Younger still favoured it. But Strang disliked the Schuman Plan and recommended that the latest proposal be rejected. Bevin agreed but, so as to give the plan one last chance, he wanted to propose an Anglo-French ministerial meeting. However, if France rejected this, Bevin, certain that Britain had behaved honourably throughout, wanted to state London's position publicly for the world to judge.

The F.G. committee under Plowden also rejected Schuman's proposal 'not because we necessarily preclude ... some surrender of sovereignty, but because we think it wrong to pledge ourselves without knowing more precisely the nature of the commitment...' Again, it was an open-ended commitment to supranationalism, not an infringement of sovereignty itself, which worried Whitehall. The committee, like Bevin, wanted to clarify Britain's position publicly, and to be positive: they even hoped to join the plan later 'in some manner'. These, and Bevin's views, were put to the Cabinet in the afternoon and were easily accepted. The few ministers present at this holiday season agreed that Britain could not join a plan whose effects were unknown but that she should not condemn Schuman's efforts. There was annoyance at the ultimatum, however, and some suggested Schuman had ulterior motives: to gain American sympathy, or to exclude Britain from Europe deliberately. The idea of joining the talks under imprecise reservations and perhaps trying to leave later, was ruled out. But the position was not yet hopeless: Bevin's proposal for an Anglo-French meeting was put to Paris and Cripps, learning of this, hoped that British membership (which he seems to have wanted more than anyone) was still possible.[24]

Cripps' hope was immediately crushed. Although Monnet later complained about the problems caused by carrying out the May–June exchanges through impersonal telegrams, he rejected the idea of ministerial talks, still fearful that Britain might undermine the precious supranational principle. The French could argue that the incompatibility of Anglo-French views was already clear and that enough delays had occurred. But the essential point was that France had the chance to pin Germany down and was not going to lose it. Among the French only Massigli saw British membership as a paramount consideration; Monnet still believed Britain would join later, once the plan had succeeded. Schuman, like Bevin, wanted to be conciliatory: he said again that British 'association' with the plan was possible, promised to liaise with Britain on developments and wanted to consider Whitehall's views on the plan. But on 3 June Anglo-French divisions were made publicly clear by communiqués from each side. A third communiqué announced that six powers, from now on 'the Six', would hold a conference on the Schuman Plan.[25]

17

After the Schuman Plan

BRITAIN's initial refusal to join the Schuman Plan conference did
not end hopes of including her in Monnet's scheme, nor did it
generate great bitterness between her and the continentals; in early
June Bevin and Schuman hoped for continuing Anglo-French
friendship. By late August, however, Britain was being heavily
criticized in Europe, all chance of her joining the Schuman Plan was
gone, and Anglo-French relations had seriously deteriorated.

   In London, in early June, the French embassy continued to hope
for British membership of the Schuman Plan, though the Foreign
Office discouraged this attitude.[1] In Paris, the British embassy
concentrated on an analysis of French behaviour since 9 May and
suggested four reasons for their insistence on supranationalism: the
nature of Cartesian logic (as opposed to British empiricism); the
need to control Germany; the encouragement from Italy and the
Benelux states; and Monnet's fear that Britain would try to blur the
plan's aims. Harvey felt that the Schuman Plan might yet fail,
allowing Britain to intervene with her own ideas, as she had with the
Council of Europe. This was not an unreasonable hope: the
Schuman Plan had been hastily developed, and still required
difficult negotiations. Bevin, of course, had already suggested that if
Britain drew up her own plan she would have a strong negotiating
position if she joined the Schuman Plan, and on 13 June he decided
that British tactics should be to prepare to intervene with a 'realistic'
scheme when the French plan failed (as he was certain it would). He
resented France's recent attitude and was determined not to be
treated as 'a Luxembourg'.[2] These tactics were encouraged by divisions within the French government, where many ministers now
criticized Monnet's 'conspiracy' of early May: Bidault resented the
destruction of his 'Atlantic' schemes; Petsche, the Finance Minister,
felt he should have been warned of the Schuman Plan; and even
René Mayer found Monnet's behaviour towards the politicians
offensive. Petsche actually contacted Cripps in early June and

suggested they maintain clandestine contacts, so as to intervene with a new plan should Monnet's ideas fail. Harvey (following traditional British opposition to intervention in French politics) rejected these suggestions, but Petsche raised them again later in June. In mid-June Massigli (who actually offered his resignation over the plan) tried to win Auriol, Bidault and others over to a plan Britain could accept, but he received little support: thanks to Monnet and Schuman the plan was then becoming firmly entrenched as part of French policy.[3]

In June events seemed to conspire to divide Britain and Europe. Inevitably the events of May had left resentment. Kenneth Younger now suspected that Monnet had deliberately excluded Britain from Europe to allow French domination (and the creation perhaps of a 'third force'). This suspicion was countered by Harvey, who saw the Schuman Plan as an understandable, radically new approach to the German problem, compatible with Atlantic co-operation and beneficial for French internal strength.[4] But Harvey's constructive view was drowned in mid-June by events which put British policy towards Europe in a poor light. The first of these events was the publication of the Labour Party pamphlet which Bevin had requested in April, to outline British policy on the Council of Europe. In May this was redrafted to cater for the Schuman Plan. The Labour Party machine was already familiar with the problem of European coal-steel industries thanks to European socialist conferences on them, and in April the party had published a pamphlet embodying the views of one Wilfred Fienburgh on international control of coal-steel. This acknowledged the need for some form of European coal-steel co-operation but, following established British policy, proposed inter-governmental, not supranational, arrangements.[5] On 24 May the N.E.C., with many ministers present, including Attlee, easily approved both the renamed 'European Unity' pamphlet, and a proposal for a new European socialist conference on coal-steel. But when the pamphlet appeared on 13 June it caused a storm. It laid down firm political and economic reasons against a European federation: on the political side it stated that Britain was a world power, with links to America and the Commonwealth, that a federation would face massive practical problems (different languages, traditions and customs) and that inter-governmental co-operation was sufficient; on the economic side it raised old Whitehall fears (that European economies were competitive, not complementary, and that federalism would ruin the sterling area) and 'socialist' considerations (principally the dis-

like of continental *laissez-faire* economics). The pamphlet still
supported extensive co-operation with Europe, through the
O.E.E.C., but its tone was distinctly more 'anti-European' than the
government wanted to appear in the light of the Schuman Plan.[6] The
press gave it full coverage and Monnet saw it as justifying his
recent policy towards Britain.[7]

Hugh Dalton, who had introduced the pamphlet at a press conference, could not understand the criticism it unleashed: the
pamphlet had Bevin's support, followed Cabinet policy and had
N.E.C. approval. But other ministers saw the damage it could do.
Attlee faced an embarrassing situation, because he was about to
make a Commons' statement on the Schuman Plan. Actually both
Attlee and Morrison, who now criticized the pamphlet, had helped
approve it, without recognizing its full significance. Cripps, who
had not seen the pamphlet in draft, and who was still positive
towards the Schuman Plan, bitterly criticized Bevin over the affair.
The problem was that 'European Unity' did broadly reflect British
policy, but in the delicate situation of mid-June its tone was in-
appropriate. Bevin should have realized this but his dislike of
European federalism, his resentment of French tactics and, probably, his illness, made him largely unrepentant.[8] In the afternoon of
13 June Attlee made his Commons' statement, saying Britain was
continuing to study the Schuman Plan and, surprisingly, he was not
criticized about 'European Unity' (instead the Conservatives pressed
the argument that Britain should have joined the Schuman Plan
conference under reservations). But on 15 June Attlee admitted to
the Commons that the pamplet was ill-timed.[9] He hoped that a
European Socialists' conference, which had been arranged for 16-18
June, would save socialist unity on the issue but (though bitter
arguments were avoided) some continental representatives at the
conference criticized the Labour pamphlet.[10] The Foreign Office had
no direct influence over these Labour Party antics, though officials
were worried by the American and French response. Interestingly,
however, the Office did not disagree with the pamphlet's contents:
Strang declared that 'European Unity' was 'in its main thesis along
the true line of British policy'.[11]

There was another opportunity to outline British policy on 26-27
June, in a debate on the Schuman Plan which the Conservatives had
pressed for. Churchill again planned to argue that Britain could
have joined the Schuman Plan under reservations. The government's majority was now so low that defeat in the debate, and
thus a general election, seemed possible. Two Cabinet meetings and

meticulous Foreign Office preparations were necessary beforehand, but Labour was confident about fighting for a 'national' cause: 'If we go down on this', remarked Lord Jowitt, 'I can't think of any better issue to go to the country on'.[12] The government's attitude, put forcefully by Cripps, was clear: Britain could not surrender control of her economy to a body whose powers were unknown; and to have joined the plan at first and withdrawn later would have offended everyone. Against these 'nationalist' arguments the Conservatives retreated. A few, including Edward Heath in his maiden speech, showed 'federalist' views, but Churchill (who had used the 'European' ideal since 1946 chiefly as a political platform) had always been vague about Britain's role vis-à-vis a European union. Like Bevin, Churchill believed in national independence, the Commonwealth and the American alliance: he could not really accept a federalist commitment for Britain. Although he, and Anthony Eden, continued to press the idea of entering the Schuman Plan talks under reservations, the Conservatives proved unwilling to support supranationalism as a general principle, and the government survived (helped, perhaps, by the coincidental outbreak of war in Korea).[13] The Foreign Office were pleased to have given a full public outline of British policy, and were quite confident that theirs was the only 'practical' approach to European co-operation, but Europeans saw the debate as further evidence of Britain's opposition to genuine European unity.

Other events at this time increased British criticism of France. The paper on French weaknesses which Strang had asked for in March was now being circulated. Called simply 'France', it was a very critical analysis. While restating France's importance to British security and Western European recovery, and while praising her pro-Western policy, rejection of political extremism, and economic rejuvenation, the paper pointed out all the old weaknesses: national demoralization; short-lived, unstable governments; a dreadful fiscal system; inadequate armed forces. The report recommended that Britain should continue to support France where possible, but preferred France to stand by herself. The paper could be seen as very positive for Anglo-French relations: it strongly reaffirmed Britain's need for a strong, friendly France, which Bevin had always wanted. But Bevin's own comment on the paper was telling: 'almost too optimistic but ... a sad story'. Since 1945 the Foreign Secretary had sought a strong France, but five years later she seemed as weak as ever. In Whitehall her support of European federalism was seen as a result of this weakness.[14]

French instability was further shown on 24 June when Bidault's government collapsed. His fall was doubly disastrous because the next day communist troops from North Korea invaded the pro-Western South and plunged the world into a new East–West crisis. That communists were now willing to use armed invasion to achieve their aims was ominous: it was widely believed that Korea was a diversionary attack, to be followed by the conquest of Western Europe. And yet, as in 1938 (when Hitler invaded Austria) France found herself without a government. All the doubts expressed in the paper on France seemed confirmed.[15] The South Koreans were saved from certain defeat by American military intervention, and in Paris, eventually, a moderate government came to power under Pleven, an experienced minister and wartime Gaullist. But Bevin remained critical of France and in August the Paris embassy prepared a very pessimistic report on French morale.[16] Inevitably these events strengthened Britain's reluctance to join the Schuman Plan: Monnet himself realized that one reason why Britain distanced herself from the plan was because she doubted the ability of the continentals to defend themselves.[17]

The conference on the Schuman Plan between France, West Germany, Italy and the Benelux countries, began on 20 June. Massigli still hoped that Britain might join the plan if it could be altered, and in late June he pressed Strang and Younger on this line. But the British rejected such ideas, recognizing that France would not dilute her supranational aims. One official criticized the well-meaning Massigili for adding confusion to a difficult situation, and Bevin especially was very cautious about seeming to sabotage the Schuman Plan.[18] The British working party, established in May, had continued to make studies on the plan, and by late June Cripps (always positive on the issue) hoped to reveal some detailed British thinking on it at a forthcoming ministerial meeting of the O.E.E.C. on 7 July. Schuman himself was keen to hear such British views, and Harvey and Hall-Patch believed this would be beneficial.[19]

A lengthy report by the F.G. committee had actually gone to the Cabinet on 22 June, covering the background to the Schuman Plan and its probable effect on British industry. It concluded that an 'International Authority' would indeed be useful for improving the efficiency of Europe's coal and steel industries, but that this need only be an inter-governmental institution, working through national delegations such as the O.E.E.C. The Cabinet liked this idea and a new Committee of Ministers was established to report on it further: the British still wanted to be ready to intervene with their own plan, at any time, should the Paris talks falter. Attlee also asked for reports on the effect of an inter-governmental authority on Commonwealth and defence considerations.[20] On 4 July, therefore, the Cabinet looked at three further reports: a paper by the new Committee of Ministers, which generally supported the F.G. committee's scheme for an International Authority; and papers on the Commonwealth and defence aspects which argued that an inter-governmental authority was much more acceptable than a supranational one. These papers showed the time and energy which the British were willing to devote to the Schuman Plan, but also revealed their continuing unwillingness to accept supranationalism. This attitude was unlikely to appeal to the French as yet, so the Foreign Office acted to scotch Cripps' hope of discussing British ideas at the O.E.E.C. The continentals, Bevin argued, would only see such ideas as an attempt to divide them, and he continued to believe that the Schuman Plan would fail by its own impracticality, when Britain could step in. The Cabinet accepted Bevin's views and the new Committee of Ministers was asked to observe the Paris Conference and look for a British opportunity to intervene there.[21]

Bevin's fear of being branded a 'saboteur', however, was not easy to escape. In early July the Secretary for War, John Strachey, made a rabidly anti-European speech, which talked of a 'plot' to overthrow the Labour government. This led to a debate in the Commons, and Attlee himself had publicly to condemn Strachey.[22] But many Frenchmen and Americans were now convinced that Britain aimed to destroy the Schuman Plan.[23] In mid-July British preparations for their own International Authority continued,[24] and for a time the Paris Conference actually seemed to falter: practical difficulties arose about putting the Schuman Plan into effect, and Schuman even considered diluting the plan to get British involvement.[25] But the O.E.E.C. conference, at the same time, showed how strongly supranationalism had caught the European imagination. Petsche, Guiseppe Pella (of Italy) and Dirk Stikker (of Holland) each put their own ideas for a functional but supranational body to cover some area of Europe's economy. The British adopted the same attitude towards these schemes as they did to the Schuman Plan: the plans could be studied (preferably slowly), but would probably be rejected for implying too close a British commitment to Europe. The continentals' desire for British leadership certainly continued: on 13 July the Italian Emanuele Grazzi begged the Foreign Office to lead a federal Europe because, he said, France was too weak to do so. But the British, while wishing to be constructive, simply could not accept the federalist principle. Cripps tried to make this clear to the O.E.E.C., with limited success.[26]

As late as 17 July British officials considered that they might be asked to put forward their own version of the Schuman Plan,[27] but the Paris Conference was now advancing successfully: on 25 July Schuman announced that the Six agreed on all major issues. This simple announcement rendered the British plan (and all the hard work on it) academic, and attention in London shifted to a different idea (first suggested, of course, in May) for *association* with a successful supranational plan. The working party was asked to look at what form such association could take, and the E.P.C. decided on Bevin's recommendation to await the French Assembly's approval of the Schuman Plan (which was several months away, at least) and then negotiate for association.[28] Bevin informed Schuman of this in August. The personal commitment of the two foreign ministers to friendly relations at this time remained strong,[29] but when the Council of Europe Assembly held its second meeting that month more strains were added to the Anglo-French alliance. There were more federalist schemes and the Labour delegation was subjected to continental criticism.[30] The Conservatives too, however, found themselves in an embarrassing position since their 'federalist' stance in 1946–9 had now been revealed as little more than a publicity exercise. The most important Conservative proposal at the Assembly was the 'Macmillan–Eccles Plan' which sought to turn the Schuman Plan into an inter-governmental scheme.[31] Monnet, unsurprisingly, rejected this, telling Schuman, with incredible exaggeration, that 'the British are waging a skilful campaign to sabotage our plan'.[32]

By late August Britain and the Six were completely divided over their vision of Europe's future. Britain's non-supranational approach to co-operation was no longer seen as a viable road to European unity. In fact Bevin's vision of Western Union, generated in the face of Soviet expansion in early 1948, and based on the hope of Western Europe's spiritual and material recovery, had itself faded by 1950. The decay of Foreign Office support for a customs union, the failure of France to achieve strength and stability, and the success of British links to America and the Commonwealth (in NATO the devaluation crisis and the Colombo Conference) had made the Atlantic community more appealing to Bevin. The obvious potential of the Schuman Plan had led certain ministers and officials to consider accepting a limited loss of sovereignty in May to join it, but French tactics helped ensure that this course was not fully explored: the French first surprised the British, then failed to give a clear impression of what the Schuman Plan intended, and finally, on 1 June, issued a virtual ultimatum. But, even with more time, the chances of developing a plan which simultaneously broke the walls of sovereignty only under strict controls (as Britain wanted), while tying Germany down (as France wanted) were virtually non-existent. True, Britain had already accepted an *implied* loss of sovereignty in the O.E.E.C., the Atlantic Pact and other bodies, and Whitehall might have been tempted to accept a *formal* loss of sovereignty in mid-1950 under strict limits. But the British certainly would not accept an *open-ended* commitment to the principle of supranationality. As decided in January 1949, Britain could not risk tying herself too closely to Europe. What happened in the weeks following 2 June was that British policy – especially as seen in the plan for an International Authority – was more closely defined as opposing any formal surrender of sovereignty, for fear of where this could lead. Behind this definition lay Britain's faith in national independence (strengthened by Labour's belief in a planned, national economy), her contempt for continental weakness and 'impracticality', and the idea that Britain could remain a world power, aided by America and the Commonwealth. In 1950 such thinking was inevitable: Britain, the victor of 1945, was psychologically incapable of surrendering her independence; Western Europe, especially France, had failed to perform well since 1947; Europe took only a quarter of British trade; and Britain still retained many global ties and commitments. But, even so, in the Brussels Pact and the O.E.E.C. London had been willing to make an unprecedented, and genuine, commitment to European co-operation. And when the Commonwealth ideal failed, when America showed that she did not need a British 'partner', and when Britain began to lose faith in herself, then, as Monnet predicted, she would turn fully towards the European community.

For France the Schuman Plan sprang from an entirely different experience. Defeat in 1940, occupation, political instability, economic weakness and the Soviet menace led France to seek security among others. More than this, a tradition of support for European unity, fear of Germany, and a history of written constitutions made France willing to accept supranational control, and her internal division between communism and Gaullism, coupled with the fear of a Soviet-American conflict, fuelled the idea that she might, in the long term, create a kind of 'third force' in the world. Important too, paradoxically, was the French desire for national status as the 'leader' of Europe. Until 1950 practical difficulties made French attempts to promote European federalism, in the Council of Europe and in Fritalux, of limited use. It took the desperate German problem and Monnet's brilliance to develop a practical initiative with the Schuman Plan. In this plan the need to control Germany and create a supranational body were of paramount importance; Monnet would not let the British dilute the supranational element. But the cost of Monnet's tactics was a limited Europe, of only six nations, based on bureaucratic, functional lines rather than an evolving, living, political organism, covering a wide area of Europe, such as Bevin had always hoped to create.

For Anglo-French relations the events of May–August left a scene of division, but there was talk of British association with the Schuman Plan, and both Bevin and Schuman hoped to preserve good relations. The Schuman Plan had, after all, only formalized a division that had been growing for years. In mid-1950 both countries had come to the point where 'functional' co-operation was accepted as the way to approach European unity, but both had come to this point from opposite directions: for Britain, functional schemes involving a loss of independence were the point at which European 'unity' must realistically end; for France functional schemes involving a loss of independence were the point at which European 'unity' really began. Britain and France were divided by a narrow but deep chasm, the chasm of 'sovereignty'.[33]

18
German rearmament

THE SCHUMAN PLAN was put forward with the laudable aims of offering Germany equality, guaranteeing French security and beginning a European federation. But in September 1950 these aims were threatened by a proposal for the ultimate step in Germany's revival, her rearmament. Until mid-1950 the old four-power aim of German demilitarization had survived, although German rearmament had been discussed frequently since 1949 and had created an emotional response in France: in October 1949 Massigli declared that the idea would antagonize Russia and bring World War Three. The French Cabinet also expressed fears over the subject and in November Bidault told Harvey of France's complete opposition to German rearmament. The British gave assurances that they too opposed the idea,[1] but some elements in Western Europe, notably the Dutch government, were quite favourable to German rearmament as a way of strengthening Western defences,[2] and Adenauer suggested that Germans could be armed as part of a 'European army'.[3] In December the Foreign Office sent its representatives a list of arguments against German rearmament, saying that it would terrify France and Western Europe, antagonize Russia and give Germany undesirable power. A similar paper was sent out in March 1950.[4] But still the issue would not die. In the Commons on 17 March Churchill and others proposed German rearmament.[5]

By the spring of 1950 Konrad Adenauer was very concerned about West Germany's defences because an armed 'police force' was being created in East Germany,[6] and most Western military chiefs were willing to consider German rearmament seriously: for American planners rearmament was a logical step in German revival and in strengthening the West; the British C.O.S. felt that a realistic European defence needed German rearmament and suggested that an armed 'police force' such as that in East Germany would make an acceptable first step towards this;[7] and even French military chiefs were willing to consider such ideas.[8] In fact, by May the Foreign

Office were quite interested in ideas for a West German armed 'police force': this could keep internal order in Germany, be useful in war, and yet avoid recreating a German army. But the Office did not know how they could establish such a force and, at the London Conferences in May, British policy was that West German defence must rely on the occupation forces.[9] German rearmament in the near future seemed unlikely.

The Korean War, however, revolutionized the whole situation, by showing that armed conflict was possible in the East–West struggle. Massigli feared that Russia would now overrun Western Europe;[10] Adenauer feared an East German invasion; and the Foreign Office began to look at the armed police force idea with greater interest.[11] Korea was in fact to bring a general militarization of NATO. A massive rearmament effort began, Greece and Turkey entered the alliance, and a full military structure was formed in Europe. This occurred despite the ill-effects of rearmament: the inflation it caused, the high spending it demanded, and the arguments it generated among the Allies. But the most controversial result of Korea, and the one which divided Britain and France most, was German rearmament.

Until early September, Anglo-French unity on the issue was maintained. In July premier Pleven told the British that German rearmament would inspire communist propaganda, and must certainly not occur before France had a strong army. Bevin was sympathetic to these arguments, though he feared that if France's military weakness continued, German rearmament would have to be considered.[12] By mid-August the C.O.S. wanted to create twenty German divisions under certain restrictions, but the Foreign Office were reluctant to move too quickly, and turned more and more to the police force idea.[13] This more cautious proposal appeared to satisfy French opinion as well. On 4 August, in special tripartite talks in Paris, the British representative mentioned the police force idea and Parodi gave a positive response to it – so long as the police were controlled by provincial, not central, government. The French believed that a provincial police force would not antagonize Russia, or give Germany as much military power as a national army.[14] The Paris embassy now reported that France could accept German 'rearmament' (a rather imprecise term)[15] and on 21 August Bevin held a meeting with his Western European representatives which confirmed that German rearmament, under safeguards, was now generally acceptable on the continent. It was decided to draft a Cabinet Paper, proposing an armed police force, for use at the next

Atlantic Council (due in New York in September).[16] The next day Schuman told his Cabinet that an armed German police force was now acceptable, though he also said that a German *army* was not.[17] The French announced their willingness to accept an armed police force in talks between Adenauer and the High Commissioners on 24 August.[18]

On 1 September the British Defence Committee accepted the Foreign Office proposal of a police force: the C.O.S. acknowledged that this was politically more acceptable than a German army. (This was very much part of a series of decisions aimed at reviving Germany and strengthening Western defences: Bevin now declared that West Germany should no longer be treated as a threat to security.)[19] All seemed to be going well for Western defence preparations when on 4 September the British Cabinet adopted the proposal for a German armed police, and Bevin informed ministers about increased French defence spending. But that very same morning, Bevin had learnt that Washington now favoured the recreation of a German army.[20] The French too had been told of this American view, and disliked it; on 5 September their Cabinet again rejected any idea of a German army. But the French did still favour the police force proposal: on 7 September Schuman told the British that he agreed with their views on this.[21] In August, a third approach to German rearmament had been raised by Churchill and others at the Council of Europe, the creation of a federal 'European army' (as Adenauer had already suggested). But the Foreign Office dismissed this as a 'nebulous' idea,[22] and the French showed no official interest in it. Thus as the New York Atlantic Council drew near a German police force seemed far more likely to emerge than either a German or a European army. Korea had made a form of German rearmament acceptable, but both Britain and France wished to avoid the creation of actual German divisions.

In tripartite talks (12–14 September) before the Atlantic Council this Anglo-French agreement was irretrievably broken. In the talks the Americans not only insisted on recreating a German army, but also made this a condition for sending more U.S. troops to Europe and appointing a U.S. commander over NATO forces there (two things which Europeans desperately wanted). This proposal, the 'one-package' deal, was put forward because Americans were unwilling to send their troops to Europe if Europe was not doing its utmost to defend itself. But this 'deal' failed to take account of the deep-seated fear of the German military menace in France and it seemed like emotional bribery, making defences against Russia conditional on the resurrection of German military power. Furthermore it meant that, if German rearmament was rejected in Europe, the other vital NATO defence arrangements which Washington had made conditional upon it would also fail to emerge.

Initially both Bevin and Schuman rejected the 'one-package' deal, but then on 13 September Bevin gave way, abandoned the police force proposal (which the Americans felt was inadequate) and asked the Cabinet to agree to the American plan. His physical weakness and pro-Americanism may have influenced this change of position, but just as important was the fact that Acheson asked only for agreement to a German army *in principle*. To Bevin this seemed reasonable enough: an actual German army would take time to form, and could be carefully controlled, and meanwhile Europe would receive U.S. troops and a U.S. commander. On 15 September, after two meetings, the Cabinet agreed to Bevin's request, though they insisted that German units must be strictly controlled, and only the C.O.S. showed any real enthusiasm for Bevin's new policy. Even Strang feared that a German army could lead to an unbridled German revival and conflict with Russia. The French felt even more strongly. French ministers were rigidly opposed to American demands: especially hard-line was the Socialist defence minister, Jules Moch, whose son had been killed by the Nazis; and Schuman began to delay the New York talks by asking endless questions. Then he suggested that the defence ministers of the three powers must meet: a move which, he believed, would dilute Moch's hard-line position. The Anglo-Americans agreed.[23] In the Atlantic Council (15–18 September) the arguments continued; France was increasingly isolated (only Belgium and Luxembourg showed sympathy for her position) but refused to retreat. Massigli told the Foreign Office that France could not accept German rearmament as a general principle for fear of where it could lead, and on 20 September, the French Cabinet ruled that though a German 'contribution to defence' by, for example, providing economic materials, was acceptable, German 'rearmament' in a broad sense was not. Talks between the defence ministers (22–26 September) failed to make headway and by the end of the month all NATO defence preparations were in jeopardy.[24]

The New York meetings had quickly destroyed any hopes of a joint Anglo-French approach to German rearmament. There were some ironic parallels in this situation to the Schuman Plan debates of May–June; but this time it was the British who had suddenly adopted a new policy, and the French who proved unable to accept the broad principle behind this (and were criticized by their allies). On 7 October, following a French Cabinet meeting, the Paris embassy reported that French opposition to German rearmament was unlikely to change.[25] On 9 October Bevin and the Defence Minister, Emanuel Shinwell, reported to their Cabinet, and Shinwell (who had argued bitterly in New York with Moch) was very critical of French policy. Bevin was still confident that a compromise might be possible,[26] and indeed, the Anglo-French division was not impossibly wide: the French could accept some German contribution to defence; and the British were willing to place limits on German rearmament. But the principle which divided London and Paris was deep. Furthermore the French felt betrayed by Bevin's about-turn in New York.[27]

In October an important new proposal emerged from Paris based on the 'European army' idea, which divided Britain and France even further. In starting on the road to European federation in May, Monnet did not foresee the creation of a supranational army for many years, but he was forced to act on the idea in the autumn because German rearmament began to undermine the Schuman Plan. The rearmament issue showed that France did not yet want genuine German equality; it also showed the Germans that they were valuable to the West and could probably bargain for equality with other powers without accepting supranational controls. Monnet simply had to act to save the Schuman Plan, keep control of Germany and reverse France's growing isolation in NATO, and he began to plan the European army in September, working, as with the Schuman Plan, on an old idea which Adenauer was known to favour, and which (it was hoped) could offer Germany equality while guaranteeing French security. Broadly the plan aimed to create a European army under a supranational body, linked to the Schuman Plan in a kind of 'community'. To weaken possible German independence further, units would joint the army not as divisions, but as mere battalions. Again as with the Schuman Plan, Monnet first won certain Americans (notably ambassador David Bruce) over to his scheme and persuaded a leading politician, this time Pleven, to sponsor it. On 19 October the Cabinet approved the plan and it was announced to the world on 24 October. Two days later the Assembly approved it by over 100 votes.[28]

Unfortunately, thereafter, the story of the European Defence Community (E.D.C.) was far from smooth. It had many problems. Not only was its preparation hasty (like that of the earlier European

parliament) but even French ministers and officials had little enthusiasm for it: Moch saw it as a way to delay German rearmament;
Monnet took little interest in it after its birth; and Massigli was
singularly unimpressed. Pleven had immediately modified the plan
to ensure that France and Germany would not enter it as equals:
there would be quite rigid controls on German units. Furthermore,
in devising it no-one considered the European army's military
efficiency: how a motley collection of small units, speaking
different languages, was supposed to resist a Soviet onslaught was
unimportant to Monnet. Finally, British membership of the plan
was not considered. This was unsurprising, since Britain had no
interest in a European federation, but ultimately it was to prove a
decisive flaw: the British were so militarily important in Europe
that only their membership could really have controlled the
German military and made the army effective.

Within days Moch presented the 'Pleven Plan' to a meeting of
NATO defence ministers, but it only aroused interest from Belgium
and Luxembourg; the Americans felt it was militarily ridiculous.
Once again no progress was possible on German rearmament, and
the issue was handed to a group of deputies, meeting in
Washington. Shinwell was again critical of Moch's policy in the
Defence Committee on 7 November, and Attlee even suggested
asking the French if they planned to surrender in the event of war.[29]
The British disliked the Pleven Plan proposal (a French official had
even admitted to the Foreign Office that it was militarily unworkable) and, on 30 October, Bevin told the Cabinet that the plan was
primarily a French domestic move, which few other countries
supported. The Cabinet decided to apply the same principles to it as
they had to the Schuman Plan: they would not join it, though
neither would they publicly oppose it.[30] Thus a few months after
devising their quite popular armed police force proposal the British
were faced by two ideas which, in early September, they had rejected: a German army and a European force. Anglo-French relations had again paid the price for Bevin's pro-Americanism and
France's fear of Germany.

It was fortuitous that in late 1950 the world situation changed in a
way that healed the Anglo-French alliance. For in November the
British came to share many French fears about the world situation
when communist China intervened in the Korean War, and drove
Western forces back. In response the Americans began to talk of
widening the Korean conflict or of using atomic weapons and even
the British were terrified that Washington might plunge the world

into war. Strang, who never liked the idea of German rearmament, advised a delay in pursuing that aim: in the delicate new world situation German rearmament might indeed spark off a Russian invasion of Western Europe. Hugh Dalton, always anti-German, shared this view, and the Foreign Office argued that German rearmament could be abandoned gracefully by arguing, as was true, that the Germans themselves did not favour it.[31] Events were complicated by a Soviet proposal, on 3 November, to hold a new four-power C.F.M. Inevitably, the French (especially Auriol) took a great interest in this: if Russia would make peace, German rearmament would be unnecessary. Bevin decided to agree to a C.F.M., so long as all East–West issues, not just those Russia wanted, were discussed. By late November (despite American doubts) tripartite talks were under way to prepare Western views for such a C.F.M.[32]

In late 1950 Bevin remained committed to the Atlantic community: he suggested that German rearmament could be solved by forming a 'NATO federated force' (an idea that appealed to none of his British colleagues) and told the Commons that European co-operation alone was 'not enough'.[33] Meanwhile the French remained opposed to German rearmament: on 6 December Socialist ministers threatened to resign if France's position weakened.[34] But despite these continuing differences the common Anglo-French interest in preserving world peace was seen in December, when Attlee decided to visit Truman in order to moderate American policy in Korea. As early as July Parodi had suggested that Britain and France could act together against any American extremism in Korea,[35] and on 2 December Pleven and Schuman visited London to discuss Attlee's mission. There was a discussion on German rearmament, in which Attlee and Bevin criticized French delays, but elsewhere the British and French reached agreement: both sides wanted to concentrate Western military efforts in Europe, not the Far East, and to resolve quickly the divisions in NATO over German rearmament. Attlee's mission to Washington went successfully, the Americans showing no real intention to extend the Korean War, and the French were kept fully informed throughout.[36]

December also saw a successful compromise on the German rearmament issue. Early in the month the Foreign Office decided to support a new American compromise on the issue (which had emerged from the NATO deputies' talks) called the Spofford Plan.[37] This sought to please everyone by beginning a NATO 'integrated force' in Europe with a U.S. commander, by starting to raise German units of 'combat team' size (less than a division, more than a battalion), and by allowing negotiations for a European army (which the Germans would join). The plan included many limits on Germany's contribution: Germans could not use aircraft, ships or heavy equipment. Given the strong views of all sides, such a complex compromise was inevitable. It answered both French fears and U.S. wishes for action. But it was a very ambiguous and awkward plan: Germany was said to be an 'equal', but clearly was not; German forces would be in the European army, but would begin to form even if the European army did not emerge; and the 'combat team' (a new idea) might prove militarily ineffective.[38] The French Cabinet, conscious of the need for American arms and fearful of becoming completely isolated, reluctantly approved the Spofford Plan on 6 December.[39] On 14 December the British Cabinet also approved the plan with reservations: because of the world situation ministers now wanted to delay the actual creation of German units, at least until after the new C.F.M. with Russia.[40] But the breakthrough was now achieved: in late December, in Brussels, the Atlantic Council held a special meeting and adopted the Spofford Plan. An 'integrated force' was to be created in Europe under General Dwight Eisenhower; France would call a conference on the European army; and German rearmament was accepted in principle.[41] After months of deadlock, and with a deepening East–West crisis, progress was again possible for NATO.

In early 1951 events were dominated by the Western rearmament effort: in Britain a massive increase in arms spending began, which soon divided the government; in France and Germany there was renewed interest in 'neutralism' to avoid rearmament; and the E.C.A. was renamed the Mutual Security Agency and became primarily a channel for U.S. military aid. But meanwhile the Brussels Council decisions were carried out. Most agreeable to everyone was Eisenhower's appointment, which became the symbol of America's commitment to European defence. In January he visited the European capitals to familiarize himself with the European situation, and he eventually took up his post in April. The European Army Conference began in mid-February in Paris, with all the Schuman Plan countries except Holland. The Dutch, always doubtful about federalism, only sent observers to the conference (as did Britain and other NATO members). Massigli continued his attempts to bring Britain into the E.D.C., but the Foreign Office still felt it to be an impractical scheme which did not offer Germany true equality and whose federal nature Britain could not accept. Nothing in the first few months of talks changed these views though the Office were impressed by increasing enthusiasm elsewhere for the Pleven Plan.[42] On 3 July Eisenhower himself spoke out publicly in favour of the E.D.C. which, he had concluded, was the only way to proceed with continental support. In Bonn meanwhile, talks were held with West Germany on the easing of Allied controls (a German foreign ministry, among other things, was now created) and on the mechanics of raising German units. In these talks the French finally agreed that for the sake of military effectiveness German divisions could be formed. With all these concessions, and the implicit promise in them of eventual German equality, Adenauer too became very well disposed to the E.D.C.[43] By August the long criticized E.D.C. was drawing support from Paris, Bonn and Washington.

Throughout early 1951 preparations were also under way for the new C.F.M. which Russia had proposed.[44] In March the foreign ministers' deputies met in Paris and began long arguments over a possible C.F.M. agenda. The French proved reluctant to end the talks before their general election (which was held in June) for fear of stimulating communist propaganda. But after the election the talks quickly broke down.[45] President Auriol, especially, was upset by this failure,[46] but the talks never even approached agreement.

By the time the conference ended Ernest Bevin was no longer Foreign Secretary. On 12 March, in the midst of these events, the strain of ministerial work and gathering illness on Bevin forced Attlee to replace him. Although he was given the post of Lord Privy Seal, Bevin felt utterly dejected and he lived for only another month. He had come to the Foreign Office in 1945 with great hopes of world peace and co-operation; when that hope was disappointed he did more than anyone else to create a new, Western security system. But in 1951 that system itself seemed to be stagnating, partly because of his own recent policies. As for Anglo-French co-operation, one of his main aims in 1945, he had created a firm military alliance with Paris, but had lost French support on his European policy. And in his last six months this division had grown, especially because of his willingness to rearm Germany despite French fears.[47] In early September an Anglo-French agreement on a German armed police force had seemed possible, but thanks to Bevin's surrender to American policy, this had not been fully explored. Within months all the main problems in Anglo-French relations had been reinforced: the British saw the problems as further evidence of French weakness; the French saw the British as unfeeling and tied to America, and adopted a new supranational scheme. Had the worsening situation in Korea not driven the two sides closer together the effect on Anglo-French relations could have been disastrous.

19

Herbert Morrison

March–October 1951

ALTHOUGH he occupied the post for only seven months Herbert Morrison quickly earned a reputation as a poor Foreign Secretary. He was a somewhat unlikely choice, having little experience in foreign policy and being disliked by Bevin, but he was a leading minister and Labour figure and he wanted the position in order to improve his hopes for the leadership. He soon faced a series of crises: the nationalization of British oil fields in Iran; pressure in Egypt for the British to leave; and the Burgess–Maclean spy scandal. The new four-power meeting and preparations for the Japanese Peace Treaty added to the usual strains of the Foreign Office, and Morrison faced other pressures: his wife was dying; he was organizing the Festival of Britain; and with Attlee ill he was acting Prime Minister. But he added to his own problems by disliking his new position: he considered his staff to be 'snobs', he made it plain that he preferred being in the Commons, or on holiday, to being at the Foreign Office, and his staff disliked him.[1] For all his poor reputation, however, Morrison's policy towards France always seems to have been very constructive, and indeed to have healed some of the wounds of Bevin's last months.[2]

Despite his experience at Strasbourg in 1949, Morrison improved Anglo-French relations noticeably on the European unity question. Since August 1950, when it became clear that Britain would associate with, but not join, the Schuman Plan, the plan's preparations in Paris had dragged slowly on. Sometimes the Foreign Office felt a coal-steel authority would never emerge: a draft treaty was not presented to the British until November.[3] The British desperately needed to know the details of the plan to prepare their own views on it, but they feared to show too much curiosity about it, since this might make the French suspect a British sabotage attempt.[4] The British sensed that the major reason for delays in Paris was Germany's pressure for greater concessions, now that the issues of Korea and German rearmament had made her more vital to the

West. This supposition was correct: the Germans hoped to put an end to the Ruhr authority and other industrial controls once they were in the Schuman Plan, but the French feared that the old Ruhr cartels would return if Germany were given complete freedom. Not until March 1950 was a decartelization agreement made which reassured France about this point.[5]

Meanwhile British policy towards Europe was again criticized during a special session of the Council of Europe in November and Harvey was very concerned about anti-British feeling in France: the French Socialists especially were disappointed with Labour attitudes.[6] But in early 1951 Whitehall no longer had any intention of harnessing the European movement. When, in January, Philip Marjolin argued that Britain could regain the leadership of Europe by supporting the reduction of tariffs in the O.E.E.C., the British replied that they were a global, not a European power, and that Europe must now concentrate on rearmament.[7] In his last Cabinet as Foreign Secretary, Bevin expressed concern about growing pressure to give greater power to the Council of Europe. The Committee of Ministers were likely to approve some reforms (by the necessary two-thirds majority) on these lines, at their next meeting on 16–17 March, and Bevin felt that this might create a situation where Britain had to leave the Council. He did wish to avoid leaving if possible: he felt the Council was needed for European morale, to tie Germany into Europe and to allow Britain to 'guide' co-operation.[8] But his old vision of a Western European 'third power' in the world had completely disappeared.

On 1 March 1951 the British finally received a draft of the Schuman Plan treaty. Even then delays continued in Paris: the treaty was signed on 18 April, but not ratified by France until December. However, the British were now able to draw up their own detailed views on the plan. Suspicions continued in Europe that Britain would try to sabotage the continental effort,[9] but on 12 March the Foreign Office sent a telegram to Paris, supporting the plan as a way to solve the German problem and hoping for association with it[10] and Morrison's attitude was, from the start, one of conciliation. He proved positive towards the Council of Europe at the Committee of Ministers on 16–17 March, and came away prepared to make some concessions to those who wanted to reform the Assembly: on 19 April he persuaded the Cabinet, against some opposition, that the Assembly should now be able to discuss defence issues.[11] Massigli even felt that, with some concessions, Morrison might negotiate for membership of the Schuman Plan, but Paris took little interest in these over-optimistic hopes.[12]

In any case a specific, new Anglo-French problem soon arose on the Schuman Plan. This centred on France's new-found willingness to free Germany of Allied industrial controls now that she was 'caught' in the Schuman Plan. On 10 April the French told London that they wanted a conference called to end the Ruhr authority and other coal-steel controls on Germany. On 16 April, the British Cabinet agreed to such a conference, so long as the French did not prejudge the results by assuring the Germans that controls would end: this condition was made because the Cabinet still wanted time to discuss their own position towards the Schuman Plan and the end of German controls. But by 19 April, not only had Schuman assured Adenauer that Allied industrial controls would end, but the story (including the British position) had reached the press. Again France's desire for a rapprochement with Germany had been allowed to upset Anglo-French relations. The British made forceful complaints to Paris.[13] But continuing his positive line Morrison did not let the disagreements last: on 24 April he welcomed the Schuman Plan treaty in the Commons, and on 1 May proposed that talks to end the Ruhr authority should begin soon.[14]

On 30 April the Foreign Office prepared a paper which largely restated their position on the Schuman Plan of a year before: officials wanted a Franco-German rapprochement and would not oppose the plan; but they preferred Atlantic co-operation and could not accept supranationalism. Among themselves officials believed that a European federation would be harmful even if Britain remained outside it because it might lead to a 'third force', separate from NATO, but they recognized the need to be positive towards European union in public if Britain were not to face international criticism.[15] In Paris Monnet himself did not believe that Britain could now join the plan, but he and Schuman were desperate to see a positive British approach to the subject, because they feared that British criticism might yet tempt certain elements to reject it.[16]

In May an exploratory tripartite meeting was held to discuss the end of Allied controls on Germany. The French were keen to progress quickly, but the British still had not fully developed their views on the Schuman Plan, and an unexpected new problem had arisen: the Ministry of Supply was reluctant to ease controls on the German steel industry, for fear of the effect on Britain's steel industry, and especially because Britain was now used to receiving huge amounts of scrap steel from Germany. On 5 June the Cabinet decided to try to secure a continuation of these important scrap supplies before they agreed to free Germany from controls.[17] This decision worried the Foreign Office, because of its likely effect on French opinion, but on 18 June ministers only slightly modified their position: they would announce their willingness to free Germany of controls in principle, but would only actually end controls if scrap supplies were guaranteed. The British put this conditional position to the French and Americans on 19 June, and to everyone's annoyance, the scrap steel issue proceeded to delay progress on decontrols for months.[18] Only in mid-September was an Anglo-German agreement on scrap supplies reached, and tripartite agreements on decontrols could not be signed until 19 October.[19] In the face of this unforeseen difficulty Morrison had to turn elsewhere to please his Allies on European unity. He did so through a declaration of support for French policy.

In April, the Permanent Under-Secretary's Committee (P.U.S.C.), established by Bevin to look at long-term policy problems, had decided to make a full analysis of the European unity issue and sent a despatch to Britain's Western European representatives requesting information on the influences behind the European movement in their particular country, how far European unity was supported in society and which type of 'unity' the country preferred (for example, full federalism, the 'functional' Schuman Plan, or what was called the 'NATO principle' – the inter-governmental approach which Britain supported). Finally the P.U.S.C. asked how London could best influence the European unity debate, and suggested that Britain might make a statement to clarify her European policy. Replies to this despatch arrived over the next two months. On 4 May Harvey reported that the French were influenced, in seeking European unity, by the need to control Germany and win U.S. approval, but that the unity ideal also had great appeal in itself in France. There was no doubt that despite different views on French society the French government supported the Schuman Plan as the best way to progress, and did not see British policy as a route to real 'unity' at all. Harvey, in conclusion, repeated his long-standing request that London should make clear in a statement that she was not 'anti-European'. He made this appeal again in early July, by which time he was concerned that the steel scrap issue, and America's growing support for the E.D.C., were emphasizing Britain's lukewarm position towards Europe.

By then the P.U.S.C. were collating the information they had received, and on 21 July produced a final paper. This noted that all Western European countries saw the value of NATO, but that France and Germany, especially, wished to go beyond this, to supranational schemes. The P.U.S.C. concluded that a careful British statement of view on Europe could have several potential beneficial effects: by increasing British influence over European co-operation; by dissuading the French and Germans from advancing too quickly; and by creating a bridge between the Atlanticists and the Europeanists, whose tensions might otherwise divide the Western alliance.[20] On 24 July the Economic Policy Committee agreed that such a statement should be made. The E.P.C. also formally and finally decided that Britain should work for association with, but not membership of, the Schuman Plan. But because the Commonwealth, and Britain's coal-steel trades unions and industrialists, had now to be consulted on this decision it would mean a further, long delay before a definitive public statement on the Schuman Plan was possible.[21]

On 30 July the Cabinet discussed the joint problems of European unity and rearmament, and Morrison presented a paper which argued that the unity movement, and Europe's reluctance to accept rearmament burdens, were both caused by a general feeling of demoralization on the continent. He wanted to counter this feeling and inspire Europe to greater self-confidence by a policy in three parts: first by arguing in favour of Western rearmament; second by encouraging more non-military European co-operation; and finally by being more positive to the continental union attempts. The Cabinet approved this policy,[22] and at the Council of Europe in August Morrison made a forceful statement, pointing to the successes of greater European co-operation thus far (in countering communism and drawing Germany into a constructive relationship) and arguing that Britain had led the way on this since 1948. But this statement, though well received, lacked impact since it was made in a closed meeting of European ministers.[23]

The feeling grew in the Foreign Office after this, that mid-October would be the optimum moment to issue a more dramatic, public statement on the Schuman Plan and European unity. By then the Commonwealth could be consulted on the Schuman Plan and the scrap steel issue would be settled.[24] But suddenly, in September, Morrison decided to act more quickly. He was then present at tripartite talks in Washington, with Acheson and Schuman, prior to another Atlantic Council. On 4 September, before these meetings, the Cabinet had confirmed its approval of greater European co-operation and also decided, because of America's new policy of support for a European army, to lend public support to the E.D.C., though British membership was still unthinkable. During the tripartite meeting the suggestion was made that a declaration of support for the E.D.C. should be issued by America, Britain and France, and Morrison immediately seized this chance, not only to show Britain's positive policy towards Europe, but also to demonstrate Anglo-Franco-American unity on the issue. A tripartite declaration on the E.D.C. was rather different to the unilateral declaration on the Schuman Plan which the Foreign Office had planned, but Morrison's decision was well rewarded: the French, especially Monnet, were delighted with this public reassurance of British support, and Oliver Harvey soon felt that the tripartite declaration had achieved all that could have been hoped.[25] When he left office a few weeks later Morrison had succeeded neither in changing Bevin's policy (which had never really been 'anti-European') nor in avoiding practical problems (the steel scrap issue was evidence of that), but he had shown British policy in a positive light, after two years in which British attitudes had caused deep offence to Europeans. His only misfortune was that some continentals believed that this signalled a British move actually to *join* the Six. When the Conservatives came to power these hopes were further increased, and then cruelly dashed.

German rearmament never became a major Anglo-French issue under Morrison. The period was more important for increasing British internal divisions on the issue. Though Morrison, Bevin, Shinwell and others were convinced of the need for German rearmament, and though Britain was committed to the idea in principle, other ministers, including Attlee, were much more doubtful, and since December Dalton had argued forcefully against German rearmament. In February, the Cabinet had expressed a desire to slow down preparations for German rearmament, and in the Commons Attlee took the opportunity to state British conditions for arming the Germans; these were that other Western nations must be rearmed first, that German units must be integrated into a wider NATO structure, and that the Germans themselves must agree with rearmament.[26] There was a bitter argument on German rearmament in the Cabinet in late July, when Dalton bluntly declared that the Germans were an aggressive people whose rearmament would antagonize Russia. Morrison and others rejected these arguments and Attlee had to act to keep the peace among his ministers.[27] Confusion was added to by disagreements on the E.D.C., because not all those who supported German rearmament liked the idea of the European army. In the Defence Committee in July Morrison argued that the E.D.C. would help to control

Germany once she was rearmed, and might be more palatable to Russia. But Attlee and Shinwell criticized the European army as an impractical scheme, and Dalton was certainly not convinced that it made German rearmament more palatable.[28] By September, as seen above, the Cabinet was more willing to give positive support to the E.D.C. (rather than simply to avoid public criticism of it) but the issue of German rearmament would continue to divide Labour in opposition.

Under Morrison the Foreign Office remained as concerned as ever about French internal problems. Another investigation into French problems late in 1950 had noted all the old faults – weak government, poor defences, demoralization in society – and Harvey expected 1951 to be a difficult year, especially since it was to see a general election.[29] Other reports on France were not as negative: the French economy was gradually improving, moderate governments had remained in office, the French were firmly tied to the Western alliance, and even their army seemed to be improving.[30] But the Foreign Office remained critical. The first months of 1951 in Paris were dominated by attempts to pass a new electoral law designed to operate against extremist parties. Arguments over this brought down Pleven's government in February, but an electoral reform was eventually passed by a new government, under Queuille, on 7 May.[31] The general election followed in June with predictable results: the extremists were limited by the electoral law, but the Communists remained the largest party and the R.P.F. took many M.R.P. votes. As a result the moderates retained a majority in the Assembly but the M.R.P. and the Socialists relied even more on support from smaller groupings.[32] This had an immediate ill-effect when, to British dismay, it took until 11 August before Pleven managed to form a new, stable government. 'Is this a foretaste of what a United Europe would be like...?' asked Strang.[33]

In August 1951 no-one was very satisfied with the state of Anglo-French relations. Massigli was exasperated with the gradual decline in their co-operation since 1949 and he begged Paris to reassert the importance of the British alliance. Maurice Schumann, the new deputy foreign minister, sympathized with Massigli's views and in early September Robert Schuman responded to them by suggesting that high-level talks should be held later in the year to repair the Anglo-French alliance. Morrison agreed with this suggestion and the British began to prepare for such talks.[34] But further dismay was caused in mid-September when Bidault and Pleven both accused Britain of rejecting co-operation with France: Pleven declared that the Treaties of Dunkirk and Brussels had been complete failures. Maurice Schumann quickly acted to reassure the British, however, saying that Bidault and Pleven were mistaken.[35] Then the tripartite declarations of support for the E.D.C. helped to restore Britain's reputation in France, indeed the Paris press expected Britain to join in supranational schemes.[36] The Foreign Office hoped to use the Anglo-French meeting to clarify their European policy to the Quai d'Orsay, but the meeting did not occur until after Labour had lost power.[37]

In September Morrison with Shinwell and Hugh Gaitskell, was in North America for various meetings, including the tripartite conference in Washington, and an Atlantic Council in Ottawa. These meetings failed to give much encouragement to the West for the future. The Canadians and others vainly tried to counter the growing Anglo-Franco-American domination of the alliance; trade deficits, inflation and raw material shortages, in the wake of Korea, were causing strains on the Western economies; and although the British, French and Americans now agreed to give nominal equality to West Germany in the alliance, differences immediately arose with Adenauer on the details of carrying this out. Britain and France, meanwhile, disagreed over appointments within the NATO command structure: the French insisted on being given command of the Western Mediterranean area, because Britain was to be predominant in a new Middle East Command. This argument could not be resolved by the time the conference ended, and marked a disappointing, but perhaps fitting end to Anglo-French relations under the Labour governments.[38] On 19 September, while Morrison was returning to London, he learnt that Attlee would be calling an election in October. Morrison could suggest no alternative, but he disliked Attlee's decision, and his doubts were soon justified. Although at the polls on 25 October Labour managed to gain a majority of votes cast, the electoral system defeated them, and Winston Churchill returned to 10 Downing Street.

Conclusion:
Labour's legacy

October 1951

DESPITE Churchill's 'federalist' attitudes of 1946–9, the new Conservative government maintained Labour's European policy. In late November Churchill presented a Cabinet Paper recalling his support for the federalist movement in the Zurich speech, but adding that 'I have never thought that Britain ... should ... become an integral part of a European Federation'. He also repeated his view that Britain should have joined the original Schuman Plan talks, but only as a way to 'steer' the plan the way Britain wanted (the very thing Monnet would never have accepted). Churchill concluded by listing the three main areas of British interest in the world: first, the Commonwealth, second, the 'English-speaking world' (that is America), and only then a 'United Europe'.[1] Already, on 22 November, the Cabinet had taken the decision both to make a favourable reference to the Schuman Plan at the Council of Europe's November session, and to make it clear that Britain would not join any supranational schemes.[2] This of course was in no way different from established British policy, and when the Home Secretary, Maxwell Fyfe, made what he thought to be a 'pro-European' speech at the Council of Europe, it was a grave disappointment to those who had hoped for a change in British policy. A speech in Rome by Eden, the same evening, bluntly announced that Britain could not join the E.D.C. and underlined the sense of disappointment on the continent. Spaak was so upset by the British attitude that he resigned from the position he had taken as President of the Consultative Assembly. It was clear that the lines established by the Labour government on European co-operation would continue to dominate British policy for many years to come.[3]

In his few months as Foreign Secretary, Herbert Morrison had striven hard to agree with France on European co-operation, but in October 1951 it was obvious that the Labour governments of Clement Attlee had failed to achieve the close co-operation with Western Europe, based on an Anglo-French alliance, which Bevin had declared to be his aim on 13 August 1945. Leaders on both sides had come to accept a fundamental division on European unity: Monnet recognized that Britain would not join the Schuman and Pleven Plans; Morrison gave his blessing to the E.D.C. The accepted interpretation of why this division came about argues that Britain, victorious in war, was loath to co-operate with Western Europe after 1945, preferring an alliance with America, co-operation with the Commonwealth, and control of her own economy. Bevin, it is said, only wanted co-operation with Europe in 1945–8 so as to win an American alliance, and the British soon wasted the goodwill they had bought in Europe with their wartime triumphs. The French, meanwhile, are said to have emerged from defeat and occupation willing to abandon the nation-state and pursue a new vision of European union.[4]

Enough of this accepted interpretation is correct to make it convincing. The British did consistently seek co-operation with areas outside Europe: in 1945–7 the Big Three relationship and the U.N. were of central importance to British foreign policy, and Bevin was cautious about pursuing a Western bloc; in 1947–9 Bevin sought the American alliance; and belief in the Commonwealth connection was always strong in the post-war Labour governments. In January 1949 it was because of the need to maintain links with America and the Commonwealth that the E.P.C. made the vital decision not to draw too close to Europe. And in France there was definitely an idealism about European union, inspired first by wartime experiences and then by the Russian threat. However, a close survey of the available evidence from the period shows that, in fact, the British did want European 'unity' in 1945–51, and that French 'idealism' about European union was strongly reinforced by national self-interest. The essential problem was that Britain and France interpreted European 'unity' in radically different ways.

In 1945, Britain and France, as Western European, democratic and colonial states, both sought similar aims, security and Great Power status, through similar methods, friendship with America and Russia, control of Germany (the accepted enemy), new Imperial arrangements and Western co-operation. The war had shown Britain's need of Western Europe, as well as her ability to stand alone, hence the idea of a British-led Western European bloc (which people like Spaak were very willing to accept). However, in 1945–6 the brave new world that everyone hoped for failed to emerge: four-power co-operation was undermined; France was forced from the Levant and failed to achieve her aims in Germany; and the

British were unable to bring France into an alliance, the vital basis of any Western bloc. However, Britain's belief in co-operation with France and Western Europe was strongly maintained. British policy was largely responsible for restoring France as a major power in 1945, and in 1946 her preservation became even more vital because of the communist threat. Geographically and historically France was the heart of Europe and her collapse would have been a decisive blow to the West. Therefore Britain tried to help the French democrats, especially with Harvey's mission in April to make a treaty. Later Bevin made a determined effort to improve Anglo-French relations with the commercial and financial talks of September 1946. Although Britain's desire to keep Russian friendship made Bevin careful about pursuing a Western bloc at this time, France, with her nationalist aims in the Levant and the Ruhr, was the more vital barrier to Western European co-operation. Bevin tried to increase links to Western Europe nonetheless: providing British military and economic supplies to Europe; associating Belgium in the occupation of Germany; and seeking to free barriers to travel in Western Europe.

In 1947–8 Bevin followed the 'grand design' with greater success: Dunkirk was signed, and Britain and France went on to lead Europe in the Marshall Plan and the Brussels Pact. In late 1947, it was Bevin who finally despaired of co-operation with Russia and who produced a blueprint of Western co-operation – the Western Union – whose central pillar was a more closely united Western Europe. And by early 1948 Britain's commitment to the continent in the O.E.E.C. and the Brussels Pact was unprecedented. The French certainly gave Bevin support in this. Paris had sought Russian friendship in 1944–7, but the Communists' departure from government, the need for U.S. aid and Russian tactics in Eastern Europe, Germany and at the Moscow C.F.M. made France very much part of the West. By 1948 she was even willing to join the Anglo-Americans in reviving Germany. But the French also showed great caution in following Western policies: in early 1948 they wanted bilateral, anti-German treaties, rather than a multilateral European pact; they almost rejected the London Accords on Germany; and when the N.A.T.O. negotiations began, they preferred a traditional automatic military alliance, accompanied by an arms build-up, to a wider Western community. As early as 1943 Frenchmen such as Monnet and Alphand wanted close economic co-operation in Europe and they pursued this aim with ever greater determination in 1946–8. But these economic schemes were not always tied to political federalism; they were not, apparently, widely supported within the French government, and they were mainly based on France's need for external economic support (especially for coal).[5] Actually, in 1946–8, Bevin and the Foreign Office were willing to investigate a customs union seriously themselves: the desire for radical economic co-operation was not one-sided. Down to mid-1948, therefore, Britain was at least as 'pro-European' as the French.

From mid-1948 to early 1950, although Britain and France remained firmly united as part of 'the West' (opposing Russia over Berlin, and building NATO) differences emerged over European unity. It became apparent that each had its own approach to European co-operation. Furthermore, Britain did begin to turn away from Western European co-operation as the centre of her foreign policy. In retrospect the period immediately after the London C.F.M. of late 1947 was rather like June 1940 when a Franco-British union was suggested. Once again the menace was enough for Britain to consider an actual political and economic union with the continent. But Britain's empirical, practical national character, and her interest in American and Commonwealth links, made her seek only a gradual advance on the way to Western Union. The Treasury and the Board of Trade came to support European co-operation, for practical reasons, in the O.E.E.C., but they had never liked the radical idea of a customs union. And after February 1948 the Foreign Office too turned back to a more cautious approach: the same cautious approach that had already led them to reject Duff Cooper's ideas for extensive Anglo-French co-operation, and to fail in following-up the Bevin–Ramadier talks of September 1947. Britain's commitment to a 'European' vision remained, nonetheless, genuine at this time. Bevin had wanted to pursue Western European co-operation for years and now, in the long term, seriously considered the creation of a Western European independent force led by Britain. He and the Foreign Office certainly cannot be accused of underestimating the vast potential of European co-operation. But that Bevin's massive vision was accompanied by 'realistic' policies was clearly seen in his insistence on inter-governmental co-operation in the O.E.E.C. and later, in the Council of Europe.

The French worked along entirely different lines. They adopted an 'instant', federalist approach to European unity. Bevin's Western Union was inevitably misread by many continentals, who did not think like the pragmatic British, in terms of an unwritten, ever-evolving constitution. To French and Belgians Western Union spoke of a precise written constitution for a European federation. The French had a history of such ideas – in Briand's schemes, and thinking in the wartime Resistance – and they had strong practical reasons for pursuing them now: to give France the leadership of Europe; to answer popular demands for a federation; and, most of all, to control Germany. Well into 1949 the idea of pressing federalist ideas without Britain was unthinkable, and the British shared French interests, such as controlling Germany and strengthening Western Europe, enough to make a division between them unnecessary. But by late 1949 the differences between France and Britain were increasingly apparent. Bevin had failed to keep the policy he had begun in January 1948 under control: Germany's gradual revitalization was still troubling France; Western Europe had failed to recover from weakness and instability; and Western European co-operation had been spoiled by federalist demands. Bevin saw federalism itself as a result of European weakness, and simply did not believe that it was practical to weld the European nations together into an actual union. This belief seemed to be borne out by the failure of the C.U.S.G., the hastily conceived European parliament, and the rather innocuous Fritalux. By early 1949 Bevin was no longer convinced that Western Europe was militarily and economically 'reliable', and the E.P.C. judged that Britain must be able to survive independently of the continent. The Foreign Office was especially exasperated with France's internal weakness and federalist tendencies. Meanwhile the creation of NATO, the success of the Commonwealth after Indian independence, and finally the devaluation crisis, convinced the British of the need to rely primarily on America and the Commonwealth.

In the spring of 1950 Britain and France were moving along different lines in their thinking on Europe, but France was still unable to devise a successful federal scheme and accepted Germany's gradual revival in the 'Petersberg policy', while Britain was still quite willing to join in 'functional' co-operation with Europe. It took the brilliance of Jean Monnet to create a practical proposal to begin a European union with the Schuman Plan, but in fact this was akin to Bevin's ideas of early 1948, in seeking a gradual approach to unity. The Schuman Plan was, in a sense, a defeat for federalism and evidence that France had learnt the impossibility of making a European constitution. Nevertheless it was a supranational scheme, put forward with little concern for Britain's reaction. Some British ministers and officials were interested in joining the plan, but could not accept the open-ended commitment to supranationalism which Monnet seemed to demand. Bevin had done immeasurable good for Western European co-operation and security with the O.E.E.C. and NATO, building up a web of military, economic, social and cultural links with the continent, but France's federalist approach was better able to solve the German problem and give Europe the genuine union which many wanted. Even so, it was a very limited 'Europe' of only six nations, unable to build a true federation, and still relying on U.S. economic and military support. In 1950–1 the Anglo-French division was reinforced by the German rearmament problem which saw Britain follow American policy and France adopt a new supranational scheme, the European army. But despite continental suspicions, the British never tried to sabotage the French efforts. From an early date Whitehall had been willing to accept continental unions, so long as they did not harm British interests, and the British were soon willing to associate with the Schuman Plan.

The reason Britain came to be seen as 'anti-European' was not only because she had a limited view of how far and how quickly European unity could progress, but also because of her *attitude* to the continental efforts. The French were always disappointed with the lack of British economic co-operation after 1945, and even after the launch of Western Union the British seemed to look to their own economic interests overmuch: in the O.E.E.C. the British were very obstructive whenever the position of sterling was threatened. Whitehall was certainly willing to do much to rebuild the European economy, but too often the Treasury and the Board of Trade seemed negative. Furthermore Bevin was often contemptuous, not just critical, of France's federalism. And there were 'anti-Europeans' in the British government, as seen in the Strachey speech. The worst example of Britain's lack of feeling towards Europe was the devaluation of sterling in September 1949. From that time, in fact, the decline in Anglo-French co-operation may be dated. In the two and a half years before then Britain and France co-operated quite closely in building up Western European links, but the devaluation stunned the continentals. Thereafter, there were many occasions when an Anglo-French 'community of interests' was seen: in the Auriol visit of March 1950, the Pleven–Attlee meeting in December 1950, and Morrisons's E.D.C. declaration in September 1951. And the two remained united as leaders of NATO (alongside America). But in general their relationship was far less close, and after 1951 the charge that the

Labour governments had been anti-European was widely accepted.

Essentially, what happened in 1945–51 was that European unity oscillated in importance for Britain: in 1945–7 the Western bloc was of secondary importance to Big Three co-operation; in 1947–8 Western Europe moved to the fore in British considerations; but by 1950 the Atlantic community was more vital. But Western Europe always remained one of the three vital areas of concern for British policy, and in the 1960s, when the American and Commonwealth links failed to provide all Britain wanted, there was no real contradiction in London looking once again to Western Europe as the centre of her policy. The reason for this oscillation was Britain's approach to her world interests after 1945: Western European policy had to be balanced against other consistent concerns. But perhaps, ultimately, Bevin's vision of realism, pragmatism and reliance on America was not far from what actually emerged: a European union did have to develop gradually, as needs arose; a U.S. military guarantee did continue to be needed; and Western European survival long relied on the system of Western co-operation which Bevin created. Both British Atlanticism and French federalism had their role to play in the advance of European unity.

Notes

INTRODUCTION: BEVIN'S INHERITANCE

1. C.de Gaulle, *War Memoirs* (3 vols, 1955–60), I, 9.
2. *362 H.C.DEB.* 5s, 301–2.
3. *392 H.C.DEB.* 5s, 101.
4. CAB.66/34, W.P.(43)75; A.Eden, *The Reckoning* (1965), 371–2, 378, 397–8.
5. CAB.66/50, W.P.(44)297; W.Churchill, *The Second World War* (6 vols, 1948–54) V, 554–6.
6. Sir L.Woodward, *British Foreign Policy in the Second World War* (5 vols, 1970–6), V, 1–18, 50–61, 89–126.
7. CAB.66/21, W.P.(42)8.
8. CAB.66/30, W.P.(42)480; P.H.Spaak, *The Continuing Battle* (1971), 76–8; F.van Langenhove, *La Securité de la Belgique* (Brussels, 1971), 98–122.
9. Woodward, *op.cit.*, V, 181–97.
10. R.Massigli, *Une Comédie des Erreurs* (Paris, 1978), 29–30, 37–42, 47–55; J.Monnet, *Memoirs* (1978), 223–3; H.Alphand, *L'étonnement d'Etre* (Paris, 1977), 161, 168–71, 179; de Gaulle, *op.cit.*, II, 203–4.
11. De Gaulle, *op.cit.*, III, 49–51.
12. J.Chauvel, *Commentaire : d'Alger à Berne* (Paris, 1972), 108–10.
13. CAB.66/63, W.P.(45)146.
14. De Gaulle, *op.cit.*, III, 53–7.
15. De Gaulle, *op.cit.*, III, 65–81 and documents 83–103; Soviet documents in *Les Entretiens de Gaulle-Stalin* (Paris, 1959).
16. R.Sherwood, *The White House Papers of Harry Hopkins* (1949), 849.
17. *The Conference of Malta and Yalta* (Washington), 1955 (government publication), 302.
18. CAB,65/48, W.M.(44)161, conf. annex; de Gaulle, *op.cit.*, III, 71.
19. Woodward, *op.cit.*, III, 95–103.
20. De Gaulle, *op.cit.*, III, 192.
21. J.Young, 'The Foreign Office and the Departure of General de Gaulle, 1945–6', *Historical J.*, xxv, 1 (1982), 209–16.

1. THE GRAND DESIGN

1. R.McCallum and A.Readman, *The British General Election of 1945* (1947), 111–12.
2. *395 H.C.DEB.* 5s, 773–5.
3. On labour policy see T.Burridge, *British Labour and Hitler's War* (1976), 159–60, 167–70.

4. CAB.66/39, W.P.(43)321; CAB.66/53, W.P.(44)414; and Burridge, *op.cit.*, 96–102, 123.
5. A.Bullock, *The Life and Times of Ernest Bevin* (1967), II, 199–205, 317–18, 341–7, 381–4.
6. J.Harvey (ed.), *The War Diaries of Oliver Harvey* (1978), 384–5; P.Dixon, *Double Diploma* (1968), 166–7; D.Dilks (ed.), *The Diaries of Sir Alexander Cadogan* (1971), 776–8.
7. H.Macmillan, *Tides of Fortune* (1969), 33–4; A.Eden, *Full Circle* (1960), 4–6.
8. On Bevin as Foreign Secretary see, for example, C.Attlee, *As It Happened* (1954), 169–70; Lord Strang, *Home and Abroad* (1956), 287–8, 293–5; Sir I.Kirkpatrick, *The Inner Circle* (1959), 202–5; Sir R.Barclay, *Ernest Bevin and the Foreign Office* (1975), 39–42.
9. F.O.371/49069/9382 and 9501.
10. F.O.371/49069/9537.
11. F.O.371/49069/9639.
12. See n. 15.
13. F.O.371/45581/6051.
14. F.O.371/45581/5904 and 5963.
15. On the 13 August meeting see F.O.371/49069/9595; Harvey diaries, 13 Aug; Cadogan diaries, 1/15, 13 Aug; A.D.Cooper, *Old Men Forget* (1953), 361.
16. F.O.371/49069/9525; Cooper, *op.cit.*, 362.
17. On Duff Cooper as ambassador see Cooper, *op.cit.*, 360–1; Diana Cooper, *Trumpets from the Steep* (1960), 213–16, 238–45; Earl of Bessborough, *Return to the Forest* (1962), 126–9; C.Gladwyn, *The Paris Embassy* (1976), 234–9; P.Ziegler, *Diana Cooper* (1981), chapters 11 and 12.
18. F.O.371/49069/9595; *413 H.C.DEB. 5s*, 292–3.
19. F.O.371/49069/9525; F.O.371/45581/6094; R.Massigli, *Une Comédie des Erreurs* (Paris, 1978), 61, 69–70, 74–6.
20. CAB.128/1, C.M.(45)25; CAB.129/1, C.P.(45)123.

2. A SETTLEMENT FOR THE LEVANT

1. F.O.371/45582/6321.
2. C.de Gaulle, *War Memoirs* (3 vols, 1955–60), III, Documents, 279–80.
3. F.O.371/45582/6321.
4. De Gaulle, *op.cit.*, III, 205–11.
5. De Gaulle, *op.cit.*, III, documents, 291–2; A.D.Cooper, *Old Men Forget* (1953), 362.
6. F.O.371/49069/10477.
7. *The Times* (10 Sept).
8. F.Williams, *A Prime Minister Remembers* (1961), 151–3; H.Truman, *Year of Decisions* (1955), 453–6; J.Byrnes, *Speaking Frankly* (1947), 102–5; CAB.129/3, C.P.(45)202.
9. F.O.371/45582/6840 and 6960; PREM.8/43; Cooper, *op.cit.*, 263–4.
10. F.O.371/45583/7203; Cadogan's diary, 1/15, 22, 25 Sept.

11. F.O.371/45582/6963; F.O.371/45583/7203; 7529 and 7549;
    F.O.371/45584/7740.
12. On Bidault's character see B.Ott, *Georges Bidault* (Annonay, 1978);
    G.Elgey, *Le République des Illusions* (Paris, 1965), 39–41, 126–30;
    P.O.Lapie, *De Leon Blum à de Gaulle* (Paris, 1971), 94–6.
13. CAB.128/1, C.M.(45)39; CAB.129/3, C.P.(45)206.
14. F.O.371/45583/7203; F.O.371/45584/7717.
15. F.O.371/45584/8308.
16. F.O.371/45584/7806.
17. F.O.371/45584/8205–7, 8308; Cadogan's diary, 1/15, 28, 29 Oct.
18. F.O.371/45585/8431, 8656, 8677, 8702, 8833; Cadogan's diary,
    1/15, 2, 8 Nov.
19. F.O.371/45587/10082 and 10091; F.O.371/52842/246;
    de Gaulle, *op.cit.*, III, 276–8.
20. De Gaulle, *op.cit.*, III, 277; J.Moch, *Recontres avec de Gaulle* (Paris,
    1971), 108–11.
21. CAB.129/1, C.P.(45)130; CAB.129/2, C.P.(45)174.
22. F.O.371/45586/9745, 9748, 9825, 9831; F.O.371/45587/9911, 9913,
    9944, 10078, 10103; C.Chamoun, *Crise au Moyen Orient* (Paris,
    1963), 163–70.
23. Cadogan's diary, 1/16, 7 Jan.
24. CAB.128/2, C.M.(45)60, and same as confidential annex CAB.128/4.
25. De Gaulle, *op.cit.*, III, 275–6; Moch, *op.cit.*, 98–106;
    F.O.371/57166/98.
26. See the discussion in J.Young, 'The Foreign Office and the Departure
    of General de Gaulle', *Historical J., xxv.* 1 (1982, 209–16; and
    F.O.800/464/46/1–4.
27. F.O.371/52843/807; F.O.371/52479/1099; Chamoun, *op.cit.*, 173–5.
28. Bevin considered holding a meeting between Britain, France, Lebanon
    and Syria at this time. F.O.371/52479/1099, 1364, 1365; Cadogan's
    diary, 1/17, for 1, 3, 9, 13, 14 Feb. Chamoun, *op.cit.*, 175–9, 182.
29. F.O.371/52843/1124; F.O.371/52844/1253, 1313, 1484.
30. CAB.128/5, C.M.(46)11.
31. CAB.128/5, C.M.(46)16; F.O.371/52843/1126; Cadogan's diary,
    1/17, 15, 16 Feb; *U.N., Official Records, First Session, General
    Assembly* (1946), 46–56, 110–13.
32. T.Lie, *In the Cause of Peace* (New York, 1954), 33–4.
33. F.O.371/52844/1561; F.O.371/52845/1680, 1681, 1726, 1728, 1729,
    1862; F.O.371/52846/1907; Chamoun, *op.cit.*, 183.
34. On British disapproval of French behaviour see CAB.128/5,
    C.M.(46)25 and F.O.371/52479/2167. On British refusal to criticize
    France publicly see *420 H.C. DEB. 55* 1854–5.

3. THE WESTERN BLOC, THE GERMAN PROBLEM AND ANGLO-FRENCH RELATIONS

1. CAB.129/3, C.P.(45)218.
2. F.O.371/59952/2411.

3. F.O.371/49070/13885; H. Alphand, *L'étonnement d'Etre* (Paris, 1977), 189; G. Catroux, *J'ai vu Tomber le Rideau de Fer* (Paris, 1952), 133.

4. C. de Gaulle, *War Memoirs* (3 vols, 1955–60), 217–19 and documents 192–7; R. Massigli, *Une Comédie des Erreurs* (Paris, 1978), 64–5; J. Dumaine, *Quai d'Orsay* (1958), 7–8.

5. On Vansittart's views see his *Events and Shadows* (1946 ?) 95–9, 161–7; and N. Rose, *Vansittart* (1978), 271–2, 282–3. On discussions of a Western bloc in the Commons see *416 H.C. DEB. 5s*, 761–2, 781–2, and *419 H.C. DEB. 5s*, 1251–3, 1345–6, 1349.

6. P.H. Spaak, *The Continuing Battle* (1971), 85–6; F. van Langenhove, *La Securité de la Belgique* (Brussels, 1971), 174–82.

7. B.R. von Oppen (ed.), *Documents on Germany under Occupation* (1955), 66–8.

8. See above, chapter 2, n. 9.

9. CAB.129/9, C.P.(46)156.

10. U.S. officials were also concerned with the French plan's economic effects: *F.R.U.S., 1945, III* (Washington, 1968), 889–913. The Russians were interested in sharing in economic control of the Ruhr under the French plan: Alphand, *op.cit.*, 188–90; Catroux, *op.cit.*, 137–47.

11. F.O.371/59911/259; F.O.371/55399/240.

12. F.O.371/59957/909m 1113.

13. F.O.371/55400/1963.

14. In the first Bevin–Bidault conversation Bevin suggested the Ruhr might be economically tied to Lorraine to strengthen the whole European economy – an idea similar to the Schuman Plan of 1950: F.O.371/55399/1407.

15. F.O.371/55400/2188.

16. *139 H.L. DEB. 5s*, 1294–5; F.O.371/59952/2780 3308; F.O.371/59953/3045, 3112, 3188, 3625, 3744; A.D. Cooper, *Old Men Forget* (1953), 366–7.

17. F.O.371/59952/3283, 3287, 3300; F.O.371/59953/3405, 3414, 3528, 3612, 3834; F.O.371/59954/4840; F.O.371/59960/3356; Harvey papers, manuscript 56402; Cooper, *op.cit.*, 367; Massigli, *op.cit.*, 82; J. Chauvel, *Commentaire: d'Alger à Berne* (Paris, 1972), 164–5.

18. CAB.129/8, C.P.(46)139; CAB.129/9, C.P.(46)156; CAB.128/5, C.M.(46)36.

19. F.O.371/55402/4620 and 4728; F.O.371/55403/4819, 4852, 4853 and 5114; CAB.129/10, C.P.(46)207; Harvey diaries, 25, 26, 28 Apr.

20. F.O.371/55403/5256 and 5375; F.O.371/55404/6073.

21. CAB.129/9, C.P.(46)197.

22. F.O.371/55402/4728.

23. On France's reaction to the East–West division in Germany see: F.O.371/59964/7441, 8040; F.O.371/59965/8729; Massigli, *op.cit.*, 83–4; Alphand, *op.cit.*, 195.

24. In September Bevin and Byrnes agreed to approve a French customs barrier round the Saar if four-power agreements was not reached soon: F.O.371/55801/11541, 11690, 12362. Such a barrier was erected in

December: F.O.371/55801/15838 and 15948; F.O.371/59967/10747; P.O. Lapie, *De Leon Blum à de Gaulle* (Paris, 1971), 25, 37–8.
25. Von Oppen (ed.), *op.cit.*, 125–8.
26. CAB.129/10, C.P.(46)223; F.O.371/55404/6081.
27. *423 H.C. DEB.* 5s, 1843–5.
28. F.O.371/59954/6814.
29. F.O.371/55407/10680.
30. Massigli, *op.cit.*, 84–5.

4. ECONOMICS, POLITICS AND AN UNEXPECTED ADVANCE

1. C. Attlee, *As It Happened* (1954), 169–70.
2. CAB. 66/61, W.P. (45) 75; CAB. 66/62, W.P. (45) 134; CAB. 66/63, W.P. (45) 159.
3. F. Donnison, *Civil Affairs and Military Government, North-West Europe, 1945–6* (1961), chapter 22.
4. CAB. 129/10, C.P. (46) 239, 240.
5. On French complaints see: F.O.371/55400/3200; F.O.371/59959/2875; F.O.371/59955/8895, 8989.
6. CAB. 128/6, C.M.(46) 89; F.O.371/55407/10680.
7. Earl of Bessborough, *Return to the Forest* (1962), 123.
8. F.O.371/59957/754; F.O.371/59958/1671.
9. F.O.371/59957/754; F.O.371/59958/1406.
10. F.O.371/59952/2780; F.O.371/59953/3625, 3744.
11. *F.R.U.S., 1946*, V (Washington, 1969), 412–13, 421–2, 440–6.
12. Bevin immediately realized that Molotov was seeking to influence the French elections through this: O. Harvey diary, manuscript 56400, 25 Apr.
13. The British were delighted with this: F.O.371/59961/4391.
14. F.O.371/59976/4579.
15. See, for example, F.O.371/59963/5777.
16. R. Massigli, *Une Comédie des Erreurs* (Paris, 1978), 80–1.
17. H. Dalton's diary, 10 Sept.; H. Dalton, *High Tide and After* (1962), 157.
18. F.O.371/59955/8895; F.O.371/59966/9765.
19. F.O.371/59978/7069.
20. A. Bullock, *The Life and Times of Ernest Bevin* (1960), I, 356–63, 386–8, 440–7, 622–3, 630–4, 648–9.
21. T.236/779; F.O.371/59953/9537.
22. F.O.371/59953/3744.
23. F.O.371/59954/6573; F.O.371/59978/7069.
24. F.O.371/59978/7069.
25. F.O.371/59978/7116.
26. CAB.129/13, C.P.(48)386; CAB.129/16, C.P.(47) 35; CAB.128/6, C.M.(46)91.
27. F.O.371/53007/4024, 4336; F.O.371/53008/4721, 4949; T.236/779; B.T.11/3152.

28. F.O.371/59979/7467, 7505; PREM 8/516; Dalton's diary, 10 Sept.
29. F.O.371/59979/7901, 7907.
30. Dalton's diary, 10 Sept.
31. Dalton's diary, 28 Sept.; CAB.128/6, C.M.(46)82; F.O.371/79979/ 7994, 8002; F.O.371/79980/8129, 8133, 8144, 8260, 8315; PREM 8/516; and *427 H.C. DEB. 5s*, 519–20.
32. F.O.371/59981/9339.

5. THE MAKING OF THE TREATY OF DUNKIRK

1. F.O.371/59955/8895, 8989.
2. On left-wing criticisms of Bevin see: F. Williams, *A Prime Minister Remembers* (1961), 169–71, H. Dalton, *High Tide and After* (1962), 168; B. Donnoughue and G. Jones, *Herbert Morrison* (1973), 387–8; and on Conservative views: *423 H.C. DEB. 5s*, 1868–9, 1946, 1949–52; *427 H.C. DEB. 5s*, 1523, 1709.
3. F.O.371/59955/8989.
4. F.O.371/67670/25; and see the discussion of Sir N.Ronald's ideas for a European arrangement, similar to Churchill's wartime Council of Europe, in F.O.371/59911/2410, 10754. Ronald's ideas were well removed from the mainstream thinking on the western bloc, and their rejection did not imply the rejection of other European co-operation.
5. P.O. Lapie, *De Lean Blum à de Gaulle* (Paris, 1971), 34; E. Depreux, *Souvenirs d'un Militant* (Paris, 1972), 229–30.
6. F.O.371/59955/10679; F.O.371/67686/119; B.T.11/3357; Lapie, *op.cit.*, 60–1; R. Massigli, *Une Comédie des Erreurs* (Paris, 1978), 87.
7. B.T.11/3357; V. Auriol, *Journal du Septennat* (7 vols, Paris, 1970–), I, 79–80.
8. F.O.371/59967/10747; F.O.371/67670/25; A.D.Cooper, *Old Men Forget* (1953), 369–70; Earl of Bessborough, *Return to the Forest* (1962), 129; Lapie, *op.cit.*, 53–7; Massigli, *op.cit.*, 88–9.
9. CAB.128/9, C.M.(47)3; PREM 8/516; F.O.371/67670/291; F.O.371/67686/269; F.O.371/67680/170; Blum papers, 4 BL 2, Dr. 2; Lapie, *op.cit.*, 54–5, 61–7.
10. F.O.371/67686/650, 654; Cooper, *op.cit.*, 371–2; Lapie, *op.cit.*, 66–70; Massigli, *op.cit.*, 90; Auriol, *op.cit.*, I, 17–18; *432 H.C.DEB. 5s*, 359–60. I am grateful to M.Pierre-Olivier Lapie for showing me his papers on the negotiations, including Massigli's report to Paris, dated 18 Jan.
11. F.O.371/67680/783; G.Bidault, *Resistance* (1967), 140–1.
12. F.O.371/67670/723. 965, 995, 1098, 1162; Cooper, *op.cit.*, 372; Massigli, *op.cit.*, 91.
13. F.O.371/67670/1215.
14. F.O.371/67671/1649.
15. F.O.371/67671/1661, 1708.
16. F.O.371/67670/1215.
17. F.O.371/67670/1135; F.O.371/67671/1777, 1853, 2051, 2316; J.Chauvel, *Commentaire: d'Alger à Berne* (Paris, 1972), 192; Auriol, *op.cit.*, 80, 87; Massigli, *op.cit.*, 92.
18. F.O.371/67671/2102.

19.   The treaty promised four-power consultation against German
      aggression, mutual aid against German attack, economic co-operation,
      and a fifty-year term. CAB.128/9, C.M.(47)25; CAB.129/17,
      C.P.(47)64.
20.   F.O.371/67671/1720, 2189, 2214; Auriol, op.cit., I, 105–6.
21.   433 H.C.DEB. 5s, 2526; Journal Officiel, Assemblée Nationale, 1947,
      538; Cooper, op.cit., 372–3.
22.   F.O.371/67671/2190, 2214; Auriol, op.cit., I, 118–19.
23.   F.O.371/67672/2525; J.Dumaine, Quai d'Orsay (1958), 109–11;
      Chauvel, op.cit., 193; Cooper, op.cit., 373; Bessborough, op.cit., 129;
      Bidault, op.cit., 142–3.
24.   C.Mauriac, The Other de Gaulle (1973), 228–9, 231, 246.
25.   Massigli, op.cit., 94–5; Dumaine, op.cit., 109.
26.   Cooper, op.cit., 373.
27.   F.O.371/67697/3066.
28.   Auriol, op.cit., I, 17–18, 56–7; Alphand, L'étonnement d'Etre (Paris,
      1977), 197.

6.   THE MOSCOW C.F.M. AND ITS AFTERMATH

1.   Dalton's diary, 17 Jan. 1947.
2.   F.O.371/67651/1468.
3.   F.O.371/67849/118, 1663.
4.   F.O.371/67849/1663; F.O.371/67651/1468.
5.   F.O.371/67663/2188, 2363, 2718; Knatchbull-Hugessen's diary,
      8 Mar.; 446 H.C. DEB. 5s, 396.
6.   On the reforms of French policy under Blum see P.O.Lapie, De Léon
      Blum à de Gaulle (Paris, 1971), 35–46. But Blum lacked time to
      reform policy on the Ruhr. Bidault changed policy here: V. Auriol,
      Journal du Septennat (7 vols, Paris, 1970–), I, 738, n. 2.
7.   W.Bedell-Smith, Moscow Mission (1950), 207–8; F.O.800/272, Bevin
      to Attlee, 16 Apr; F.Williams, A Prime Minister Remembers (1961).
      154–9.
8.   Auriol, op.cit., I, 89, 113–18; G.Catroux, J'ai vu Tomber le Rideau de
      Fer (Paris, 1952), 211–20.
9.   Bedell-Smith, op.cit., 209; C.Bohlen, Witness to History (1973), 262.
10.   Auriol, op.cit., I, 131, 673–6; F.R.U.S., 1947, II (Washington, 1972),
      187–95.
11.   F.O.371/67663/2712; F.O.800/465/47/10.
12.   F.O.371/65020–2; F.O.800/272, Harvey to Sargent, 1 Apr.; F.R.U.S.,
      1947, II, 241–2, 265–6, 274, 346–7, 485–8.
13.   CAB.128/9, C.M.(47) 43; Dalton's diary, 15 May.
14.   For example, R.Murphy, Diplomat among Warriors (1964), 376.
15.   G.Elgey, La République des Illusions (Paris, 1965), 276; Auriol,
      op.cit., I, 224–4.
16.   For the effect of Moscow on the French see: R.Massigli, Une Comédie
      des Erreurs (1978), 98; H.Alphand, L'étonnement d'Etre (Paris, 1977),
      198; G.Bidault, Resistance (1967), 144–9.

17. For a full discussion see Elgey, *op.cit.*, 278–85.
18. The British had been expecting trouble from the communists for some weeks: F.O.371/67680/3210, 3253.
19. F.O.371/67663/2363 and 3323; *F.R.U.S., 1947, III* (Washington, 1972), 713–15.
20. Bidault made such a remark to Bevin *before* the communists left the government : F.O.371/67663/3744; see F.O.371/67663/4289 on the Belgians.
21. F.O.371/67854A/2875.
22. F.O.371/67724/4644.
23. F.O.371/67724/4670.
24. F.O.371/67724/4816.
25. *437 H.C.DEB.* 5s, 1718–43, 1789–90, 1821–2, 1950.
26. F.O.371/67727A/5031.
27. F.O.371/67724/5705.
28. F.O.371/67724/5971.
29. F.O.371/67724/6143.
30. F.O.371/67724/5529; Knatchbull-Hugessen's diary, 11 June; P.H.Spaak, *The Continuing Battle* (1971), 90.

7. THE MARSHALL PLAN

1. The French were able to present some ideas in Washington very quickly: *F.R.U.S., 1947, III* (Washington, 1972), 251–2; Bidault to Bonnet (10 June), in *Documents de la Conference ... a Paris du 27 Juin au 3 Juillet* (Paris, 1947); H.Alphand, *L'étonnement d'Etre* (Paris, 1977), 198–200; J.Monnet, *Memoirs* (1978), 264–6, 268–9.
2. The British had received details of the American plan from the Canadians on 2 June, but Bevin's determined response seems no less surprising because of this : T.236/782; C.Attlee, *As It Happened* (1954), 170; Lord Strang, *Home and Abroad* (1956), 289; Lord Gladwyn, *The Memoirs of Lord Gladwyn* (1972), 202–3; and, in general, F.O.371/62398–62400.
3. On early considerations about the plan in Paris see: V.Auriol, *Journal du Septennat* (7 vols, Paris, 1970–), I, 266–7, 274–5, 277–8; Alphand, *op.cit.*, 200–1.
4. F.O.371/61399/4689; D.Acheson, *Sketches from Life* (1961), 150; C.Bohlen, *Witness to History* (1973), 264–5.
5. CAB.128/10, C.M.(47)55; CAB.129/19, C.P.(47)188; F.O.371/62400/4863; F.O.371/62402/5062; A.D.Cooper, *Old Men Forget* (1953), 375; J.Dumaine, *Quai d'Orsay* (1958), 127–8; Auriol, *op.cit.*, I, 284–5.
6. On the conferences see especially the French 'Yellow Book', *Documents de la Conference ... a Paris ...* (Paris, 1947).
7. F.O.371/62403/5262; F.O.371/62404/5303, 5312; F.O.371/62409/5676.
8. F.O.371/62402/5234, 5159; F.O.371/62403/5219, 5259; F.O.371/62404/5329; CAB.128/10, C.M.(47) 56, 60; CAB.129/19, C.P.(47)197.

9. G.Bidault, *Resistance* (1967), 150–2; Auriol, *op.cit.*, I, 296, 303, 311–13, 319–25, 338–41, 351–3; Dumaine, *op.cit.*, 128–30.
10. CAB.128/10, C.M.(47)60; CAB.129/19, C.P.(47)197.
11. F.O.371/67724/6791, 7008; F.O.371/73045/322.
12. On the C.E.E.C. work see: CAB:128/10, C.M.(47)76; CAB.129/20, C.P.(47)260; *F.R.U.S.*, 1947, III, 331–439; *C.E.E.C. Report* (Paris, 1947).
13. F.O.371/62407/5572.
14. CAB.128/10, C.M.(47)49; CAB.129/19, C.P.(47)163.
15. CAB.128/10, C.M.(47)63, 76; CAB.129/30, C.P.(47)209, 210.
16. On American ideas see: M.Beloff, *The U.S. and the Unity of Europe* (1963), 1–25; F.Dobney (ed.), *Selected Papers of Will Clayton* (1971), 201–4; G.Kennan, *Memoirs 1925–50* (1968), 337.
17. Cooper, *op.cit.*, 376.
18. Dalton's diary, 27 June; F.O.371/62552/5132; *F.R.U.S.*, 1947, III, 268–93.
19. F.O.371/62552/5263; B.T.11/3152.
20. Alphand, *op.cit.*, 203–4; Auriol, *op.cit.*, I, 391; R.Massigli, *Une Comédie des Erreurs* (Paris, 1978), 102.
21. F.O.371/62552/7147; Cooper, *op.cit.*, 376.
22. F.O.371/62416/7440, 7709.
23. F.O.371/62553/8020, 8089, 8122; F.O.371/62580/7497, 7779.
24. F.O.371/62553/8359.
25. *T.U.C. Report*, 1947, 420–2.
26. F.O.371/62553/8360; CAB.128/10, C.M.(47)77.
27. F.O.371/62553/8089, 8213, 8529.

8.   THE BEVIN–RAMADIER TALKS

1. F.O.371/67673/8461, 8579, 8652; V.Auriol, *Journal du Septennat* (7 vols, Paris, 1970–), I, 468–9; A.D.Cooper, *Old Men Forget* (1953), 377–8; R.Massigli, *Une Comédie des Erreurs* (Paris, 1978), 104.
2. F.O.371/67673/8579.
3. F.O.371/67673/8717, 8821, 8828.
4. F.O.371/67673/9053.
5. F.O.371/67674/10270; Cooper, *op.cit.*, 378–80.
6. Although London saw Indo-China as being of central importance in the fight against Communism, the issue did not become vital to Anglo-French relations until Eden returned to the Foreign Office.
7. F.O.371/72946/81; E.Depreux, *Souvenirs d'un Militant* (Paris, 1972), 296–304; J.Moch, *Une si Longue Vie* (Paris, 1976), 252, 269; N.Bethell, *The Palestine Triangle* (1979), 319–21, 334–6, 340–1.
8. F.O.371/41935/5355, 6078, 6552; F.O. 371/49119/133, 657, 1330, 7895.
9. F.O.371/49119/12226; F.O.371/59999/479, 1114.
10. CAB.129/9, C.P.(46)197.
11. F.O.371/67671/1649.
12. CAB.129/19, C.P.(47)191; F.O.371/67697/4983;

F.O.371/67698/6681.

13. F.O.371/67673/9054; F.O.371/67674/9164.

14. F.O.371/68997/2761.

15. G.Rendel, *The Sword and the Olive* (1957), 299–310; Auriol, *op.cit.*, I, 220; R.Delavignette in L.Gann and P.Duignan (eds), *Colonialism in Africa* (2 vols, 1970), 277.

16. F.O.371/60021/3136, 3363; CAB.129/1, C.P.(45)101, 134; CAB.129/7, C.P.(46)95.

17. F.O.371/49135/13379; Revers to Teiten (10 Jan. 1948), Daladier papers, 5 DA 12, Dr 1.

18. The British still feared de Gaulle's return while acknowledging he could bring strong government: F.O.371/67681/6622; F.O.371/67682/8619, 9772; F.O.371/67683/10555.

19. On Auriol's hopes for peace see Auriol, *op.cit.*, I, 419, 426–7, 444–6, 512–13, 516, 521–2.

20. C.Sulzberger, *A Long Row of Candles* (Toronto, 1969), 361.

21. Sulzberger, *op.cit.*, 357–8.

22. F.O.371/67674/9376, 10271, 10554, 10907; Cooper, *op.cit.*, 380–2.

23. Cooper, *op.cit.*, 376–9; Diana Cooper, *Trumpets from the Steep* (1960), 245; F.O.371/67674/10271, 10504.

24. Sir W.Hayter, *A Double Life* (1974), 84–5; J.Dumaine, *Quai d'Orsay* (1958), 147, 152–3; G.Brown, *In My Way* (1971), 131–3.

25. G.Bidault, *Resistance* (1967), 149.

26. F.O.371/67673/8908, 9053; F.O.371/67674/9443, 9527, 9992; F.O.371/64633; Auriol, *op.cit.*, I, 444, 500.

9. THE LONDON C.F.M., BRUSSELS PACT AND WESTERN UNION

1. F.O.371/67683/10262; CAB.128/10, C.M.(47)90; V.Auriol, *Journal du Septennat* (7 vols, Paris, 1970–), I, 629.

2. E.Shinwell, *I've Lived Through it All* (1973), 188–9; H.Macmillan, *Tides of Fortune* (1969), 118–9.

3. F.O.371/67674/11010; R.Massigli, *Une Comédie des Erreurs* (Paris, 1978), 105–6.

4. On Bevin's vision see: Lord Strang, *Britain in World Affairs* (1968), 343; and C. Attlee, *As It Happened* (1954), 171.

5. Auriol, *op.cit.*, I, 637–9. The French premier, Schuman, may already have approached Marshall about an alliance : M. and S.Bromberger, *Les Coulisses de l'Europe* (Paris, 1968), 78–81.

6. F.O.371/64250/16541; *F.R.U.S., 1947, II* (Washington, 1972), 811–30; *F.R.U.S., 1948, III* (Washington, 1974), 1–2; J.Smith (ed.), *The Papers of General Lucius Clay* (2 vols, Bloomington, 1974), 501–2, and 513–18.

7. CAB.128/12, C.M.(48)2, CAB.129/23, C.P.(48)6. Even Bevin's former left-wing critics now pressed him to build a Western European union: letter to Bevin (9 Jan. 1948), R.W.G. Mackay papers.

8. CAB.134/215, E.P.C.(47) 6th meeting and E.P.C.(47)11.

9. CAB.133/38, 39; F.O.371/62555/11958; F.O.371/62754/11983, 116701, 12224.
10. F.O.371/62555/12502; F.O.371/68957/1307.
11. F.O.371/67674/11009.
12. The C.O.S. suggested America should launch a 'military Marshall plan'. F.O.371/67674/11125–7; Montgomery of Alamein, *Memoirs* (1958), 456–7.
13. F.O.371/67674/11127; F.O.371/73045/353.
14. Auriol, *op.cit.*, I, 57, 64–6.
15. F.O.371/67669/10969; F.O.371/72979/212; F.O.371/73045/321–3, 353–4; Sir I.Kirkpatrick, *The Inner Circle* (1959), 205; Auriol, *op.cit.*, II, 28.
16. F.O.371/73045/273, 372, 373, 592.
17. F.O.371/73045/273, 480, 554, 561; *F.R.U.S., 1948, III*, 3–12; H.S.Truman, *Years of Trial and Hope* (1956), 257; G.Kennan, *Memoirs, 1925–50* (1968), 397–8.
18. *446 H.C.DEB. 5s*, 387–409.
19. Massigli, *op.cit.*, 107–9.
20. F.O.371/73045/809.
21. F.O.371/69002/1761.
22. F.O.371/72979/687.
23. F.O.371/73046/894; F.O.371/73047/1117, 1118, 1250; CAB.128/12, C.M.(48)13; CAB.129/24, C.P.(48)46; Auriol, *op.cit.*, II, 51, 69–70, 72–3; Massigli, *op.cit.*, 109–10; P.H.Spaak, *The Continuing Battle* (1971), 145–6.
24. F.O.371/73046/894, 976; F.O.371/73047/1148, 1251, 1271; F.O.371/73048/1404; Auriol, *op.cit.*, II, 70–1.
25. F.O.371/73046/1061; F.O.371/73047/1270, 1308; F.O.371/73048/ 1317, 1345, 1455, 1457, 1501; F.O.371/73049/1528; Auriol, *op.cit.*, II, 107; Massigli, *op.cit.*, 110–11; Spaak, *op.cit.*, 146–8.
26. F.O.371/73050/1763, 1864, 1865.
27. F.O.371/73050/1930, 1931, 1933; F.O.371/73051/1934, 1999, 2029, 2030; F.O.371/73052/2119, 2163; F.O.371/73053/2411; Auriol, *op.cit.*, II, 123, 137–8; Massigli, *op.cit.*, 111–13; G.Rendel, *The Sword and the Olive* (1957), 178–9; J.Chauvel, *Commentaire : d'Alger à Berne* (Paris, 1973), 195–8.
28. CAB.128/12, C.M.(48)22; CAB.129/25, C.P.(48)83.
29. Spaak, *op.cit.*, 87.

10. THE WESTERN UNION IN OPERATION

1. CAB.128/12, C.M.(48)24; CAB.129/26, C.P.(48)96; F.O.371/73054/2557; F.O.371/73055/2559; G.Rendel, *The Sword and the Olive* (1957), 281.
2. F.O.371/73054/2429, 2456; F.O.371/73055/2573, 2574, 2609, 2646, 2786; R.Massigli, *Une Comédie des Erreurs* (Paris, 1978), 114; V.Auriol, *Journal du Septennat* (7 vols, Paris, 1970–), II, 165.
3. Originally Britain and France wanted to call a new C.E.E.C. meeting,

but the Americans opposed this: F.O.371/68868/224, 251, 302, 414, 416, 495; F.O.371/68869/587, 594, 754.

4. F.O.371/71809/192; and in general F.O.371/68869–68872A (the Berthoud–Marjolin mission).

5. F.O.371/68926/2419; CAB.134/216, E.P.C.(48) 9th; CAB.134/217, E.P.C. (48)13; CAB.128/12, C.M.(48)20; CAB.129/25, C.P.(48)75; Sir R.Clarke, *Anglo-American Co-operation in War and Peace* (1982), 190–201.

6. F.O.371/71809/133, 219, 335, 336; *F.R.U.S., 1948, III* (Washington, 1974), 384–8.

7. F.O.371/68926/2421.

8. F.O.371/71809/348, 350, 416, 458, 518; CAB.129/26, C.P.(48)98; and P.Gore-Booth, *With Great Truth and Respect* (1974), 164–6. Ironically American pressure for a strong permanent organization seems to have only really begun on 18 Mar. too late to succeed: F.O.371/71809/368, 509, 587.

9. F.O.371/73055/2852–3; F.O.371/73056/2948, 3034, 3161, 3100.

10. F.O.371/73089/3587; CAB.128/12, C.M.(48)29; CAB.129/26, C.P.(48)108; J.Dumaine, *Quai d'Orsay* (1958), 163; Massigli, *op.cit.*, 115.

11. F.O.371/67687A/9811, and see 6030 on earlier concern at France's sterling position.

12. CAB.128/12, C.M.(48)7; CAB.134/216, E.P.C.(48) 3rd; PREM.8/789.

13. CAB.134/216, E.P.C.(48) 12th, 13th; CAB.128/12, C.M.(48)26; CAB.129/26, C.P.(48)101.

14. CAB.128/12, C.M.(48)31; F.O. 371/71767; Auriol, *op.cit.*, II 215–16; H.Alphand, *L'étonnement d'Etre* (Paris, 1977), 208.

15. F.O.371/71766/802.

16. Montgomery of Alamein, *Memoirs* (1958), 457–61; F.O.371/73058/3780; F.O.371/73059/4324, 4617; G.Mallaby, *From My Level* (1965), 150–3; Massigli, *op.cit.*, 118–22; On the payments problem regarding French air force equipment see: F.O.371/72970/99, 3186, 5299; F.O.371/73071/4910, 5023, 5227.

17. F.O.371/73053/2338, 2340; F.O.371/73057/3411, 3413, 3442; Auriol, *op.cit.*, II, 150, 195; G.Bidault, *Resistance* (1967), 155–6; Sir N.Henderson, *The Birth of NATO* (1982), 19–34.

18. G.Kennan, *Memoirs, 1925–50* (1968), 93, 397–46; H.S.Truman, *Years of Trial and Hope* (1956), 255–60.

19. F.O.371/68067; F.O.371/68068A/1412; F.O.371/73069/2642, 3650; E.Reid, *Time of Fear and Hope* (Toronto, 1977), 45–54, 71–2, 102–12; Henderson, *op.cit.*, 14–19; *F.R.U.S., 1948, III*, 52, 59–61, 64–7, 69–75. Actually Bevin did warn the French that Britain would be holding talks in Washington but the French apparently missed the significance of this: F.O. 371/72979/2560.

20. F.O.371/72979/212. 1120; Auriol, *op.cit.*, II, 26, 34–5, 39, 66, 73; G.Elgey, *République des Illusions* (1965), 383–4.

21. *Journal Officiel, Assemblée Nationale, 1948,* 745–6.

22. CAB.128/12. C.M.(48)2; CAB.129/25, C.P.(48)5.
23. CAB.129/25, C.P.(48)78; CAB.128/12, C.M.(48)20, 21;
F.O.371/70581/1689; F.O.371/70582/1939; Auriol, *op.cit.*, II, 106–7,
119, 122, 135–7, 151; Alphand, *op.cit.*, 205–6.
24. Auriol, *op.cit.*, II, 66–8, 84, 164, 171–4, 185–8, 211, 214–15, 219, 245,
248–9, 263, 266, F.O.371/73057/3412; Alphand, *op.cit.*, 207–10.
25. CAB.128/12, C.M.(48)34; CAB.129/27, C.P.(48)134; Auriol, *op.cit.*,
II, 174–80, 190–2, 212–14, 218, 232, 238–44; Alphand, *op.cit.*, 209;
J.Chauvel, *Commentaire : d'Alger à Berne* (Paris, 1972), 199–200;
26. F.O.371/72947/4772, 4788, 4819; F.O.371/70592/4360, 4414, 4432;
F.O.371/70593/4469, 4497–9, 4595, 4623; F.O.371/70594/4702, 4710,
4772; CAB.128/12, C.M.(48)37, 39; CAB.129/27, C.P.(48)138;
Bidault, *op.cit.*, 158–9, 161–2; Chauvel, *op.cit.*, 200–2; Alphand,
op.cit., 209–10; Auriol, *op.cit.*, II, 255–6, 258–60, 263–6, 268–71, 275.
27. Bidault, *op.cit.*, 164; Chauvel, *op.cit.*, 202–3; J.Dumaine, *Quai
d'Orsay* (1958), 171–2, 175; Elgey, *op.cit.*, 390–1.

11.   THE CREATION OF NATO

1. F.O.371/73060/5995; F.O.371/73061/6559, 6634; F.O.371/73072/
5260; F.O.371/73073/6053; F.O.371/73074/6218, 6278.
2. F.O.371/73072/5612; F.O.371/73073/5640, 5652, 5818; F.O.371/
73074/6123, 6141; E.Reid, *Time of Fear and Hope* (Toronto, 1977),
113–21; V.Auriol, *Journal de Septennat* (7 vols, Paris, 1970–), II, 318;
Sir N.Henderson, *The Birth of NATO* (1982), 30–1, 36–40; *F.R.U.S.,
1948, III* (Washington, 1974), 82–9, 92–7 100–8, 140–3, 206–8.
3. F.O.371/73060/5521.
4. F.O.371/73060/5521, 5995; F.O.371/73074/6142; R.Massigli, *Une
Comédie des Erreurs* (Paris, 1978), 135–6.
5. F.O.371/73074/6278; F.O.371/73075/6632, 6826;
F.O.371/72949/6448.
6. F.O.371/73075/7002–4; Henderson, *op.cit.*, 42, 46–50, 52–4.
7. F.O.371/73075/6947–8; Henderson, *op.cit.*, 54–5.
8. On Foreign Office views of this crisis see: F.O.371/72949/6170;
F.O.371/72951/7217, 7269, 7363.
9. F.O.371/73075/7003, 7032.
10. F.O.371/73076/7092, 7197; Reid, *op.cit.*, 121.
11. F.O.371/73076/7380; F.O.371/73077/7530, 7698.
12. F.O.371/73079/8708, 8876, 8931; Auriol, *op.cit.*, II, 501; Massigli,
op.cit., 136–7; P.H.Spaak, *The Continuing Battle* (1971), 150.
13. F.O.371/73074/6142; F.O.371/73062/7475; CAB,131/5, D.O.(48)
20th.
14. F.O.371/73080/9136.
15. F.O.371/73081/9295; F.O.371/79225/885; F.O.371/79231/1991;
Auriol, *op.cit.*, III, 71, 82; Massigli, *op.cit.*, 136, 138; J.Chauvel,
Commentaire: d'Alger à Berne (Paris, 1972), 208–9.
16. F.O.371/73081/9294–5.
17. F.O.371/73083/10302, 10345, 10510, 10525–6; Henderson, *op.cit.*,

67–75; Reid, *op.cit.*, chapter 18.
18. F.O.371/73083/10566; F.O.371/79218/56, 57, 77; CAB.131/6, D.O.(48)88; CAB.131/8, D.O.(49) 1st.
19. F.O.371/79220/260; F.O.371/79221/363, 364, 366.
20. F.O.371/79072/341, 680; F.O.371/79222/608, 667.
21. F.O.371/79221/364, 422; F.O.371/79222/519, 681; F.O.371/79223/866, 970, 971; Henderson, *op.cit.*, 80–1.
22. F.O.371/79224/1053, 1055, 1161; Henderson, *op.cit.*, 81.
23. F.O.371/79224/1246; F.O.371/79225/1414; F.O.371/79226/1463; F.O.371/79227/1629.
24. F.O.371/79225/1414; F.O.371/79228/1742, 1753/5; Auriol, *op.cit.*, III, 116, 118–19; Henderson, *op.cit.*, 94–6.
25. F.O.37/79228/1773.
26. F.O.371/79229/1806, 1807, 1840; F.O.371/79230/1958–9; F.O.371/79231/1960, 1991, 2023; F.O.371/79234/2177–8; Henderson, *op.cit.*, 96–7.
27. F.O.371/79224/1335, 1401, 1402; F.O.371/79226/1497; Auriol, *op.cit.*, III, 124.
28. F.O.371/79226/1465–8, 1544–5, 1584; F.O.371/79227/1630; F.O.371/79228/1718; Auriol, *op.cit.*, III, 127; Massigli, *op.cit.*, 139–41; Reid, *op.cit.*, 143–56; Henderson, *op.cit.*, 89–93.
29. F.O.371/79231/2018, 2022.
30. F.O.371/79231/2022; F.O.371/79232/2061, 2107; F.O.371/79233/2143, 2148.
31. *462 H.C.DEB. 5s*, 2533–6.
32. *Journal Officiel, Assemblée Nationale, 1949*, 5064–74, 5092–5102, 5224–74.
33. Auriol, *op.cit.*, II, 474, 502; III, 11–23, 53, 144–7, 151, 158–61, 173.
34. Auriol, *op.cit.*, III, 397–8.
35. F.O.371/73079/8714; and on 1949 see CAB.131/7, D.O.(49)33, 59.
36. On the new military organization see F.O.371/73077/7852; F.O.371/73078/8089; CAB.128/13, C.M.(48)62; Montgomery of Alamein, *Memoirs* (1958), 461–2; Auriol, *op.cit.*, III, 446–7, 459–61; Massigli, *op.cit.*, 122–31; G.Mallaby, *From My Level* (1965), 150–69.
37. F.O.371/73077/7852; F.O.371/73078/8024, 8029; Auriol, *op.cit.*, III, 459–60, 483–4, 495; Maréchal Juin, *Memoires* (2 vols, Paris, 1960), II, 165–71.
38. F.O.371/73079/8047; F.O.371/73081/9495; Auriol, *op.cit.*, III, 42, 71, 213–14, 422–3; Mallaby, *op.cit.*, 174–5; S.de Lattre, *Jean de Lattre* (2 vols, Paris, 1972), II, 145–51.
39. Reid, *op.cit.*, chapter 10; G.Kennan, *Memoirs, 1925–50* (1968), 457–8.
40. Reid, *op.cit.*, 69, 134–5; Massigli, *op.cit.*, 137–8.

12. THE COUNCIL OF EUROPE

1. R.Churchill (ed.), *The Sinews of Peace* (1948), 198–202.
2. N.E.C. minutes, 22 Jan. 1947, minute 111; N.E.C. International Sub-committee, 14 Jan. 1947, minute 28; F.O.371/67670/25.

3. N.E.C. minutes, 28 Jan. 1948, minute 182; N.E.C. International Sub-committee, 20 Jan. 1948, minute 45 and 17 Feb. minute 46.
4. F.O.371/73095/4416.
5. Lord Strang, *Home and Abroad* (1956), 290.
6. CAB.134/216, E.P.C.(48) 13th.
7. F.O.371/73095/4418; F.Ritsch, *The French Left and the European Idea* (New York, 1966), 152–70.
8. CAB.129/28, C.P.(48)162; F.O.371/73095/4418; F.O.371/73096/5378.
9. F.O.371/73096/5782.
10. F.O.371/73060/5995; G.Bidault, *Resistance* (1967), 164–5; R.Massigli, *Une Comédie des Erreurs* (Paris, 1978), 145, 152, 156; J.Chauvel, *Commentaire : d'Alger à Berne*, (Paris, 1972), 189–90; and see F.O.371/72946/1859.
11. F.O.371/73096/5856.
12. Bidault, *op.cit.*, 166, 174–6; P.H.Spaak, *The Continuing Battle* (1971), 202–3; R.Hostiou, *Robert Schuman et l'Europe* (Paris, 1964); Schuman's own *Pour l'Europe* (Paris, 1964).
13. F.O.371/73097/6787, 6808, 6809, ; V.Auriol, *Journal du Septennat* (7 vols, Paris, 1970–), II, 368; Massigli, *op.cit.*, 157; Chauvel, *op.cit.*, 210.
14. F.O.371/73097/6809, 6885, 6889, 7005, 7234.
15. F.O.371/73097/6926, 6972, 7201, 7250.
16. F.O.371/73097/7219, 7327, 7504; Massigli, *op.cit.*, 158–9.
17. F.O.371/73097/7235; CAB.128/13, C.M.(48)59; *456 H.C.DEB. 5s,* 96–107.
18. F.O.371/73098/7996, 8040, 8186–7, 8265, 8560; Massigli, *op.cit.*, 159–60.
19. F.O.371/73109; F.O.371/73063/8037, 8093.
20. F.O.371/73098/8363, 8442, 8815, 8935, 9355; Massigli, *op.cit.*, 160–1; Spaak, *op.cit.*, 204.
21. F.O.371/73098/8796–7, 8917.
22. CAB.128/13, C.M.(48)69; CAB.129/30, C.P.(48)249.
23. Dalton's diary, 17 Nov. 1948.
24. CAB.129/32, C.P.(49)3; F.O.371/73100–1; Dalton's diary, 25 Nov. and end of 1948; Massigli, *op.cit.*, 162.
25. F.O.371/73063/8037–8; F.O.371/73064/8418.
26. F.O.371/73101/10348, 10350; CAB.128/13, C.M.(48)78; *459 H.C.DEB 5s,* 581–7, 710–14, 727–32.
27. F.O.371/73101/10350.
28. F.O.371/79212/67.
29. CAB.128/15, C.M.(49)2; Dalton's diary, 12 Jan. 1949.
30. F.O.371/79213/590; F.O.371/79072/341; Massigli, *op.cit.*, 162–3, 167; Auriol, *op.cit.*, III, 9, 32.
31. F.O.371/79214/586, 605–6; F.O.371/79261/936; Massigli, *op.cit.*, 163; H.Dalton, *High Tide and After* (1962), 315–16; Spaak, *op.cit.*, 204–5; Inverchapel to Bevin (20 Jan.) and Bridges to Inverchapel (27 Jan.), Box 14, Inverchapel Papers, Bodleian Library.
32. CAB.128/15, C.M.(49)8; CAB.129/32; C.P.(49)18; Massigli, *op.cit.*,

163–4; Auriol, *op.cit.*, III, 72, 81–2; Spaak, *op.cit.*, 205–6.

33. For the text see M.Carlyle (ed.), *Documents on International Affairs, 1949–50* (1953), 348–58.
34. On the First Assembly see especially Dalton, *op.cit.*, 319–25; H.Macmillan, *Tides of Fortune* (1969), 164–83; Massigli, *op.cit.*, 171–6; Spaak, *op.cit.*, 207–10.
35. CAB.128/16, C.M.(49)62; CAB.129/36, C.P.(49)200; CAB.129/37, C.P.(49)204.
36. CAB.128/16, C.M.(49)67; CAB.129/37, C.P.(49)230.
37. F.O.371/69002/2411; F.O.371/71766/542.
38. F.O.371/73106/8921, 10087–8.
39. Spaak, *op.cit.*, 203.

13. THE ECONOMIC UNIFICATION OF EUROPE

1. F.O.371/71766/9. 73, 641.
2. F.O.371/68920/853.
3. F.O.371/68957/1951; F.O.371/69008/1982; F.O.371/71766/73.
4. T.236/788.
5. F.O.371/68957/399; F.O.371/68940; F.O.371/71853/1068–9.
6. F.O.371/71887/1595.
7. B.T.11/3883; T.236/780; F.O.371/71887/2368.
8. CAB.134/216; E.P.C.(48) 23rd; CAB.134/217, E.P.C.(48)34, 37.
9. Marjolin, Head of the O.E.E.C., also wanted to base European co-operation on the Anglo-French alliance. V.Auriol, *Journal du Septennat* (7 vols, Paris, 1970–), II, 81–2, 144–5, 193–4; J.Monnet, *Memoirs* (1978) 271–4, 278; F.O.371/72946/1859.
10. B.T.11/3883; F.O.371/71854/4459; CAB.134/216, E.P.C.(48) 31st; CAB.134/219, E.P.C.(48)78.
11. Sir R.Clarke, *Anglo-American Collaboration in War and Peace* (1982), 201–8.
12. F.O.371/71768/6337.
13. Labour Party, *Feet on the Ground* (1948); *Labour Party Conference Report, 1948*, 117–19, 172–9.
14. *456 H.C.DEB. 5s*, 96–106, 256–66; *457 H.C.DEB.5s*, 28–9, 523–32.
15. F.O.371/71768/7285; CAB.130/56, Gen.304/1st and Gen.304/1; F.O. 371/71856/8161.
16. F.O.371/71857/8647, 8661.
17. CAB.134/220, E.P.C.(49) 5th; CAB.134/221, E.P.C.(49)6.
18. The E.P.C. paper was the product of an inter-departmental meeting on 5 Jan., on which see Clarke, *op.cit.*,208–10.
19. CAB.128/15, C.M.(49)15; CAB.129/32, C.P.(49)27.
20. F.O.371/79072/61.
21. F.O.371/79931/1430; F.O.371/79932/2151, 2886.
22. F.O.371/77933/3322; T.229/207; Monnet, *op.cit.*, 277–81; R.Mayne, *The Recovery of Europe* (1970), 175–6; M. and S.Bromberger, *Les Coulisses de l'Europe* (1968), 96–8.

23. CAB.128/16, 50–5.
24. F.O.371/78094, 78099; CAB.128/16, C.M.(49)59; Auriol, *op.cit.*, III, 324–9; J.Dumaine, *Quai d'Orsay* (1958), 219–20; G.Elgey, *La République des Illusions* (Paris, 1965), 437; *F.R.U.S., 1949, IV* (Washington, 1975), 651–2, 841–3, 848–9.
25. F.O.371/79076/6560–1; F.O.371/79099/6345; Auriol, *op.cit.*, III, 330–2, 336–7.
26. F.O.371/79076/7039; Auriol, *op.cit.*, III, 377, 463.
27. F.O. 371/79076/6600, 7067, 7366, 7503.
28. F.O.371/79058/7558, 7736.
29. On the Hoffman speech see: M.Beloff, *The U.S. and the Unity of Europe* (1963), 38–45; E.van der Beugel, *From Marshall Aid to Atlantic Partnership* (Amsterdam, 1966), 178–87; and *F.R.U.S., 1949, IV*, 412–15, 419–21, 429–9, 438–40, 445–7, 456–8.
30. Marjolin at first feared the Hoffman speech would raise expectations about European unity too high, and sought Anglo-French co-operation against it: F.O.371/78134/10741–2, 10753.
31. F.O.371/78134–5; *F.R.U.S. 1949, IV*, 415–16, 421–6, 429–32, 440–3, 447–56, 462–8; P.H.Spaak, *The Continuing Battle* (1971), 196–7.
32. F.O.371/78134/10815; *F.R.U.S., 1949, IV*, 435–7.
33. CAB.128/16, C.M.(49)62; CAB.129/37, C.P.(49)203. Bevin put these views to Acheson in November: F.O. 371/78134/11438.
34. CAB.129/37, C.P.(49)208.
35. F.O.371/78111/9528, 9711, 10044, 10088; F.O.371/78112/10388.
36. F.O.371/78112/11696, 11779, 11816.
37. F.O.371/78113/12428, 12489, 12535, 12943; Auriol, *op.cit.*, III, 438–9.
38. F.O.371/87083/3, 9; Monnet, *op.cit.*, 281–2.

14. FRENCH INSTABILITY AND THE GERMAN PROBLEM

1. F.O.371/72946/2538; F.O.371/72947/3541, 3582; F.O.371/72948/5751; Sir W.Hayter, *A Double Life* (1974), 90–1.
2. F.O.371/73105/8829; V.Auriol, *Journal du Septennat* (7 vols, Paris, 1970–), II, 466.
3. F.O.371/72954/9700; CAB.134/216, E.P.C.(48) 37th; CAB 134/219, E.P.C.(48)102.
4. F.O.371/72954/10139.
5. F.O.371/72979/10188; Auriol, *op.cit.*, II, 568.
6. F.O.371/79054/2543, 2547, 2756, 3562; F.O.371/79049/2853.
7. F.O.371/79058/8120
8. *F.R.U.S., 1948, II* (Washington, 1973), 381–413; L.Clay, *Decision in Germany* (1950), 409–12; Auriol, *op.cit.*, II, 276–7, 280–1, 316–17, 339–40.
9. CAB.128/13, C.M.(48)82; CAB.129/30, C.P.(48)51; CAB.129/31, C.P.(48) 304; F.O.371/70632/9845, 9929; Auriol, *op.cit.*, 276, 516–17, 521, 524–5, 527, 531–2, 539, 542–3, 545. 554–5, 559–60, 582–3.
10. CAB.128/13, C.M.(48)81; CAB.129/31, C.P.(48)301; Clay, *op.cit.*,

412–19; *F.R.U.S., 1948, II,* 423–8, 432–8, 432–41, 630–64.

11. CAB.128/13, C.M.(48)56, 63, 74, 82; CAB.129/39, C.P.(48)203; CAB.129/30, C.P.(48)234, 259; CAB.129/31, C.P.(48)303.
12. CAB.128/13, C.M.(48)82; CAB.129/31, C.P.(48)303, 306; Dalton's diary, entry of Dec. 1948.
13. F.O.371/73954/9700.
14. F.O.371/79072/187, 680; Auriol, *op.cit.,* III, 10.
15. F.O.371/76694/640, 1623, 2657.
16. CAB.128/15, C.M.(49)10; CAB.129/32, C.P.(49)23; CAB.129/34, C.P.(49)76; Auriol, *op.cit.,* III, 173.
17. CAB.128/15, C.M.(49)19; CAB.129/33, C.P.(49)50.
18. CAB.128/15, C.M.(49)26; CAB.129/34, C.P.(49)79, 87; Auriol, *op.cit.,* III, 188, 195–9, 207–8; D.Acheson, *Present at the Creation* (1970), 270–3, 286–9.
19. Acheson, *op.cit.,* 291–301; I.Kirkpatrick, *The Inner Circle* (1959), 214–15; R.Barclay, *Ernest Bevin and the Foreign Office* (1975), 60–4; H.Alphand, *L'étonnement d'Etre* (Paris, 1977), 213; Auriol, *op.cit.,* III, 195–9, 219–20, 226–7, 238–9.
20. CAB.128/16, C.M.(49)67, 68; F.O.371/76601/8745, 8779, 8780, 8806, 8810–12; F.O.371/76602/8909; Kirkpatrick, *op.cit.,* 216–17; Acheson, *op.cit.,* 326, 337–9, 342; Auriol, *op.cit.,* III, 397, 401–5, 417–20; A.Bernard, *Un Ambassadeur se Souvient 1945–55* (Paris, 1978), 242–3, 245–6, 250–6.
21. See below, chapter 15, n. 17.
22. CAB.129/37, C.P.(49)204.

15. BEFORE THE SCHUMAN PLAN

1. F.O.371/88930/1; F.O.371/89166/1; V.Auriol, *Journal du Septennat* (7 vols, Paris, 1970–); III, 401–5, 417–20, 437–8, 451–2, 460–2; R.Massigli, *Une Comédie des Erreurs* (Paris, 1978), 178, 180–1.
2. F.O.371/85147/1476.
3. F.O.371/89189/7; F.O.371/89190–5; V.Auriol, *Mon Septennat* (Paris, 1970), 257–8; J.Dumaine, *Quai d'Orsay* (1958), 228–9, 249–60; Kenneth Younger's diary, 12 Mar. 1950.
4. F.O.371/89189/5–6.
5. F.O.371/89185/2.
6. F.O.371/89246/1; F.O.371/89250/1; F.O.371/89253/1.
7. F.O.371/85147/2149, 2157.
8. *473 H.C. DEB* 5s, 192–7, 214–15, 319–23, 330; Younger diary, 8 Apr.
9. F.O.371/85148/2260.
10. On planning for the London Conference see: CAB.128/17, C.M.(50)15, 29; CAB.129/39, C.P.(50)80, 92.
11. CAB.129/38, C.P.(50)18.
12. CAB.128/17, C.M.(50)15; CAB.129/38, C.P.(50)40; CAB.129/39, C.P.(50)82.
13. N.E.C. International Sub-committee, 20 Apr. 1950; Ernest Davies' memorandum, Dalton Papers; Dalton's diary, 16 June 1950.

14. F.O.371/89189/9.
15. G.Bidault, *Resistance* (1967), 177; Auriol, *Mon Septennat*, 259–60; M. and S.Bromberger, *Les Coulisses de l'Europe* (Paris, 1968), 110; D.Acheson, *Present at the Creation* (1970), 383; F.O.371/89173/4; F.O.371/89189/9. Earlier in the year, Schuman and his officials had assured Bevin they would not act without him on Germany and European unity: F.O.800/460/50/6; F.O.800/465/50/6.
16. On Monnet's fears about East–West tension see: E.Bjol, *La France devant l'Europe* (Copenhagen, 1966), 373; Bromberger, *op.cit.*, 99–100; H.Alphand, *L'étonnement d'Etre* (Paris, 1977), 217.
17. Schuman's sense of mission was strengthened in September 1949 when Acheson said that France should frame Allied policy towards Germany: Massigli, *op.cit.*, 190; Acheson *op.cit.*, 326; G.Elgey, *La République des Illusions* (Paris, 1965), 440.
18. On Franco-German problems see: J.Monnet, *Memoirs* (1978), 283–7; A.Berard, *Un Ambassadeur se Souvient* (Paris, 1978), chapter 10; K.Adenauer, *Memoirs* (1966), 232–56.
19. Bjol, *op.cit.*, 371, 373, 375–6, 378–80, 382 (Monnet's advisers play down the importance of old ideas for a Ruhr–Lorraine combine); Massigli, *op.cit.*, 192–5; *F.R.U.S., 1948, II* (Washington, 1973), 533–4; and see above, chapter 3, n. 14.
20. Auriol, *Journal*, III, 401–5, 419–20, 451–2, 460–2; A.Philip, *The Schuman Plan* (1951), 3–6.
21. N.E.C. International Sub-committee, 17 May 1949, and 20 Apr. 1950.
22. Massigli, *op.cit.*, 191–2; Adenauer, *op.cit.*, 165–6; and Monnet, *op.cit.*, 285–7.
23. On the forging of the Schuman Plan see: Monnet, *op.cit.*, 288–304; G.Bidault, *Resistance* (1967), 174, 176–7; Massigli, *op.cit.*, 185–7; Alphand, *op.cit.*, 217; J.Dumaine, *Quai d'Orsay* (1958), 263–4; Bjol, *op.cit.*, 377–9, 381–2; Bromberger, *op.cit.*, 116–25.
24. Monnet, *op.cit.*, 304–5.
25. Massigli, *op.cit.*, 183–4, 195–6; Monnet, *op.cit.*, 308; Bjol, *op.cit.*, 374, 377–8, 381; Dumaine, *op.cit.*, 264–5; R.Schuman, *Pour l'Europe* (Paris, 1964), 167.
26. Acheson, *op.cit.*, 382–4; Monnet, *op.cit.*, 301–2; Massigli, *op.cit.*, 187–8, 190, 194–5.

16.   BRITAIN AND THE SCHUMAN PLAN

1. F.O.371/85841/2318; R.Massigli, *Une Comédie des Erreurs* (Paris, 1978), 185–90, 195–6.
2. See *The Times* (11 May), although some newspapers, notably the *Daily Express*, were always anti-European.
3. F.O.371/85841/2141, 2320–1.
4. CAB.130/60, Gen.322/1st; F.O.371/85841/2328; D.Acheson, *Present at the Creation* (1970), 386–7.
5. CAB.130/60, Gen. 322/1st and Gen.322/1–3; F.O.371/85841/2330.

6. *475 H.C. DEB.* 5s, 587–8. On conservative support for the plan see H.Macmillan, *Tides of Fortune* (1969), 186–9; and the letter from Macmillan and others, including non-conservatives, to *The Times* (22 May).

7. F.O.371/85841/2324, 2329–30; F.O.371/85842/2342; F.O.371/85843/2446; Sir W.Hayter, *A Double Life* (1974), 92; Younger diary, 14 May.

8. The conference also saw more concessions to Germany: CAB.129/40, C.P.(50)115, 118; Younger diary, 14, 20 May.

9. CAB.134/293, F.G.(50)1st; CAB.134/224, E.P.C.(50)13th; F.O.371/85842/2338. On the signs of labour's approval of the Schuman Plan at this point see: Massigli, *op.cit.*, 199; J. Monnet, *Memoirs* (1978), 305; R.Schuman, *Pour l'Europe* (Paris, 1964), 167.

10. F.O.371/85841/2297; F.O.371/85842/2340.

11. CAB.134/293, F.G.(50)2nd; F.O.371/85842/2358–9.

12. Dalton to Mollet (3 May), Dalton Papers, 9/8.

13. F.O.371/85842/2362, 2365, 2374, 2376; F.O.371/85843/2465, 2460, 2470, 2502; Monnet, *op.cit.*, 307.

14. CAB.134/224, E.P.C.(50)14th; CAB.134/226, E.P.C.(50)55; CAB.134/293, F.G.(50)3rd.

15. F.O.371/85843/2465.

16. Monnet, *op.cit.*, 308.

17. The French draft communiqué of 25 May began: 'The Governments ... are resolved to carry out a common action ... by pooling their coal and steel production.' F.O.371/85844/2521, 2537, 2543; CAB.134/224, E.P.C.(50)15th; Massigli, *op.cit.*, 203–4.

18. F.O.371/85843/2499; F.O.371/85844/2520; Massigli, *op.cit.*, 236–7, Monnet, *op.cit.*, 312.

19. F.O.371/85843/2500, 2504; F.O.371/85844/2525.

20. F.O.371/85844/2524, 2526; Monnet, *op.cit.*, 311–13; G.Elgey, *La République des Illusions* (Paris, 1965), 448–9; M. and S.Bromberger, *Les Coulisses de l'Europe* (Paris, 1968), 129–30.

21. F.O.371/85843/2499; Massigli, *op.cit.*, 204.

22. F.O.371/85844/2552; F.O.371/85845/2587.

23. The British proposed an addition to the communiqué, beginning: 'The ... United Kingdom will participate ... in a constructive spirit.... But they cannot at this stage enter into any more precise commitment.' The French, on 1 June, redrafted their original communiqué, so it began: 'The Governments ... in their determination to pursue a common action ... have assigned to themselves as their immediate objective the pooling of coal and steel production.' F.O.371/85844/2568–9; F.O.371/85845/2592, 2615–17; Monnet, *op.cit.*, 312–14; Massigli, *op.cit.*, 205–6.

24. CAB.128/17, C.M.(50)34; CAB.129/40, C.P.(50)120; CAB.134/293, F.G.(50)5th; F.O.371/85846/2677, 2765, 2772; D.Jay, *Change and Fortune* (1980), 198–200; Massigli, *op.cit.*, 206–7; Younger Papers, memorandum of 2 June.

25. F.O.371/85844/2520; F.O.371/85845/2617, 2658;

F.O.371/85846/2660, 2667–8; F.O.371/85848/2826;
Massigli, *op.cit.*, 207–8, 221–2; Monnet, *op.cit.*, 312–14.

17.   AFTER THE SCHUMAN PLAN

1.   F.O.371/85848//2843, 2853; R. Massigli, *Une Comédie des Erreurs* (Paris, 1978), 208–9.
2.   F.O.371/85846/2765; F.O.371/85847/2804; F.O.371/85854/3355.
3.   Paris to F.O.151 (10 June), Dalton Papers, 9/15; F.O.371/85853/3280; Massigli, *op.cit.*, 212–14, and on V.Auriol's doubts about the plan see his *Mon Septennat* (Paris, 1970), 269–70.
4.   F.O.371/85850/3068.
5.   W.Fienburgh, *International Control of Basic Industries* (1950).
6.   N.E.C. minutes, 24 May 1950, minutes 237–8; Labour Party, *European Unity* (1950).
7.   On French reaction see: J. Monnet, *Memoirs* (1978), 314–15; Massigli, *op.cit.*, 209–11; Auriol, *op.cit.*, 268.
8.   Dalton diary, 14–19 June; Younger diary, 6 July. A week after 'European Unity' was published, Bevin said it had been a mistake to revise it with references to the Schuman Plan, and added that its timing and presentation could have been better. Private information.
9.   Dalton diary, 14–15 June; *476 H.C. DEB.* 5s, 35–47, 551–3.
10.   Dalton diary, 16, 18 June; Dalton to Attlee (18 June), Dalton Papers 9/9; N.E.C. International Sub-committee, 15 June 1950, minute 34.
11.   F.O.371/89189/10. The Foreign Office had suggested in May that the release of 'European Unity' should be delayed to give more time to consider British policy towards the Council of Europe. Private information.
12.   CAB.128/17, C.M.(50)38, 39; CAB.129/40, C.P.(50)133; D.O.371/85852/3173; Dalton diary, 27, 28 June.
13.   See especially *476 H.C.DEB.* 5s, 1907–24, 1933–48, 2140–72.
14.   F.O.371/89173/10; F.O.371/89174/15.
15.   F.O.371/89175/32.
16.   F.O.371/89175/45; F.O.371/89176/47.
17.   Monnet, *op.cit.*, 316–17.
18.   F.O.371/85851/3165, 3175, 3274; F.O.371/85853/3310, 3313; F.O.371/85854/3354; Massigli, *op.cit.*, 217.
19.   F.O.371/85854/3353, 3356, 3397.
20.   CAB.135/293, F.G.(50)6th and F.G.(50)38, 40; CAB.128/17, C.M.(50)38; CAB.129/40, C.P.(50)128.
21.   CAB.128/18, C.M.(50)42; CAB.129/40, C.P.(50)149; CAB.129/41, C.P.(50)153–4.
22.   F.O.371/85857/3559, 3573–4; *477 H.C. DEB.* 5s, 472–4, 1155–221; Younger diary, 6 July; H.Thomas, *John Strachey* (1973), 262–3.
23.   F.O.371/85858/3625.
24.   A draft treaty was prepared embodying the British plan: F.O.371/85856/3505; F.O.371/85859/3730.
25.   F.O.371/85858/3647; Massigli, *op.cit.*, 222; Monnet, *op.cit.*, 318–33.

26. CAB.134/224, E.P.C.(50)17th; T.232/194; D.Stikker, *Men of Responsibility* (1966), 166–7.
27. F.O.371/85859/3718.
28. CAB.130/60, Gen.322/4th; CAB.134/224, E.P.C.(50)20th, CAB.134/226, E.P.C.(50)81.
29. F.O.371/85861/3897) F.O.371/89189/13.
30. H.Dalton, *High Tide and After* (1962), 327–34; N.E.C. International Sub-committee, 19 Sept; minute 44 and Report by D.Healey.
31. H.Macmillan, *Tides of Fortune* (1969), 201–9, 201–19; Massigli, *op.cit.*, 223; Monnet, *op.cit.*, 313–16.
32. Monnet, *op.cit.*, 334–5.
33. On the last two chapters the established accounts are usually very favourable to Monnet, and have clearly been over-influenced by his views: R.Mayne, *The Recovery of Europe* (1970); N.Beloff, *The General Says No* (1963), 52–60; M. and S.Bromberger, *Les Coulisses de l'Europe* (Paris 1968).

18. GERMAN REARMAMENT

1. F.O.371/79070/7039; F.O.371/79058/7736; V.Auriol, *Journal du Septennat* (7 vols, Paris, 1970–), III, 418–19, 437, 463–4.
2. F.O.371/85087/57.
3. M.Carlyle (ed.), *Documents on International Affairs, 1949–50* (1953), 310.
4. F.O.371/85087/57 and 2436.
5. *472 H.C.DEB. 5s*, 1288–90, 1320–2, 1392.
6. K.Adenauer, *Memoirs* (1966), 267–70.
7. F.O.371/85048/2416.
8. General Bethouart, *La Bataille pour l'Autriche* (Paris, 1966), 162; G.Elgey, *La République des Illusions* (Paris, 1965), 459–60.
9. F.O.371/85048/3136, 3183.
10. F.O.371/89186/11, 14.
11. F.O.371/85049/4272, 4343, 4553, 4573–4; Adenauer, *op.cit.*, 271–4.
12. F.O.371/89175/40; F.O.371/85050/4807.
13. F.O.371/85050/4582; F.O.371/85051/5096, 5371.
14. F.O.371/89201/12.
15. F.O.371/89185/16; F.O.371/85088/5307.
16. F.O.371/85052/5425.
17. P.O.Lapie, *De Léon Blum à de Gaulle* (Paris, 1971), 351–2; Lapie Papers, notes on Cabinet meeting of 22 Aug. 1950.
18. F.O.371/85052/5400, 5408–9.
19. F.O.371/85051/5375, F.O.371/85052/5541; CAB.131/8, D.O.(50) 16th, 17th; CAB.131/9, D.O.(50)63, 66, 67.
20. CAB.128/18, C.M.(50)55.
21. F.O.371/85052/5541; F.O.371/85053/5679, 5691; Lapie Papers, notes on Cabinet meeting of 5 Sept.
22. F.O.371/89189/13; F.O.371/85052/5492; *Consultative Assembly, Second Session, Reports* (Strasbourg, 1950), 45–57, 222–8.

23. CAB.128/18, C.M.(50)58, 59; CAB.129/42, C.P.(50)210;
     F.O.371/85054/5999; D.Acheson, *Present at the Creation* (1970), 422;
     H.Truman, *Years of Trial and Hope* (1956), 268–71; J.Moch, *Histoire
     du Réarmament Allemand* (1965), 43–9.
24. CAB.129/42, C.P.(50). 220, 223; F.O.371/85055; Acheson, *op.cit.*,
     442–5; Moch, *op.cit.*, 49–87;
     H.Alphand, *L'étonnement d'Etre* (Paris, 1977), 220.
25. F.O.371/85056/6424; Lapie Papers, notes on Cabinet meeting,
     6 Oct. V.Auriol, *Mon Septennat* (Paris, 1970), 293–4.
26. CAB.128/18, C.M.(50)63; CAB.129/42; C.P.(50) 220 and 223.
27. F.O.371/85089/65934 and 6690; R.Massigli, *Une Comédie des Erreurs*
     (Paris, 1978), 251.
28. On the Pleven Plan see: Auriol, *Mon Septennat*, 293, 298–9; E.Bjol, *La
     France devant l'Europe* (Copenhagen, 1966), 360–2, 365–6;
     M. and S. Bromberger, *Les Coulisses de l'Europe* (Paris, 1968),
     132–40; Massigli, *op.cit.*, 252–9; J.Monnet, *Memoirs* (1978), 336–49;
     Moch, *op.cit.*, 92–3, 97, 104, 131–7.
29. CAB.131/8, D.O.(50)21st; CAB.131/9, D.O.(50)95.
30. CAB.128/18, C.M.(50)69; F.O.371/85089/6862;
     F.O.371/85090/6925.
31. F.O.371/85058/7934, 7955, 8028; Dalton diary, 9, 20, 21 Dec.
32. CAB.129/34, C.P.(50)266, 294, 312, 319; F.O.371/85058/7691, 8057;
     Moch, *op.cit.*, 229–32.
33. CAB.131/8, D.O.(50)22nd; CAB.131/9, D.O.(50)100;
     481 H.C.DEB.5s, 1172–4.
34. F.O.371/89177/73.
35. 371/89185/14.
36. F.O.371/89186/26-34; PREM.8/1206; Massigli, *op.cit.*, 264–5;
     Auriol, *Mon Septennat*, 309–12.
37. F.O.371/85058/7989, 8026, 8057.
38. CAB.129/34, C.P.(50)311; Acheson, *op.cit.*, 485–6; Alphand, *op.cit.*,
     217–21; Moch, *op.cit.*, 234–6.
39. Lapie papers, notes on Cabinet, 6 Dec. Lapie, *op.cit.*, 356–62;
     Moch, *op.cit.*, 239–44.
40. CAB.128/18, C.M.(50)86; CAB.129/34, C.P.(50)311.
41. CAB.129/44, C.P.(50)1; Acheson, *op.cit.*, 485–8;
     Moch, *op.cit.*, 244–56.
42. CAB.129/45, C.P.(51)128.
43. Adenauer, *op.cit.*, 307–28, 344–64.
44. CAB.129/44, C.P.(51)33, 48, 60.
45. CAB.128/19, C.M.(51)43, 44, 46.
46. On Auriol's interest in a four-power meeting see *Mon Septennat*,
     293–4, 302–4, 313–14, and *Journal, V*, 5–8, 19, 65–6, 72, 142–3, 198,
     216, 226–7.
47. On Bevin's demise see: C.Attlee, *As It Happened* (1954), 202–5;
     Lord Strang, *Home and Abroad* (1956), 296–8; 'Ernest Bevin : a radio
     portrait', *B.B.C., R.P. Library*, L.P. numbers 23605–6.

19. HERBERT MORRISON

1. On Morrison's reputation see especially A.Schlaim *et al*, *British Foreign Secretaries since 1945* (1977), 73–9; and B.Donnoughue and G.Jones, *Herbert Morrison* (1973), 479–80, 484–500.
2. When Morrison became Foreign Secretary, Anglo-French relations were disturbed by France's exclusion from an Anglo-American meeting in Malta, on Middle East defence. But this problem was solved quickly when tripartite talks on the Middle East began in NATO.
3. F.O.371/85865/5299; F.O.371/85866/5593.
4. F.O.371/85867/5735; F.O.371/85868/5894, 5963.
5. F.O.371/85863/4918, 4978, 5065; R.Massigli, *Une Comédie des Erreurs* (Paris, 1978), 225–8; J.Monnet, *Memoirs* (1978), 350–3.
6. See especially N.E.C., International Sub-committee, 16 Jan. 1951, minute 11, and report by Healey; and F.O.371/89189/14.
7. F.O.371/94135/23.
8. CAB.128/19, C.M.(51)19; CAB.129/44, C.P.(51)72.
9. See, for example, F.O.371/93827/63, 68.
10. F.O.371/93827/49.
11. Donnoughue and Jones, *op.cit.*, 480–3; CAB.128/19, C.M.(51)29; CAB.129/45, C.P.(51)105.
12. Massigli, *op.cit.*, 229.
13. F.O.371/93831/157; CAB.128/19, C.M.(51)28; CAB.129/45, C.P.(51)108.
14. F.O.371/93830/151; F.O.371/93831/161, 167; 487 *H.C.DEB. 5s*, 49.
15. F.O.371/93832/188.
16. F.O.371/93833/201.
17. CAB.128/19, C.M.(51)40; CAB.129/45, C.P.(51)147; CAB.129/46, C.P.(51)152.
18. CAB.128/19, C.M.(51)44; CAB.129/46, C.P.(51)164; F.O.371/93837/317, 323, 327, 330.
19. F.O.371/93841/435, 447; F.O.371/94356/3–4.
20. Private information.
21. CAB.134/228, E.P.C.(51)18th; CAB.134/230, E.P.C.(51)85; F.O.371/93839/367, 379, 380; F.O. 371/93840/391.
22. CAB.128/20, C.M.(51)56; CAB.129/47, C.P.(51)230.
23. CAB.129/47, C.P.(51)236.
24. F.O.371/93840/407–9.
25. CAB.128/20, C.M.(51)58; CAB.129/47, C.P.(51)239, 240, 266; F.O.371/96036/21; F.,O.371/93841/445; F.O.371/96057/9–11.
26. Dalton diary, mid-Feb. 1951; Donnoughue and Jones, *op.cit.*, 483, 494–5, 529; CAB.128/19, C.M.(51)12; CAB.129/44, C.P.(51)43; 484 *H.C.DEB.5s*, 67.
27. CAB.128/20, C.M.(51)56; CAB.129/47, C.P.(51)230.
28. CAB.131/10, D.O.(51)20th.
29. F.O.371/89177/65, 78.
30. F.O.371/96035/1; F.O.371/96041/5; F.O.371/96037/1.

31. On British analyses of these problems: F.O.371/96036/6–8, 10; F.O.371/96041/17; F.O.371/96042/21–4.
32. For F.O. analyses: F.O.371/96036/13; F.O.371/96042/28, 38.
33. F.O.371/96036/15–17; F.O.371/96043/54. 58, 60.
34. Anglo-French relations were currently upset by a visit of the Tunisian nationalist, Bourguiba, to London. F.O.371/96057/3, 4, 6; Massigli, *op.cit.*, 286–9.
35. F.O.371/96057/7–8.
36. F.O.371/96057/9.
37. F.O.371/96057/10, 12, 13.
38. CAB.128/20, C.M.(51)60; CAB.129/147, C.P.(51)251, 266; D.Acheson, *Present at the Creation* (1970), 555–61, 569–71; Donnoughue and Jones, *op.cit.*, 500–1.

CONCLUSION: LABOUR'S LEGACY

1. CAB.129/48, C.(51)32.
2. CAB.128/23, C.C.(51)10.
3. A.Eden, *Full Circle* (1960), 32–3; A.Nutting, *Europe Will Not Wait* (1960), 40–1; P.H.Spaak, *The Continuing Battle* (1971), 219–26.
4. On this interpretation see, for example, Nutting, *op.cit.*, 1–38; N.Beloff, *The General Says No* (1963), 50–60; A.Sked and C.Cook, *Post-war Britain* (1979), 76–81.
5. F.Lynch, *The Political and Economic Reconstruction of France* (Ph.D. Thesis, Manchester University, 1981) draws out the importance of coal supplies to France.

Select bibliography

OFFICIAL, TRADE UNION AND PARTY SOURCES

British Government
Command Papers (CMD), Fourth Series
Hansard, debates of the Lords and Commons (H.S. and H.L. DEB. 5s)
Public Record Office, Kew:
  B.T.11 : Board of Trade, Commercial Department
  CAB.65, 66 : War Cabinet minutes and memoranda
  CAB.128, 129 : Cabinet minutes and memoranda 1945–51
  CAB.130 : Cabinet committees
  CAB.131 : Defence committee
  CAB.133 : Customs Unions
  CAB.134 : Economic Policy Committee
  F.O.800 : Foreign Office, private paper collections
  PREM.8 : Premier's office, 1945–51
  T.209, 232 and 236 : Treasury series

French Government
Documentation Française, Textes Diplomatiques, Journal Officiel,
  Assemblée Nationale

U.S. Government
F.R.U.S. : Foreign Relations of the United States (volume published by
  the U.S. Government Publishing Office)

International
Council of Europe, Consultative Assembly, Official Records
  (Strasbourg)
O.E.E.C., Report (2 vols, Washington, 1947)
O.E.E.C., Report to E.C.A. (Paris, 1948)
United Nations, Official Records (New York)

Party and Trades Union
Labour Party, Conference Reports
National Executive Committee, minutes and documents
Trades Union Congress, Annual Report

PRIVATE PAPERS COLLECTIONS

A.V.Alexander   Churchill College, Cambridge
C.Attlee   Churchill College, Cambridge and Bodleian Library, Oxford

E.Bevin   Churchill College, Cambridge and Public Record Office
L.Blum   Foundation Nationale des Sciences Politiques, Paris
A.Cadogan   Churchill College, Cambridge
S.Cripps   Nuffield College, Oxford
E.Daladier   Foundation Nationale des Sciences Politiques, Paris
H.Dalton   British Library of Political and Economic Science, London
A.Eden   Public Record Office
O.Harvey   British Library
Lord Inverchapel   Bodleian Library, Oxford, and Public Record Office
Sir H.M.Knatchbull-Hugessen   Churchill College, Cambridge
P.O.Lapie   Archives National, Paris
R.W.G.Mackay   British Library of Political and Economic Science,
    London
H.Morrison   Nuffield College, Oxford
O.Sargent   Public Record Office
Lord Strang   Churchill College, Cambridge
K.Younger   by kind permission of Lady Younger

PUBLISHED MEMOIRS AND DIARIES

D.Acheson, *Sketches from Life* (1961)
—   *Present at the Creation* (1970)
K.Adenauer, *Memoirs, 1945–53* (1966)
H.Alphand, *L'étonnement d'Etre* (Paris, 1977)
C.Attlee, *As It Happened* (1954)
—   *Granada Historical Records Interview* (1967)
V.Auriol, *Mon Septennat* (Paris, 1970)
—   *Journal du Septennat* (7 vols, Paris, 1970–)
Sir R.Barclay, *Ernest Bevin and the Foreign Office* (1975)
N.Beloff, *Transit of Britain* (1972)
A.Berard, *Un Ambassadeur se Souvient, 1945–55* (Paris, 1978)
Earl of Bessborough, *Return to the Forest* (1962)
General Bethouart, *La Bataille pour l'Autriche* (1966)
G.Bidault, *Resistance* (1967)
L.Blum, *L'Oeuvre de Léon Blum* (several vols, Paris, 1955–)
C.Bohlen, *Witness to History* (1973)
J.Byrnes, *Speaking Frankly* (1947)
—   *All in One Lifetime* (1958)
G.Catroux, *J'ai vu Tomber le Rideau de Fer* (Paris, 1950)
C.Chamoun, *Crise au Moyen-Orient* (Paris, 1963)
J.Chauvel, *Commentaire : d'Alger à Berne* (Paris, 1972)
Sir W.Churchill, *The Second World War* (6 vols, 1948–54)
Sir R.Clarke, *Anglo-American Co-operation in War and Peace* (1982)
L.Clay, *Decision in Germany* (1950)
A.D.Cooper, *Old Men Forget* (1953)
D.Cooper, *Trumpets from the Steep* (1960)

H.Dalton, *High Tide and After* (1962)
E.Depreux, *Souvenirs d'un militant* (Paris, 1972)
D.Dilks (ed.), *The Diaries of Sir Alexander Cadogan* (1971)
P.Dixon, *Double Diploma* (1968)
F.Dobney (ed.), *Selected Papers of Will Clayton* (1971)
J.Dumaine, *Quai d'Orsay* (1958)
A.Eden, *The Reckoning* (1965)
— *Full Circle* (1960)
C.de Gaulle, *War Memoirs* (3 vols, 1955–60)
Lord Gladwyn, *Memoirs* (1972)
P.Gore-Booth, *With Great Truth and Respect* (1974)
W.A.Harriman, *Special Envoy* (1976)
J.Harvey (ed.), *The War Diaries of Oliver Harvey* (1978)
Sir W.Hayter, *A Double Life* (1974)
Sir N.Henderson, *The Birth of NATO* (1982)
Lord Ismay, *Memoirs* (1960)
D.Jay, *Change and Fortune* (1980)
Maréchal Juin, *Memoires, 1944–58* (1960)
G.Kennan, *Memoirs, 1925–50* (1968)
Earl of Kilmuir, *Political Adventure* (1964)
I.Kirkpatrick, *The Inner Circle* (1959)
F.Van Langenhove, *La Securité de la Belgique* (Brussels, 1971)
P.O.Lapie, *De Léon Blum à de Gaulle* (Paris, 1971)
S.de Lattre, *Jean de Lattre* (2 vols, Paris, 1972)
H.Macmillan, *Tides of Fortune* (1969)
G.Mallaby, *From My Level* (1965)
R.Massigli, *Une Comédie des Erreurs* (Paris, 1978)
C.Mauriac, *The Other de Gaulle* (1973)
J.Moch, *Histoire de Rearmement Allemand* (Paris, 1965)
— *Recontres avec de Gaulle* (Paris, 1971)
— *Une Si Longue Vie* (Paris, 1978)
J.Monnet, *Memoirs* (1978)
Montgomery of Alamein, *Memoirs* (1958)
H.Morrison, *An Autobiography* (1960)
L.Pearson, *Memoirs* (2 vols, Toronto, 1974)
E.Reid, *Time of Fear and Hope* (Toronto, 1977)
Sir G.Rendel, *The Sword and the Olive* (1957)
R.Schuman, *Pour l'Europe* (Paris, 1964)
E.Shinwell, *I've Lived Through It All* (1977)
J.Smith, *The Papers of Lucius D.Clay* (2 vols, Bloomington, 1974)
W.Bedell Smith, *Moscow Mission* (1950)
P.H.Spaak, *The Continuing Battle* (1971)
D.Stikker, *Men of Responsibility* (1966)
Lord Strang, *Home and Abroad* (1956)
C.Sulzberger, *A Long Row of Candles* (Toronto, 1969)
H.Truman, *Year of Decisions* (1955)
— *Years of Trial and Hope* (1956)
F.Williams, *A Prime Minister Remembers* (1961)

OTHER PUBLISHED WORKS

E.Barker, *Britain in a Divided Europe* (1971)
— *Churchill and Eden at War* (1978)
P.de Beaumont, *La Quatrième République* (1960)
M.Beloff, *New Dimensions in Foreign Policy* (1961)
— *The U.S. and the Unity of Europe* (1963)
N.Beloff, *The General Says No* (1963)
E.van der Beugel, *From Marshall Aid to Atlantic Partnership*
    (Amsterdam, 1966)
E.Bjol, *La France devant l'Europe* (Copenhagen, 1966)
M. and S.Bromberger, *Les Coulisses de l'Europe* (Paris, 1968)
A.Bullock, *The Life and Times of Ernest Bevin*, (2 vols, 1960, 1967)
T.Burridge, *British Labour and Hitler's War* (1976)
P.Calvocoressi, *Survey of International Affairs, 1947–51* (3 vols, 1952–4)
M.Carlyle, *Documents on International Affairs, 1947–8* (1952),
    1949–50 (1953)
G.de Carmoy, *The Foreign Policies of France* (1970)
B.Criddle, *Socialists and European Integration* (1969)
W.Diebold, *Trade and Payments in W. Europe* (New York, 1952)
F.Donnison, *Civil Affairs and Military Government in N.W. Europe*
    (1961)
B.Donnoughue and G.Jones, *Herbert Morrison* (1973)
G.Elgey, *La République des Illusions* (Paris, 1965)
M.Fitzsimons, *The Foreign Policy of the British Labour Government*
    (Indiana, 1953)
J.Frankel, *British Foreign Policy* (1975)
E.Furniss, *France, Troubled Ally* (Princeton, 1954)
E.Fursdon, *The E.D.C.* (1980)
J.Gimbell, *The Origins of the Marshall Plan* (Stanford, 1976)
C.Gladwyn, *The Paris Embassy* (1976)
B.Graham, *French Socialists and Tripartisme, 1944–7* (1965)
A.Grosser, *La IVe République et sa Politique Extérieure* (Paris, 1961)
K.Harris, *Attlee* (1982)
H.Heiser, *British Policy with Regard to the Unification Efforts on the*
    Continent (Leyden, 1959)
R.Hostiou, *Robert Schuman et l'Europe* (Paris, 1969)
G.Kirk, *The Middle East, 1945–50* (1954)
W.Lipgens, *A History of European Integration, 1945–7* (1982)
S.Longrigg, *Syria and Lebanon under French Mandate* (New York, 1972)
R.McGeehan, *The German Rearmament Question* (Urbana, 1971)
R.McKay, *Heads in the Sand* (1950)
R.Manderson-Jones, *Special Relationship* (1972)
C.Mayhew, *British Foreign Policy* (1950)
R.Mayne, *The Recovery of Europe* (1970)
W.Medlicott, *British Foreign Policy since Versailles* (1968)
F.Northedge, *Descent from Power* (1974)
B.Ott, *Georges Bidault* (Annonay, 1978)

A.Philip, *The Schuman Plan* (1951)
D.Pickles, *French Politics* (1953)
A.de Porte, *De Gaulle's Foreign Policy, 1944–6* (Cambridge, U.S., 1968)
H.Price, *The Marshall Plan and its Meaning* (New York, 1955)
R.Quilliot, *La S.F.I.O. et l'Exercice de Pouvoir* (Paris, 1972)
F.Ritsch, *The French Left and the European Idea* (1966)
V.Rothwell, *Britain and the Cold War* (1982)
B.Ruhm van Oppen (ed.), *Documents on Germany Under Occupation* (1955)
A.Schlaim, P.Jones and K.Sainsbury, *British Foreign Secretaries Since 1945* (1977)
S.Serfaty, *France, de Gaulle and Europe* (Baltimore, 1968)
Lord Strang, *British in World Affairs* (1961)
H.Tint, *French Foreign Policy Since the Second World War* (1972)
N.Waites (ed.), *Troubled Neighbours* (1971)
A.Werth, *France 1940–55* (1956)
P.Williams, *Hugh Gaitskell* (1979)
F.Willis, *France, Germany and the New Europe* (1968)
C.Woodhouse, *British Foreign Policy Since the Second World War* (1961)
Sir L.Woodward, *British Foreign Policy in the Second World War* (5 vols, 1970–6)
P.Ziegler, *Diana Cooper* (1981)

North Sea

Baltic Sea

Kiel

Hamburg

to U.S. ZONE

BRITISH ZONE

Berlin (in sectors)

(under Polish administration: eventually became part of Poland)

Holland

Polar

R. Rhine

Essen

Dortmund

SOVIET ZONE

Dusseldorf

Cologne

Leipzig

Belgium

Bonn

Dresden

FRENCH

Luxembourg

Frankfurt

France

Czechoslovakia

N

AMERICAN ZONE

ZONE

Stuttgart

Freiburg

Munich

Switzerland

Austria (also under four-power occupation

| 0 | 100 miles |
| 0 | 160 KM |

Italy

French plans

——— area of four-power occupation

The Ruhr: to be politically separate, under international controls

—·—· under Polish administration

possible extension of Ruhr state

·········· other international borders

The Rhineland: to be politically separate and occupied by Allies

– – – zonal boundaries

The Saar: to be economically united with France

Map 1. Germany after 1945, illustrating the zonal occupation and French plans for its future. (For a map of French proposals in the Rühr, see P.R.O. CAB.129/9, C.P. (46) 156 (15 April).

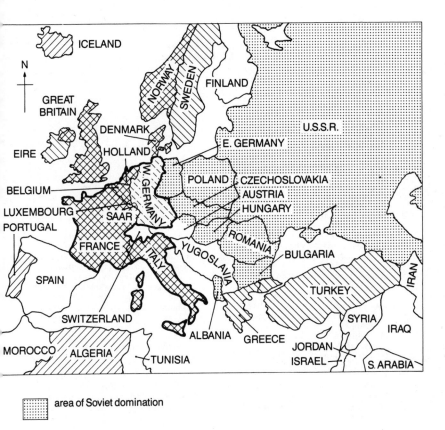

ICELAND

N

GREAT
BRITAIN

EIRE

NORWAY SWEDEN FINLAND

DENMARK

HOLLAND

E. GERMANY

U.S.S.R.

BELGIUM

W. GERMANY

POLAND   CZECHOSLOVAKIA

LUXEMBOURG

PORTUGAL

SAAR

AUSTRIA

HUNGARY

FRANCE

ITALY

YUGOSLAVIA

ROMANIA

BULGARIA

TURKEY

IRAN

SPAIN

SWITZERLAND

ALBANIA   GREECE

SYRIA

IRAQ

JORDAN

MOROCCO   ALGERIA   TUNISIA

ISRAEL

S. ARABIA

area of Soviet domination

members of the Atlantic
Pact, April 1949

members of the Council of
Europe, May 1949

joined the Council of
Europe, 1951

members of the Schuman
Plan, April 1951

Map 2.   Europe 1949–51

Index

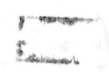